NAXALISM
At a Glance

NAXALISM
At a Glance

P.C. Joshi

KALPAZ

Naxalism—At a glance

ISBN : 978-81-7835-921-2

Published in 2013 in India by
Kalpaz Publications
C-30, Satyawati Nagar,
Delhi - 110052
E-mail: kalpaz@hotmail.com
Ph.: 9212729499

Lasser Type Setting : Rajender Vashist, Delhi
Printed at : Chawla Offset Printers, Delhi

Dedicated to all those, alive or in their heavenly abode, who helped me in one way or the other during my university days at Allahabad.

Also with very special regards and thanks to Ms. S. Nisha to whom I owe a lot and cannot repay her debt.

Communism is not love. Communism is a hammer which we use to crush the enemy.

Chairman Mao Tse Tung

Contents

Preface

After a violent agrarian uprising in Naxalbari village in 1967, CPI–Marxist Leninist Party took birth in 1969 under the leadership of Charu Mazumdar, Kanu Sanyal and Jangal Santhal. Inspired by Mao Tse Tung, they broke up from CPI–Marxist and formed a more radical outfit. In the decade of seventies, the Naxal movement weakened because of Emergency clamped by the Centre but once it was lifted, it resurfaced. Naxal group known by name of 'Dakshin Desh' emerged as Maoist Communist Centre (MCC) in Bihar and soon got strengthened. People's War Group (PWG) led by armed rebels raised its head in Andhra Pradesh making the landlords their target and aiming at snatching the land from them. In 1980s and 1990s around 30 groups surfaced here and there across the country. All these outfits kept on differing on one point or the other with each other and there was hardly any unity among them though some of the Naxal groups did try to achieve it. Most of the Naxal groups got themselves engaged in land grabbing and extortion to raise party funds. In 2000 they chose parliamentary path, participated in election process and adopted mass line approach. Yet some of the outfits remained underground in their activities and identity. A new party was formed after People's War and MCCI merged in the year 2004 under the name of Communist Party of India (Maoist)–CPI–Maoist– which is threating the internal security of the country. It has links with foreign militant outfits and is capable of producing certain category of arms etc. It has large amount of funds and enough space in jungles. The menace has to be curbed now before it is too late.

Naxalities of all hues are well-read, learned and practical people but itching to snatch state power by revolutionary and violent methods over parliamentary path which India opted for in the year 1950 while adopting a constitution for itself and making the country a democratic republic. In their estimation, the parliamentary democracy is not able to solve multifarious problems concerning, social conditions like exploitations, hunger, discrimination, corruption, injustices based on caste system, in securing socio-economic justice for the oppressed and downtrodden class. Punishment for the oppressor is warranted. But the major question was what happens when the state itself becomes the oppressor and there is no remedy left with the citizens. Naxals probably thought that the remedy lies in confronting the state or oppressor (class enemy) with violent (annihilation) means and in the process they abandoned the mainstream politics. They think of confronting the state by adopting guerilla tactics with the help of their cadre without considering the fact whether they can sustain the movement against the state machinery i.e. police and other para-military forces and for how long ? It seems they are succeeding. In almost 13 states of India they have a sizeable following. Civil liberty groups, as rightly said by Arun Shourie in Raipur in February 2007 while speaking at a security conference, are mostly populated with Naxalites. But if the state adopts a strict posture of repressive machinery against these Naxals and becomes determined to eliminate them, is it at all difficult for the state ? But the government does not want to be oppressive against its own citizens and views Naxals also as its citizens. In the process the government either avoids stern actions or reacts mildly which, in turn, helps Naxal movement survive and grow. Some say Naxalism is anger of the exploited lot. The state is duty bound to mitigate the genuine grievances of its citizens.

If one is unjustly victimised, in all probability, he is bound to turn violent and adopt means which can't be said to be democratic to give vent to his anger. The tribals who are original inhabitants of various regions of India are being victimised and deprived of land by way of taking it away from them under one pretext or the other which gives them reason to adopt violent means to give vent to their anger. But the Naxalites are also doing the same to tribals now. For example, in Bastar they have forbidden the villagers to pluck tendu leaves and monopolised the Tendu leaves business themselves. The plight of these tribals was described by the Supreme Court in Samatha vs. State of Andhra Pradesh and others (AIR 1997 JJ, SC 3292 para 12 to 15). Markandey Katju and Gyansudha Mishra, while delivering the judgement observed "It is the duty of all people who love our country to see that no harm is done to the scheduled tribes and that they are given all help to bring them up in their economic and social status, since they have been victimised for thousands of years by terrible oppression and atrocities. The mentality of our countrymen towards these tribals must change and they must be given the respect they deserve as the original inhabitants of India".

But in Naxalites cadres, consist of highly educated, and rich people also. When Dr. Biyanak Sen was convicted, there were people who spearheaded signature campaign and demonstrated seeking his release. They do it only for Naxalites cadres—underground or overground –not for others even if they are convicted on wrong notes.

Almost all Naxal parties of all shades thriving in India, consider 'Chairman Mao/Communist Party of China as their own Chairman, and party despite of Mao's dictat to act according to ground conditions of their country. Yet they derive inspirations from China only. They forget that China has trampled the ethnic minorities, suppressed the liberation movements, crushed the uprising at Tiananmen Square, adopted the capitalist economy under the garb of socialism. How China has adopted expansionist designs by grabbing Indian territory is simply forgotten and even negated by these Communists. They would do well to recall what Sardar Vallabhbhai Patel wrote in December 1950 "Chinese imperialism ...conceal racial national and historical claims ....while our western and north-western threats to security are still prominent as before, a new threat has developed from the north and north-east........ India's defence has to concentrate itself on two fronts simultaneously. Our defence measures have so far been based on the calculations of a superiority over Pakistan." (*The Pioneer*, March 18, 2011 article by Premen Addy "The Path to Democracy").

Consider what Shri Prakash Singh has to say in his book "The Naxalite Movement in India" — "The Chinese actually follow a subtle design in pursuing their imperialist ambitions. First they manipulate historical accounts to show that a particular area was part of the Chinese kingdom during some period in the past. In the second stage, they start showing that area as part of their territory in their maps — this is, cartographic aggression. And in the third stage, they start staking their claim by sending patrols and throwing their weight around."

March 31, 2011

P.C. Joshi

Acknowledgements

My special thanks to :

1. Late Shri Rama Shankar Sanwal of Lucknow.
2. Late Shri Purnanand Sanwal and his daughter late Smt. Ganga Joshi of Anand Niwas, Nainital.
3. Late Shri Lalta Prasad Gupta of Karkhana Bazar (my classfellow), Almora.
4. Dr. R.K. Agarwal D.Litt., Asstt. Professor in Commerce in 1958 in Allahabad University, his mother and wife.
5. Capt. Dewak Ram OC of 8 UP Bty. NCC in early sixtees and a visiting examiner, Major Sharma of Arty from Ranchi. Both of them postponed NCC 'C' certificate examination by one day at their own risk when it clashed with my SSB Interview for a Commission in the Army. They took the risk only to make my career.
6. The late Maharajkumar of Sikkim.
7. Late Rajarshi Purushottam Das Tondan.
8. Kashi Naresh (late).
9. Late Jagdeesh Prasad Marwari, my B.Com. classfellow.
10. Late Shri Shyam Bihari Tiwari and his late parents of Aihar, Raibareli, U.P.

P.C. Joshi

1

Red Terror and Bleeding Hearts

The world Communist movement started when Communist League was formed in December 1847. Manifesto of the Communist Party appeared in German in 1872 but English edition appeared in 1888. Before 1917 Communist Parties were named Social Democratic or Labour Parties. But their ideologies were based on Manifesto of the Communist Party. Even under the banner of Communist League, Social Democratic Parties or labour parties the communist movement started in 1847. The word "Communist" was coined from the word 'commune'. The Czar was made to quit in February 1917 revolution. Soviet Democratic movement in October–November 1917, was led by Bolsvicks (i.e. Communists). The Communist movement spread so fast that by 1982 the number of communist parties swelled to 19 from only 1 in 1917. The Russian revolution had its repercussions on India as well when Communist Party of India (CPI) was proposed to be formed in October 1920 in Tashkent in Communist International Meeting attended by M.N. Roy, Ambani Mukherjee etc. and it (CPI) was established on December 26, 1925. The first conference of Communist Party of India was held in 1925 in Kanpur as an underground party. In 1942 it was allowed to function openly. CPI held its first congress in 1943. In 1946 it was again banned. CPI had launched the Peasants armed struggle in Telengana. B.T. Ranadiv wanted to oppose the government of India whereas P.C. Joshi was for support to the Indian government. For this nationalist stand P.C. Joshi was branded as 'nationalist communist'. As such, he did not survive long as general secretary of the Communist Party of India, so much so, when P.C. Joshi was underground in 1948-50, Ranadiv denied him even soap and a shaving kit. (The Indian Express (Sunday edition) March 4, 1999 article by K.R. Malkani "Does Communists have a future in India?"). In 1948 Congress party was characterised as a stooge of British Imperialism. In 1952 a tactical line was adopted under the advice of the Communist Party of Soviet Union (CPSU) to strike a balance between these two groups – one with the rural-oriented approach and the other with Urban-oriented one. People, throughout the world got fascinated and attracted towards Communist ideology since it appealed to them in the fiftees and sixtees – probably because of success of Russian revolution on economic front benefits.

In 1951 Indian National Congress was branded by them as one representing a bourgeois – landlord clique. In 1956 it was branded as national bourgeois. 1957-59 first communist government came into power in Kerala. In the 20th Congress of CPSU, Nikita Khruschev proclaimed the revisionist thesis of "peaceful co-existence", "peaceful competition" and "peaceful transition". In 1956 "Moscow Revisionism" line was adopted by Khurschov who took the stand that a peaceful transition was the way to achieve socialism. Till then the Russian thinking was that socialism can be achieved by way of violence and use of force. But the CPC, Albanian Communist Party and other leftist groups did not agree with Khruschov, sixth Party Congress of CPI was held at Vijaywada in 1961 where differences among party leadership surfaced and three groups emerged. The first group was in majority. The second group was led by B.T. Ranadiv and P. Sundariah. The third one was led by EMS Namboodripad. Second and third groups were in minority. This party congress was attended by Michel Suslov USSR leader. The differences among the leadership was basically on their attitude towards Indian National Congress. Earlier they had already characterised INC as stooge of British Imperialism. The second point of ideological difference of opinion developed after 1962 on Sino-Indian border conflict. B.T. Ranadiv and P. Sundariah held the opinion that a socialist country like China cannot attack India. It was their anti-nation stand. The other group supported India and resultantly, rightist groups started aligning with Moscow whereas the Leftist group with China. In the beginning of 1962 Ajoy Ghosh died and a new general secretary had to be elected.

A compromise formula was arrived at and S.A. Dange was elected Chairman and E.M.S. Namboodripad was made general secretary. There was no formal split in the party at this juncture inspite of differences. In 1962 a charge was made in the Central Committee against chairman Dange whose context was that in 1924 he had, during his detention, volunteered to cooperate with the British government. The leftist group played it timely and said that person of such a dubious personality should not be Chairman. The ideological differences following Chinese aggression in 1962 forced the party to hold a meeting and the meeting was held at the Thyagraja Hall in Calcutta on April 11, 1964. The consequence was the party CPI split. In 1962 most of the comrades who were against Dange were put in Jail. In 1965 EMS went with B.T. Ranadiv and Sundariah.

The split group that walked out of the present and existing one met at Tenali (Andhra Pradesh) and spelt out their ideological concepts. They characterised Indian Congress and bourgeois landlord clique as led by big landlords and advocated 'people's democracy' through People's Democratic Fronts where the leadership is vested in workers. The Rightist group (Moscow–oriented) wanted to establish Nationalist Democracy by National Democratic Front where big landlords were included but big bourgeoises were excluded. The Leftist group at Tenali congress did not agree to peaceful transition to socialism as advocated by Khurschov. They did not compromise and held that collaboration with national bourgeois i.e. Congress was not possible and issued a call to the followers of the party to follow a violent path i.e. the Chinese line. In October 1964 a party congress was held and a new name to the party CPI–Marxist was adopted. Now there were two Communist Parties – CPI and CPI-Marxist – the former Moscow-oriented and the later, China-oriented. Charu Mazumdar who had joined the banned CPI in 1938 quit it in 1964 and joined CPM which was more radical but maintained their party's commitment to agrarian, soviet and democratic movement and toed the line of class struggle in conformity with Marxist Leninist ideology. In December 1964 thousands of CPM workers were arrested. Although they believed in violence yet they were willing to participate in mid-term election in Kerala. Many CPM workers were in detention in Kerala yet CPM won 46 seats. No party came in majority. As such no government could be formed. In 1965 China's Great People's Cultural Revolution had also its impact on CPM. In 1966 party leaders were released in West Bengal and Kerala. CPM participated in elections and won. EMS Namboodripad became Chief Minister of Kerala whereas Jyoti Basu took over as Home Minister in West Bengal representing United Democratic Front (UDF) government formed on March 2, 1967 led by CPI–(M).

Meanwhile the political scenario at national as well as international level changed fast. At international level a great debate started in Communist movement. CPSU under the leadership was heading the revisionist line while Mao Tse Tung Chairman of CPC was leading the revolutionary line.

Coming back to national level, the Congress government in West Bengal led by Ajoy Mukherjee of Bangla Congress came to power with the support of left parties. Ajoy was the brother of CPI leader Bishwanath Mukherjee. The United Front government favoured and granted the working class the right to 'Gheraos, which had became quite common in those days, the industrialist till their demands were met. It also encouraged the oppressed peasants to behave in a similar fashion while dealing with 'Jotedars' (land owners) who were mostly Hindus. Peasants were, in fact, itching to take revenge. On the system of crop-sharing also there used to be hurt-burning among peasants who were mostly tribal Santhals. They had no land or held small land holdings and they used to work on the land of 'Jotedars' on the basis of crop-sharing. Half of the produce or two third of the produced grain, as per agreement, was to be given to the Kulak/ Jotedar. (Kulak – a Russian word for rich landlord peasant). But the crux is that the peasants were unhappy with Jotedars, harboured a grudge against them and wanted to regain the possession of vested land. On the question of land reforms, differences among CPM were voiced by Charu Mazumdar who was the then District Committee member in Darjeeling. Ultra left in CPM who were not following the Parliamentary path openly fell out and gradually formed Revolutionary Councils – mainly by Charu Mazumdar. Sushital Chowdhury had set his eyes on Marx-Angel institutions. Both of these groups were not aligning with CPM.

On March 2, 1967 when a tribal youth was ploughing his land in Naxalbari under judicial orders, he was attacked by men of local landlords. On March 3, three share croppers refused to give the share to the landlord whose land they were cultivating and removed whole crop, again in Naxalbari itself. The problem was initially tribal-based whose land holdings used to be usurped by the Jotedars during the past several years. 'Kisan Organisations' were active in Naxalbari area. Over land disputes often violence ensued. Tea garden workers and tribal peasants were organised and united by the CPI trade union movement in fiftees. Kanu Sanyal was associated with this type of work since then. The leadership of peasants agitation was with Charu Mazumdar and Kanu Sanyal. 'Landless Peasant's Revolt' took place on March 2, 1967 at Naxalbari, Kharbari and Phansidewa. On March 3 the day after UDF government came to power in West Bengal, there was forced occupation of government land by the Charu Mazumdar, Kanu Sanyal, Kokan Mazumdar and Jangal Santhal. They created a sort of lawlessness in Naxalbari by firing first shot in a village situated nearby and attacking Naxalbari Police station calling it liberating these areas through armed struggle following Mao Tse Tung's line. These CPM leaders seem to have been influenced by an article written by Marshal Lin Piao in 1965 captioned "long live the victory of Peoples' War". Charu's thoughts were "annihilation of class enemies by squads of peasant guerillas to achieve liberation" and "victory certainly belongs to us because China's chairman is our chairman and Chinese Communist Party is our Party".

On March 18 a convention was held which aroused a general feeling of upsurge among landless peasants. They set up Peasants/ Kisan Committees, who got armed and spread terror. Red Flag were furled all over. Violent clashes followed when the armed agents of a local Jotedar thrashed a share-cropper Bigul Kisan, looting of foodgrains and killing of a few landlords took place.

On May 18, 1967 the Siliguri Kisan Sabha of which Jangal Santhal was President declared their readiness to go for armed struggle to re-distribute land to the landless. Annoyed by this declaration, after a week, a sharecropper was beaten by landlord's men over a land dispute.

People's Daily and Peking Radio came out with news bulletin headlined "Red era in India has begun". Soon fissures within the newly born CPM were felt. The year 1965-66 also witnessed growth of various groups within CPM viz Chinta group led by Kanai Chatterjee and Dakshin Desh by Amulya Sen. The armed peasant's uprising organised by Kanu Sanyal was modeled on Maoist line since he was very influenced by Chinese Revolution of 1950. He and Charu Mazumdar together launched the Naxalbari movement instigating landless peasants to forcibly occupy and cultivate the land that simply did not belong to them. On May 22, 1967 the Santhals in Naxalbari village rose in revolt on the issue of land under the leadership of Charu Mazumdar.

CPM leadership noted that the hard line Marxists like Charu, Kanu, Sadhan Sarkar, Sourin Bose, Sushital Roy Chowdhury, Parimal Dass Gupta and Sunity Ghosh etc. were defying party line and directives. As such, they were not liked by party leadership and were expelled alongwith about 400 other members of the party. Darjiling District Committee of the party was also dissolved. Almost all of them were brilliant people, genius, courageous and mental giants. Charu Mazumdar, himself a symbol of sacrifice and courage was a sort of magnet that attracted people to his ideology at initial stages.

In their estimation and analysis, India was a semi-feudal country for which a protracted people's was required and that peaceful transition was not possible, rejected parliamentary process and boycotted elections, supported the right of nationalities to self-determination. It was essential, in their analysis, to fight against revisionism and all forms of bourgeois ideology and wanted to tread the path of Marxism – Leninism – Mao Tse Tung thought.

Meanwhile Police received a report that the leaders of the Naxalbari uprising were hiding in village Boro Jhorojote. Police party went to the village on May 24 to arrest those leaders who could not be found there. Only tea garden workers and peasants had assembled agitating for land ownership. They gave stiff resistance to the police and in the process someone shot an arrow which hit Police Inspector Sonam Wangdi resulting in his death. Policemen escaped in the face of stiff resistance and tough response from armed tribal villagers led by Jangal Santhal just to return the following day i.e. May 25 with more and full preparations. The women activists had organised a secret meeting by the Mechi river on Nepal border. Police waited for them at Prasad Jote village and shot dead 11 people including two children. Police action added fuel to fire. Kanu Sanyal termed it as "Revenge killing". The uprising remained confined to the area under the jurisdiction of three police stations – Naxalbari, Kharibari and Phansideva. The morale of the agitators was so high that the police could not enter the village of Jharu Jote near Naxalbari till August 1967. Naxalbari was an Agrarian Movement against injustices perpetrated by land owners (Jotedars and Kulaks). There existed a Land Reform Act 1954 which had abolished Zamindari system. Since CPM wanted People's Democratic state, they launched a land movement in Naxalbari whose inhabitants were mostly landless Santhal tribals but landlords were Hindus. CPM had alliance with bourgeois government whereas ultras or extremists wanted armed peasants' movement for the emancipation of people. Anarchic situation continued to be created by tribal Santhals. On June 10, 1967 a mob of about 150 CPM supporters raided the house of Nagen Roy Chowdhury in Kharibari village and looted paddy, gun, ornaments and abducted him and later on killed him. Between March and August 1967 peasants captured land and looted grain from the landlords and distributed it, burnt land records, formed revolutionary squads/committees which directed all the villagers to arm themselves in self defence. In fact, the Naxalbari process had started right from the early fiftees with the mobilisation carried out by Communist at ground level but the simmering larva, burst that day i.e. on 24 May 1967. Charu Mazumdar had given a slogan "land to the tillers" and it had done miracles. But when the state government decided to take police against them, all the agitators, leaders of naxalbari movement simply disappeared. They simply dithered away. Although police had arrested many persons in continuous raids, the leadership simply went underground. Only Jangal Santhal was caught by police and it was learnt that he was hungry for two days.

On July 5, 1967 the People's Daily of China in its editorial under the caption 'a peal of spring thunder' wrote : "Revolutionary, peasants in the Darjeeling area have risen in rebellion. Under the leadership of a revolutionary group of Indian Communist Party, a red area of rural revolutionary armed struggle has been established in India. This is a development of tremendous significance for the Indian people's revolutionary struggle ....." Liberation, November 1968 issue, highlights the gains of Naxalbari uprising as seen by Kanu Sanyal who said the achievements were as follows :

(i) the old feudal structure which had existed for centuries was smashed.

(ii) fraudulent deeds and documents were burnt.

(iii) unequal agreements between the peasants and Jotedars were all declared null and void.

(iv) Hoarded rice was confiscated.

(v) Open trials of tyrannical Jotedars were held.

(vi) Gooda elements attached to the Jotedars were suitably dealt with.

(vii) Armed groups of peasants were organised with traditional weapons and guns snatched from the Jotedars.

(viii) nightwatch was arranged to maintain law and order.

(ix) revolutionary committees were set up to establish peasants political power, and

(x) the existing bourgeois laws and courts were declared inoperative.

Whatever Kanu might have written in appreciation of his Naxal movement but the fact is the moment West Bengal government ordered police action against them, they simply whithered away. It fizzled out : Now the ground situation has changed. Old naxalite hands are no more there. Khokan Mazumdar of Janshakti group of CPI-ML claims that there is not even a book on the 1967 rural uprising in the local Subroti Sena library. He points out that sons of former CPI-ML workers have joined CPM and that they have now become prosperous political elite'. Abhijit Mazumdar left for Peking via Kathmandu to meet Chinese Chairman Mao. They were picked up by Chinese Comrades at Kathmandu who drove them to Peking by a jeep reaching there on September 30, 1967. They saw China celebrate National Day. On October 1 and people weeping at the site of Chairman Mao. Kanu and others met Mao, Chou-en-Lai, and the Commander-in-Chief. According to Kanu, Mao's 'over the years Darjeeling district general secretary of CPI-ML (Liberation) says that there has been a systematic witch-hunt-against anybody who opposes the CPI-M. The demography of the area has changed now. A lot of Bangladeshi have entered India and settled in these areas. Biharis, Nepalese have also overtaken the earlier adivasis inhabitants like Mundas, Oraons, Santhals and Rajbongshis (they are not tribals but Scheduled Castes). A shopkeeper Manoj Shah of Prasad Jote village gives a rough estimate of the number of families in the village as : 2 Biharis, 2 Bengalis, 10 Nepalis, 20 Rajbongshi and 50 Bengladeshis. CPM leader takes them (Bangladeshis) under his wing because it helps him gain bulk votes. They get land and ration card. In return it is a relationship of convenience.

During the Naxalbari struggle there were differences within party (CPM) and Kanu thought that the Chinese leaders could help in clearing the confusion of right or wrong lives. Kanu and few others were advised : "whatever you learn in China try to forget it. Go to your own country, try to understand the specific situation and carry the revolution forward . . ."

Communism was described by Mao in his book "Communism is not love. Communism is a hammer which we use to crush the enemy." The origin of the word Naxalism is based on the uprising in 1967 in a village called Naxalbari in West Bengal where a few radical revolutionaries led by Charu Mazumdar and Kanu Sanyal staged a violent and revolutionary opposition against CPI-M leadership with the help of peasants against Jotedars and Kulaks since they were dispossessed of their landholdings by them over decades.

Charu Mazumdar had provided ideological, cover for the Naxalbari movement and converted the peasants struggle into a militant movement, of course with active participation of Kanu Sanyal. When major police action was ordered by the State government, militant students and CPI(M) rebels set up Naxalbari Peasants Struggle Aid Committee, United Front government with the help of CPM tried to curb the Naxal uprising and the leaders were arrested by July 20. Charu Mazumdar and Kanu Sanyal analysed the sudden failure of the movement by way of writing two documents : One by Charu on "Naxalbari Siksha" and the other by Kanu on "Report on Tarai Peasants movement." Both the leaders concluded that no peasant's movement can succeed unless it was led by a genuinely revolutionary Communist Party. The Naxalbari Peasants Aid Committee took a shape of broad based All India Krishak Sangram Sahayak Samiti to forge Unity amongst Marxists who subscribed to Mao Tse Tung's line. In order to rally round Mao's party line, the radicals who had been thrown out of CPM decided to form an all India Coordination Committee on November 12 and 13, 1967 of communist Revolutionaries which was later renamed as AICCC in May 1968. AICCR itself passed into oblivion on April 22, 1969 after giving birth to CPIML based on Mao's thoughts.

In the estimation by China's Peoples Daily, a single spark could start a prairie fire in India. They wrote it in their editorial of July 5, 1967 under the caption "Spring thunder over India". Radio Peking on June 28, 1967 calling it the spring Thunder said "A phase of peasants armed struggle led by the revolutionaries of the Indian Communist Party has been set up in the countryside in Darjeeling district of West Bengal state of India. This is the front paw of the revolutionary armed struggle launched by the Indian people under the guidance of Mao Tse-Tung's teachings." The crux is that the Naxalbari happened because the land ceiling laws and redistribution of land remained on papers only. Had the redistribution of land been done and land ceiling laws applied in right earnest, probably the Naxals would not have born to survive and flourish. Soon after that People's Daily, run by the Communist Party of China, the centre for world revolution, wrote an article in 'People's Daily' under the title "Spring thunder over India" which stated : "A peal of spring thunder has crashed over the land in India. Revolutionary peasants in Darjeeling are have risen in rebellion. Under the leadership of a revolutionary group of the Indian Communist Party, a red area of rural revolutionary armed struggle has been established in India. The Chinese people joyfully applaud this revolutionary storm of the Indian Peasants in the Darjeeling area as do all the Marxist-Leninist and revolutionary people of the world".

The spark and heat of Naxalbari peasant's uprising carried and sustained by 'Naxalbari Peasants struggle Aid Committee' reached areas like Srikakulam, Birbhum, Debra-Gopiballavpur, Mushahari (Bihar) and Lakhimpur– Kheri (UP).

In order to propogate their revolutionary line, AICCCR whose convenor was Sushital Roy Chowdhury started a party-magazine by name of "Liberation" on November 11, 1967. "Deshbrati" was brought out in Bengali. Liberation was edited by Suniti Kumar Ghosh.

Government raided offices of both of these periodicals/party organs in April 1970.

Açharya Vinoba Bhaweji had realised or sensed the importance of land distribution and launched a movement which came to be known as "Bhoodan Movement". It was, of course, very successful but greater and larger efforts were needed in order to transform the society, landless class continued to be exploited and suffered at the hands of landlords. In West Bengal the then revenue minister Hare Krishan Konar did try to improve the prevalent situation and re-distribute the land but without support from all elements, the desired results could not be achieved by him. Naxalites who deprived Jotedars of their peddy and land to till it themselves actually fought an unequal war with the police. Naxalites were armed with bows and arrows whereas Police and Eastern Frontier Rifles were armed with weapons. After the Communist Party of India (Marxist) split and CPI-ML was born on 22 April 1969, the latter's task/objects were "to rouse the peasants masses in the countryside to wage guerrilla war, unfold agrarian revolution, build rural base areas, use the country side to enricle the cities and to liberate the whole country….." Without bothering for the unequal war, Charu Mazumdar was over enthusiastic with leading the landless peasants and believed "that the first rays of the red sun have already lit up the coast of Andhra and will tinge the other states before long …..making a people's democratic India …..no longer a distant objective."

But the assessment of China proved wrong. The strong hands of state power trampled the uprising and suppressed them ruthlessly. Naxalbari uprising/revolt obliterated and gone into oblivion. So happened with Srikakulam. Midnapore and Birbhum struggles also disappeared. Of course, Mazumdar shifted the struggle to Calcutta in 1970 i.e. from rural areas to urban cities.

To begin with, Naxalites identified 4 major oppressors : American Imperialism, Soviet Imperialism — Indian big business characterised as "Comprador" capital owing to its reluctance to fight imperialism and feudalism public sector or bureaucratic capital. Feudalism was the main enemy and the rural masses main force of revolution. This was in accordance with Chinese path which involved waging guerilla war in the countryside establishing liberated zones and thereby encircling and capturing the cities.

The forerunner of Naxalbari movement could safely be said to be Tebhaga movement in East Bengal during 1945-47 where Bhowani Sen had involved and ensured the participation of middle class peasants in a big way. Under the 'Tebhaga' scheme, the share of the landlord who demanded one half of the crop produced was reduced to one third from one half. Kisans forcibly started taking away rather looting two thirds, of the harvested crop from grain-stores of 'Jotedars' which brought peasants and landlords in clash with each other. The movement died down because landlords with the help of administration and police dealt with peasants with a heavy hand.

The movement was crushed by the police in 52 days only. Naxal or Naxalism happens to be a movement that took birth in Naxalbari village of Darjeeling in West Bengal which was inspired and led by Charu Mazumdar, Kanu Sanyal etc. in 1967 with the main aim to grab land belonging to landlords and withholding the produce from such land taken by tillers under contract. Some intellectuals thought it better to name the movement as agrarian movement instead of Naxal movement. But their main aim remains to capture state power through revolutionary means.

In the year 1969 itself the united front government had started receiving messages from the peasants that the consent of the people was not there regarding what the party was doing, rural peasantry was unhappy with those who came from urban areas to guide the destiny of Medinipur district, nor the CPI-ML leaders were able to carry local leaders with them. Soon the stage of 1969 was over. In March 1970 Charu Mazumdar gave a call to the students and youth and suddenly the clarion call had its electrical effects in urban areas. Groups of students started hoisting red flags, attacking police etc. Even the vice chancellor of Jadavpur University was attacked. This sort of situation lasted almost till 1973. Charu's penchant for annihilation continued. His dictum always used to be "Cut the Jotedar's throats, kill them". This led to differences amongst the leaders of the party. Even Kanu was against such annihilations which was the highest form of class struggle for Charu Mazumdar. In 1969 Charu wrote in 'Liberation' (party journal). "The act of annihilations of class enemies through guerrilla activities is the primary stage of guerrilla struggle". His annihilations policy led to frenzy in Calcutta creating panic and terror even shocking Chinese. Kanu sanyal described it as a fundamental deviation from Marxism-Leninism and Mao's thoughts. Kanu claims only one landlord was killed during the Naxalbari struggle. In practice the annihilations line was first followed in Srikakulam in late 1969, Kanu claims.

The annihilation programme of Charu Mazumdar created differences among party members. Even Chinese were taken aback by what Charu was propagating and the consequent and resultant panic generated among masses in West Bengal. There was constant criticism of Charu Mazumdar. Radio peking which had hailed the Naxalbari uprising all of a sudden fell silent causing worry to Charu himself. He dispatched his associate Soren Bose to Peking to find out their reaction. As said, Naxalites are secretive, Charu sent Suren Bose to Peking via London instead of sending him straight from Calcutta to Peking. Bose met Chou-en-Lai, the then Premier who scolded the CPI-ML starting "You seem to have opened a secret assassination club...?".

In March 1970, the centre took over West Bengal administration and ordered a crackdown on the Naxalites. Calcutta urban cadres working in Debra and Gopiballavpur area including Ashim Chatterjee, Santosh Rana etc. fled the village to start guerilla warfare in cities, particularly in Calcutta. The walls of the city of Calcutta were pasted with red quotations of Chairman Mao Tse Tung. Agents of the bourgeoise government." There was pandemonium and panic in Calcutta. Industries closed themselves and shifted outside West Bengal, life was at the mercy of Naxalites. In 1970 April a conference was held where it was stated that Charu Mazumdar wants to become Mao of India but Charu did not pay any heed. Communist party of China was also not endorsing the line adopted by Charu Mazumdar.

The communist movement was split from CPI to CPM and again the split was from CPM to CPI-ML and then burst into so many splinters. Though they realised the importance of remaining united but personality cult refrained them as much as their thinking on the line of annihilation adopted by Charu Mazumdar. In order to distinguish their party from CPI and CPM, it was named as CPI-ML. 8th congress of CPI-ML was held in Calcutta on May 15/16,1970 maintaining utmost secrecy. It was attended by about 35 delegate from all over the country. It elected 21 member central committee and 9 member politburo. Charu Mazumdar was made general secretary. Apart from him, other members of politburo were Sushital Roy Choudhury, Saroj Dutt, Souren Bose, S.N. Singh, Shiv Kumar Mishra, R.P. Sharoj, Appu and 2 others from Andhra Pradesh.

The extremist movement that was build on landless peasants anger against landlords with Naxalbari uprising in May 1967 kept on flourishing in West Bengal, Bihar, Andhra Pradesh and Kerala etc. under the leadership of Charu Mazumdar. Naxalite movement that acquired the status of almost armed mass uprising, might have taken a serious armed revolt but the movement was quelled with a heavy hand by the police. An atmosphere of terror had been created by Charu's bands/squads by annihilating the class enemies secretly who according to him consisted of rich landlords, Jotedars, money lenders, big businessmen, policemen and government servants. Most unprecedented phase of the movement was in between March 1970 and May 1971 during which about 400 naxalite incidents were reported. During 1969-72 in West Bengal alone, over 700 CPI-ML squads were believed to have operated. The west Bengal–Bihar–Orissa border region committee headed by Ashim Chatterjee was involved in 120 annihilation in November 1970. The violence spread to other areas as well—villages as well as Calcutta city itself where some policemen were also killed in pursuance of annihilation policy of Charu Mazumdar. The middle class, which indeed was the backbone of the naxalite movement expressed anger over such senseless killings. Even Charu's own colleagues started questioning him on his policy of annihilation of class enemies. But Charu reported stating that "a revolution should soak his hands in the blood of the class enemy" and that the violence should be carried out by mass actions and not through selective annihilation. Though party received support from the Communist Party of China (CPC) at its initial stages but later it also became concerned on the annihilation policy of Charu. Still Charu Mazumdar elected general secretary of the party in the secretly convened 1st party congress held on May 11,1970 in Garden Reach area of Calcutta under the camouflage of a wedding ceremony.

Ashim Chatterjee who claimed to have carried out 120 annihilations and opined that the annihilation should have raised the number of peasants supporters from 20,000 from 20,00,000 gave up the policy later taking a fresh look at the whole thing after the Chinese suggested a reassessment.

Meanwhile, United Front Government in West Bengal fell which had the support of CPI and CPM, Government of India decided to strike the naxalite because of their senseless policy of annihilation and operation "Steeplechase" was undertaken from July 1 to August 15, 1971 jointly with the Army, para-military forces and the state police in West Bengal, Bihar, Orissa. A number of top leaders were arrested. Ashim chatterjee who had opposed the annihilation line in March 1971 itself but not totally rejected it, was among those who were arrested on November 3,1971. He later on went to the extent of branding the CPI-ML as a 'social terrorist party' and not a communist party.

On the issue of his policy, of annihilation which was at its peak in 1970-71, stand on CPC and the attitude of the party towards the liberation struggle of Bangladesh, S.N. Singh, the leader of the party in Bihar developed differences with the central leadership in the year 1971. Differences of Charu Mazumdar with S.N. Singh also cropped up because once S.N. stayed at the house of a rich landlord and, Charu objected to it but in the initial stages of Naxalbari peasants uprising S.N. Singh was one of the closest associate of Charu Mazumdar. A section within the CPI-ML led by S.N. Singh criticised Charu for attacking policemen, traffic constables for branding them as class enemy. Soren Bose who was sent to China by Charu on his return said that CPC thinks Charu had ignored real thing, the party was not organising as it should have been i.e., to bring masses into its fold is not being done. CPC also opined that Charu is taking too many premature action in West Bengal which should be stopped. But he did not improve and nothing changed. He planned much more refined and ferocious attacks in the rural areas of the state through guerilla squads. Government was compelled to bring in Army. Charu maintained "....anyone who opposes the battle of annihilation cannot remain with us...."

And in order to curb indiscipline and maintain unity, Charu Mazumdar removed S.N. Singh, Shiv Kumar Mishra, Gurbax Singh, Ashim Chatterjee from the central committee of the party. Not only that he also removed Sushital Roy Choudhary from Liberation (mouth piece of the party) from the position of its editor. He also dismissed UP and Bihar state committee and Bengal-Bihar-Orissa Border Regional Committee.

Meanwhile, in retaliation, in November, 1971 in a secret Anti-Charu meeting, S.N. Singh passed a resolution against annihilation in the Bihar state committee of CPI-ML which caused 1st split in CPI-ML. S.N. Singh was elected general secretary and Charu Mazumdar Suniti Ghosh etc. were expelled from the party. Resultantly a new central committee by the name of PROVISIONAL CENTRAL COMMITTEE (PCC-CPI-ML) emerged.

Charu Mazumdar, who had come to Calcutta to meet his daughter who was studying MBBS, was arrested from his hideout on July 16,1972. He died in Lal Bazar police lock up within a week on July 28, 1972. It is believed that one Deepak Biswas led the police to Charu's hideout. Deepak was shot dead for his perfidy on July 3, 1981. With the death of Charu Mazumdar and separation of S.N. Singh from Charu's CPI-ML, violent incidents came down and with this, the violent phase of the Naxalite movement also came to an end. In fact CPI-ML began breaking up albeit temporarily.

It is not that Charu always wanted to annihilate the landlords or rich people. One of the incidents where Charu showed his inner-self was that Nawab Musharraf Hussain of Jalpaiguri who lived in Calcutta opened his doors to everyone during the 1943 Bengal famine. In 1967 during the Naxalbari revolution Charu Mazumdar remembered this and did not touch his 'estate'. (Indrajit Hazra in the *Hindustan Times* of October 25, 2009 article "Among the real Naxal's").

The movement was started with violence in Agrarian sector whose main characteristics were:

1. Forcible occupation of land.
2. Attack on government machinery mainly police.
3. Murder to create terror among the class enemy but to create sympathy among people.
4. To create demoralisation among the law and order machinery.
5. To get more people committeed to the cause of extremists/ Naxalites.

6. To conduct silent invisible activities which were more dangerous.

In the 1967 general elections, United Front government was voted to power. Alongwith CPM when peasants rose against the landlords under the leadership of Charu and Kanu, they expected support to peasant-working class-poor masses friendly government. But when the police suppressed their armed uprising, many CPM cadres questioned the action of the revolutionary party i.e. CPM. Those who split in the communist movement and gave birth to CPI-ML they rejected electoral politics.

A joint statement by the delegations representing the Kerala State Committee of CPI-ML and state Re-organising Committee of CPL-ML of Andhra Pradesh described the first phase of Naxal uprising as follows:

Quote "**8 :** By the end of 1970 at a time when the movement in many parts of India was facing set backs renegades like Satya Narayan Singh came out in open against the proletarian revolutionary line of comrade Charu Mazumdar. Next year some other opportunists like Ashim Chatterjee joined the camp of S.N.S. to form a parallel CPI (ML) just before Com. Charu Majumdars Martyrdom another set of opportunists under Kanu Sanyal's leadership came out in open with a statement challenging the leadership of Com. Charu Majumdar.

9. While all these renegades and opportunists were making attempts to disrupt the party from within and without revolutionary landless and poor peasant masses were making history by snatching rifles from the enemy forces at Magurjan and organising peoples army and building up liberated areas in Birbhum. Though these struggles suffered Indian revolutionaries to a higher level Com. Charu Majumdar pointed out that after Majurgan the struggle has entered a new stage of attacking the state machinery.

10. Facing all sorts of attacks from within and without by various types of renegades and opportunists and ruthless suppression at the hands of the reactionary ruling classes, the movement suffered serious setbacks. Revolutionary concious caders and rank and file of the party all over India, under the leadership of Com. Charu Majumdar were trying to overcome these difficulties and to build the party deep among the masses of workers and peasants. It was at this moment

that com. Charu Majumdar was arrested and became a martyr consequent to police torture. This was the most severe blow received by the revolutionary movement in India.

11. After the martyrdom of comrade Charu Majumdar the leadership of the party was usurped by the Mahadev Mukherjee clique which tried to distort Charu Majumdars Proletarian revolutionary line saying that it is invariably connected with Lin Piao who was declared to be a careerist and double-dealer by the tenth congress of CPC and this clique upheld Lin Piao (i.e. they became Pro Lin Piao). At that time when all these opportunists were making confusion, cadres and rank and file of the CPL-ML in different parts of India including some state committees like those of Kerala, Andhra Pradesh, Bihar etc. took a firm stand upholding the line of the tenth congress of CPC at the international level and comrade Charu Majumdar's Proletarian line as the guideline for Indian revolution. These state Committees and cadres independently came to the correct conclusion that only a leadership which upload the above mentioned line can lead the Indian revolution successfully throughout the end. Later events proved that this evaluation was absolutely correct (Anti-Lin Piao faction was formed by Vinod Mishra in 1974 who branded it as revisionist).

12. In Bihar, the movement was developing defeating the Lin Piaoist clique and upholding Com. Charu Majumdars proletarian Revolution line. They were trying to build up a peoples army and red areas. But comrade Subrato Dutta (Johar) who led the movement became a martyr in the end of 1975, the leadership of this movement slipped into the hands of revisionists who treacherously led that movements to the camp of Teng Hua Clique and subsequently to the revisionist camp of SNS Chandra Pulla Reddy Clique". Unquote.

The CPI(ML) Programme of 1970 described the state power in India as being in the hands of 'feudalism' comprador - bureaucrat - capitalism, imperialism and social imperialism. The twentieth Congress of CPSU advanced the formulation that in certain conditions a peaceful transition to socialism was possible. The CPC rejected this thesis. In India, the left faction of the CPI also questioned it. When the CPI (M) was formed, it asserted the classical Marxist idea that the ruling classes defend their power by force and that therefore, they cannot be overthrown by peaceful means. This affirmation of the notion of armed revolution was one of the ideological issues which differentiated the CPI(M) from CPI. (Manoranjan Mohanty - article Ideology and Strategy of the Communist Movement in India).

While Naxalites of different shades started regrouping and stepping up their class struggle, S.N. Singh who was almost isolated and had shattered health, had lost all hopes. Yet he organised a first ever public meeting in village Ekwari of Bhojpur district which was the operational area of Anti-Lin-Piao group of CPI-ML led by Vinod Mishra. The meeting of April 18, 1979 was presided over by Ashok Chatterjee of West Bengal and surprisingly attended by good number of Bhumihars of Bihar including one S.P. Singh who only a few years back had sought JP's help to quell or tame the Naxalites of the area. S.N. Singh actually planned to throw a surprise to Vinod Mishra by holding this public meeting. Singh gave a call for liberation of the exploited but rejected the theory of individual killing and violence. In early 1977 (after polls of March 1977) Singh was deputed by Janata Party leaders to rope in Kanu Sanyal and his friends to bring them to the fold of Parliamentary democracy by setting up Umadhar Singh as his Party's candidate for Lok Sabha election from Samastipur.

Difference within the PCC CPI-ML led to the resignation of S.N. Singh, General Secretary and the election of Chandra Pulla Reddy in his place. Difference arose on the question of identification of 'main enemy' a crucial aspect in determining the strategy of Marxist–Leninist party. S.N. Singh and his group insisted that the Soviet Social imperialism should be identified as the 'main enemy', which was also the position taken by the Chinese Communist party. This group also held the view that Soviet Social Imperialism had gained 'strong hold' over country's economy and the exploiting classes had sided with it. US Imperialism was less relevant in that context. But C.P. Reddy group held the view that both Soviet Social Imperialism as well as US Imperialism are two sides of the same coin though the former poses a greater threat than western imperialism. The word 'main enemy' had important and practical significance for both SN Singh faction as well as that of C.P. Reddy faction of CPL-ML. If the Soviet Social Imperialism is identified as the 'main enemy', then the Janata Party which had defeated the Congress Party headed by Mrs. Indira Gandhi had close relations with the Soviets – could be regarded as one with which the PCC CPI-ML need not engage in total confrontation and hence adopt an all out armed struggle programme. Instead, they thought, that was the time when the party could try and exploit opportunities for mass mobilisation in preparation for a 'people war' in the future when the contradiction between the Janata Government and the people become acute. But on the other hand, if both Soviet Social Imperialism and US Imperalism were regarded as 'principal enemies' though the former may be a greater threat, of the two threats the PCC CPI-ML would be expected to follow the more orthodox policy of making preparation for waging 'protracted warfare' in the immediate future. S.N. Singh faction and C.P. Reddy faction differed on the 'past attitude' also. While S.N. Singh united CPI-ML gave it board base anti-fascist party involving various components of Janata Party who later on threw Congress-I off the seat of power and expected the Janata Party to do good to the masses and changed its tactics in the sence that he never wanted violent activities in party, C.P. Ready group followed a line of armed violence in the forest areas of Godavari Valley in Andhra Pradesh. S.N. Singh followers were lesser in number in the Central Committee but more in Polit Bureau. Civil liberties movement also cropped up during this period. Bihar State Committee in its meeting on June 30-July 2, 1979 held at Bahragora (Singhbhum) decided by a majority to support Chandra Pulla Reddy. But S.N. Singh resigned on health ground. He was opposed by S.R. Bhaiji and Gurbux Singh both powerful central committee members. Even Moni Chakravorti another central committee member criticised him for carrying out armed action in Singhbhum district. Yet S.N. Singh was invited to attend the next meeting of the state committee at which his thesis 'on the present situation and the task of the party' was discussed but Andhra State committee member Pyala Vasudev Rao, CCM propagated against his views. Because of serious differences within the CPI-ML, S.N. Singh was, in fact, ousted from post of General Secretary of the Party. Two documents namely (a) 'A self-critical analysis of the evolution of the movement since its inception, following Naxalbari movement and (b) 'The People's Democratic Revolution and other immediate tasks' were also in circulation. The documents were basically critique of the policies followed by Charu Mazumdar and that there had been 'left deviation' in following the party line. Around this time China came out with "three world theory". They gave a call to make the decade of seventies as decade of liberation and to make the country 'liberated' by 1975, the failure to follow mass line and mobilise the people for a protracted people's war, overlooking the role of the national bourgeois in carrying forward the democratic revolution, different tactics to be applied to different areas according to the ground situation, realisation of importance of forest areas as 'Base areas', to realise the importance of snatching land to carry agrarian revolution to take necessary steps to form guerilla units and involve them directly in the struggles to convert them into People's Liberation Army (PLA), not to give importance to annihilation programme, training in the tactics of self defence, reject the United Front tactics and utilise contradictions among the ruling classes. Yet the documents paid tribute to Charu Mazumdar for generating the revolutionary movement which had resulted in rethinking process during his lifetime resulting in rejecting the left deviation by majority of revolutionary groups with the exception of Pro-Lin Piao faction. Bhaskar Nandy, central committee member of PCC CPI-ML had met the representatives of anti-Lin Piao faction to discuss the program to be launched jointly by both the parties. A joint meeting held in June 1979 issued a joint communique opposing the hegemony of the two super powers, countering aggressive designs of Soviet Social Imperialism preventing Indian expansion against its neighbours (reference was India's Bangladesh war against Pakistan) seeking normalisation of Sino-India's relations etc. Exhorting the need to organise the struggle of broad masses of peasantry against landlords and support to the movement of policemen for their democratic rights and better living conditions.

S.N. Singh was a strong follower of a broad based 'Anti-fascist front' involving several groups, which ultimately culminated in forming Janata party. When Janata Party actually came to power, S.N. Singh asked them that the masses had expectations of doing good for masses and therefore was of the opinion that now was the time when they should give up violence and instead work for mass organisations. S.N. Singh desired forging of a broad patriotic united front with Janata Party which actually meant, joining forces which were against Pro-Soviets.

S.N. Singh faction consisted of Santosh Rana, Bhaskar Nandi, Khokan Mazumdar, Dhrub Chaudhury etc. Around 1984 there was vertical split even in S.N. Singh group which will be taken up later. C.P. Reddy group consisted of S.R. Bhaiji, K.D. Sethi, Gurbax Singh, Baldev Singh, P. Vasudev Rao, Moni Chakravarti etc. After CP's death in 1985, the leadership of his group was taken over by his wife Nirmala Reddy but in that group also split took place.

Both the above referred documents desired unity of communist revolutionaries of all hues since all of them believed in common ideology of Marxism-Leninism Mao's thoughts with Socialist China as the base of world revolution, carrying on armed agrarian revolutionary struggle and Soviet Social Imperialism, Feudalism and Compradore Bureaucratic monopoly capitalism—as the main enemy, which needs to be crushed by main allies like peasants' workers and national bourgeoise knitted in People's Democratic Front. Their main task was to carry on armed agrarian revolution in concentrated rural areas of strategic importance by carefully chosen armed units of poor and middle class peasants who would create ground situation for a people's war to be carried for a long period of time with the main aim of destroying the authority of big landlords rather than annihilating them and establish authority of peasants and workers. Emphasis was also laid on creating a carefully chosen network of self defence staff etc. The documents also cautioned against S.N. Singh's line of joining parliamentarism which would be equally detrimental to the revolutionary tendencies as was the adventurist line of annihilation propounded by Charu Majumdar. C.P. Reddy branded the line taken by S.N. Singh as right deviation. But S.N. Singh, united CPI-ML maintained that the Janata party government was "patriotic and democratic" regime which had respected Civil liberties and as such deserved his party's support. He or his faction i.e. united CPI-ML did not entertain the call by other Naxal groups during mid 1977 to overthrow Janata Government and branded such moves as "sheer madness and left adventurism." He opined that participation in parliamentary election was on the basis of Com. Lenin's advise where in he said that in order to serve party's long-term goals, it should be combined with other goals. The united CPI-ML led by S.N. Singh exhorted its cadres to continue carrying on systematic campaign at all level for civil liberties by way utilising all legal opportunities to open up movements against anti-imperialists and anti feudal struggles with the sole aim of building a strong monolithic party. The party desired to widen and strengthen its mass base. A few important colleagues of S.N. Singh like Bhaskar Nandi, Dhrub Chowdhury and Khokan Majumdar who had formed a Unity Committee also desired to return to the fold of United CPI-ML on these stands and desired unity of all CPI-ML faction as a historic necessity.

United CPI-ML (formed in 1975), Unity Committee of the CPI-ML, unity centre of communist revolutionaries of India (UCCRI-ML) (formed in April 1975) and central organising committee of the CPI ML (COC-CPI-ML) were by and large, against Congress and Mrs. Gandhi. UCCRI-ML and the COC-CPI (ML) termed the above said strategic line of S.N. Singh and branded it as revisionist. But UCCRI-ML also split into Moni Guha @ Apurba Roy group having influence in West Bengal and Devullpalli Venkateshwar Rao group in Andhra Pradesh, D.V. Rao had been expelled from the secretaryship of the party in August 1976.

Earlier a small group known as 'Daksin Desh' converted itself on October 20,1969 into a group known as Maoist Communist Centre (MCC) led by Kanai Chatterjee and Amulya Sen who were also founding members. Later on in November 1987 there was a merger between People's War Group (PWG) and MCC. PWG was formed in March 1980 by Kondapalli Seetharamaiah in Andhra Pradesh. He was earlier a Lieutenant of Charu Mazumdar but formed PWG having followers in Maharashtra, Tamil Nadu and Andhra Pradesh.

The uprising in Naxalbari in 1967 was quelled by the police within two months. But it was emulated in Srikakulam in 1969 when red corridors were created in about 300 villages, again to be destroyed by the police by early 1970. The movement was crushed in Behra Gopiballabhpur in West Bengal in 1969-70 by the police but in case of Birbhum in West Bengal, Army was roped in since the police did not prove to be that effective. In 1971 CPI-ML developed differences among themselves and fissiparous tendencies surfaced. Differences over the question of annihilation of the class enemies which existed right from its birth in 1967 mainly led to the split of the movement through there were other factors like stand on China-India border dispute, question of the CPI-ML's participation in the elections and

Charu Majumdar positioning himself above the party and his dictatorial attitude, anarchism and terrorism propounded by Charu's line also contributed their bit towards split in the CPI-ML. Different leaders had different ideas of the movement and accordingly they started forming their own groups" faction. In July 1979, Kanu Sanyal said "the /party that we established is no longer there". It has been totally splintered. Now everyone wants to be a leader and each group is aiming to be the real CPI-ML. S.N. Singh had started questioning the wisdom of Charu Majumdar's approach of annihilation of class enemy. In November 1971 S.N. Singh split the party over this question only with which he did not agree and passed a resolution in the Bihar state committee against annihilation policy. He also had differences over the attitude of central leadership over the question of the liberation struggle in Bangladesh. S.N. Singh formed a provincial central committee of CPI-ML. With the formation of this PCC, CPI-ML had begun cracking up. Now there were two groups/factions of CPI-ML–one led by Charu Majumdar and another one led by S.N. Singh.

Soon after the death of Charu on July 28, 1972 not only the most violent phase of Naxal movement from 1967 to 1972 came to an end but the whole movement passed into a total state of collapse. The Marxism-Leninism inspired and influenced movement participated by peasants adopting hit and run tactics for land and dignity got consigned to the closed doors. The concept of liberation through annihilation of class enemies by squads of peasants guerillas went into oblivon. Yet the movement was not completely wiped out. It remained dormant for sometime and then saw further fragmentations and splits. The morale of the movement and the organisation suffered a blow because of various incidents. The massacre of naxalite youths in the Cossipore-Baranagore area and the failure to offer any resistance to it, the killing of 178 young men in that area (unofficial account raises this number to 500), the divisions within the naxalite movement/organisation and fratricidal clashes with CPM caders while both were under attack from the ruling party were some of the factors that weakend the movement both organisationally and politically. Mrs. Indira Gandhi swept polls in 1971 and 72 soon after the liberation of Bangladesh. The outcome of Bangladesh strengthened the ruling Congress. The 10th party congress of Communist Party of China CPC declared Lin Piao an outcast and surreptitiously mounted an attack on the cultural revolution striking at the very basis of Naxalism. The thesis had to be reformulated. Naxals who entered cities were arrested. Finally the death of Charu Majumdar brought down the curtain on the first phase of Naxal movement in India. (A.K. Roy in the Telegraph, June 2, 1987). By first halve of 1973 the movement had collapsed but towards the end of 1974 it showed signs of revival. Mr. Sumant Banerjee gives additional reasons (New Delhi, Sept 29–Oct 12,1980 issue) as: since CPI-ML ignored the important role of the industrial workers, they did not raise any echoes in the industrial areas and the government forces could swoop down the red bases in the villages and destroyed CPI-ML pockets. CPI-ML leadership also neglected the task of mobilising the wider masses – both in the villages and cities through the mass fronts and movements. Movements on economic issue like higher wages for agricultural labourers, forcible harvesting of crop etc. were ignored. In October 1970 Charu Majumdar underrated the power of the central government by stating "once the landless agricultural labourer's takes up a rifle in his hand, the panicky reactionary police and military will come en mass to surrender their rifles to the guerillas". The fact was that the reality did not conform to the leadership's naive expectations".

In West Bengal the developments of Chinese communist party's 10th congress held in July 1973 had is impacts. It had posthumously disgraced, denounced and branded Lin Piao, Mao's heir – appearant, as traitor Chou-en-Lai had derided him as the 'super traitor' who had planned to usurp Mao. In the 9th party congress of CPC, which can be said to be purely Lin Piao congress, Lin Piao was designated as heir–appearant to Mao. The 10th party congress deliberations had its impacts/repurcussions in CPI-ML and it split in Pro-Lin and Anti-Lin factions. CPI-ML leaders refused to toe the Peking line. Those who supported Lin Piao started forming separate committee and were known as Pio-Lin in December 1973. Y.S. Murthi group, Mahadev Mukherjee, Prof. Nishit Bhattacharya and Azizul Haq etc. followed Pro-Lin line. Anti-Lin line was followed by Vinod Mishra, K. Venu, K.N. Ramachandran, Swadesh Bhattacharya etc. They were called Anti Lin simply because they supported Mao and criticised Lin. In was only Charu Majumdar group formed in 1971 which got seperated from S.N. Singh, split into Anti and Pro-Lin groups. It had no impact on S.N. Singh group of PCC-CPI-ML whose leaders were S.N.

Singh himself, Chandra Pulla Reddy, Santosh Rana, Gurbux Singh, Khokan Majumdar, Baldev Singh and Bhaskar Nandi. Charu Majumdar group also splintered in a third group besides pro and Anti-Lin known as COC CPI-ML in Sept 1973. Even Pro-Lin group split into sub groups one known as Y.S. Murthi group, second as Mahadev Mukherjee group (formed in 1978) and Azizul Haq group (formed in 1978). Shanti Pal group which was formed in 1973 and was Pro-Lin maintained its independent identity. Anti-Lin Piao group led by Vinod Mishra, Swadesh Mukherjee, Anil etc also developed splits – the Kerala group whose leaders were K. Venu, K. Ramachandran, Aiynoor Vasu and K. Murthi. COC CPI-ML also split into Suniti Ghosh group Sohal group, K. Sitaramaih group, Rawoof group, and CLI (February 1979) group led by Ray Bahadur Rai and Dayanand. To begin with Prof. Suniti Ghosh, Kondapalli Sitaramaiah and K.G. Satyamurthi were together in Central Organising Committee (COC) CPI-ML but later on they split and formed their own groups.

S.N. Singh group which was formed in November 1971 merged in UNITED CPML and APRCP also merged into it in December 1974. In December 1977 it formed PCC CPI-ML after merger with UNITY COMMITTEE. Its leaders were S.N. Singh, Santosh Rana, Chandrapulla Reddy, Gurubux Singh, Khokan Majumdar, Bhaskar Nandi etc and had influence in Andhra Pradesh, West Bengal, UP, J&K, Orissa, Delhi, HP, Maharashtra, Assam,Tripura, Tamil Nadu and Kerala.

Andhra Pradesh Coordination Committee of Communist Revolutionaries (APCCCR) (formed in February 1969) with Tarimala Nagi Reddy as its convenor also split - APRCP formed in 1971 got merged with united CP, Marxist Leninist in December 1974. Six of Nine members of APCCCR were arrested in Madras in 1971 and it split into 3 main groups in 1973. APCCCR with C.P. Reddy as secretary, united centre for communist revolutionaries UCCRI led by D. Venkeshwar Rao and Revolutionary Organisation of Communists (ROC). Kondapalli Sitaramaiah broke away from ROC in 1975 and formed People's War Group (PWG). ROC further split into Pro-Lin Piao group of Mahadev Mukherjee and IPF Indian People's Front of Vinod Mishra, Nagbhushan Patnaik. In 1982 UCCRI was divided into 2 factions—original one led by Kenkeshwar Rao and the other by

Manan Rama Rao. APCCR itself turned into UCCRI-ML, WBCCR and CUC-ML also merged into it in April 1975. UCCRI -ML later on split into Anil Mukherjee group and D.V. Rao group in August 1976. APCCCR had taken a stand that was strategically different from that of CPI-ML.

After Charu Mazumdar's death, Mahadev Mukherjee took over the leadership of the party which came to be known as CPI-ML (Pro Lin Piao). But over the damning of Lin Piao by the Chinese Communist Party in 1973, SUBRATO DUTTA@ JOHAR took over as General Secretary of the Pro-Charu and Anti-Lin Piao Maoists. Both Anti and Pro Lin Piao factions, were formed in 1973, Subrato Dutt known to the police as 'Kolika' and christianed by the peasants of Bhojpur, where he consolidated Naxalite successes as 'Comrade Johar' (sacrifice). Subrato Dutt was killed in a police encounter in the village of Babubandh in Sahar Block of Bhojpur on November, 29-1975. His bleeding body was removed by the peasants without enabling police to lay its hands on the body, and secretly cremated it on the banks of some river. Mahadev Mukherjee followed the line of Lin Piao. The leadership of Charu's group after Subrato Dutt's demise passed on to Vinod Mishra in 1975. Mahadev Mukherjee had resigned in August 1978 over the annihilation issue.

S.N. Singh etc had formed a United CPI-ML in the year 1975 but on the question of participation of in the elections, besides stand on China, this group also developed cracks in the party. The group led by S.N. Singh was opposed to Vinod Mishra and Mahadev Mukherjee though Mishra and Mukherjee were also ranged across each other on the question of Lin Piao. S.N. Singh group which was known as pro-election group showed sympathy with the CPM government of West Bengal which was not liked by Chandra Pulla Reddy. He separated and ousted S.N. Singh etc from his group. It had influence in the hilly trijunction of Tamil Nadu, Andhra Pradesh and Karnataka. Reddy had maintained the strategy of keeping his party underground and that of carrying on armed revolution.

Imposition of emergency in June, 1975 saw large scale arrests of CPI-ML cadres of all the groups. Many top leaders of CPI-ML were killed in encounters with the police in Bihar and Andhra Pradesh. Emergency was lifted in early 1977 and general elections were held in March. S.N. Singh on April 10, 1977 declared that CPI-ML would participate in the coming Assembly elections. Soon after, Kanu Sanyal, Jangal Santhal, Ashim Chatterjee and Souren Bose who were in Jail found merit in S.N. Singh's thinkings and called upon people of West Bengal to vote and support CPI (M) led UF candidate in election. However, UCCRI-ML and Unity Committee (ML) did not agree with S.N. Singh proposition. Masses unhappy with Emergency Excesses did not vote for Congress Party which had been ruling the country uninterruptedly for thirty years and instead a loose conglomerate under the banner of Janata Party was voted to power. Naxalites took advantage of the situation and gave a call to boycott the elections and incited their cadres to create violence, disturb elections, kill policemen and snatch their weapons etc. All the tirade was directed against the Congress Party in general and Mrs. Gandhi in particular.

In West Bengal the party split in 7-8 groups, in Kerala into four major factions and in Andhra Pradesh in eight groups. Though all the groups drifted form the parties original ideological moorings, all of them retained their anti-Soviet and anti-authoritarian stance. Some of them even accepted electoral politics which was against the tenets of CPI-ML. Santosh Rana of S.N. Singh faction of CPI-ML had participated in West Bengal Assembly elections in June, 1977 and won. This set the course in favour of Ballot Box. Comparatively, most of naxalite groups discarded violence and individual annihilation. S.N. Singh groups known as PCC CPI-ML, encouraged by Santosh Rana's Victory, set up other candidates in Lok Sabha elections in January, 1980 PCC CPI-ML group and that of Vinod Mishra's central committee were the major ML parties in West Bengal. Charu's group was led by Mahadev Mukherjee whereas Lin Piao group was led by Aziz-ul-Haq. The central committee of communist revolutionaries led by D.V. Rao formed in August , 1976 and Shanti Roy toed the lines of Maoist Communist Centre (MCC). On the formation of left front government in West Bengal in mid 1977 about 200 Naxals were arrested and 11 cadres members of PCC CPI-ML were killed.

In the year 1977 there were 69 violent incident involving Naxalites and 21 deaths. In 1978, 163 incidents took place wherein 40 deaths occurred. In 1979, 233 incidents and 62 deaths and in 1980, 305 incidents and 84 deaths occurred. But West Bengal government released those Naxalites held in detention without specific charges. In February, 1981 in West Bengal there were a number of cases of gun snatching incidents in West Dinajpur district (77 gun were snatched but 55 recovered). On September 26, 1981 a special branch sub-inspector of police was killed by Naxalites near Calcutta.

Though Naxalbari movement took its birth in West Bengal state, it became fragmented and disorganised force soon after but it spread to other states of Indian Union. A group known as Provisional Central Committee (PCC CPI-ML) came into existence which was more known than others. Since 1977 most of the Naxalite factions had given up violence and the policy of individual or class enemy annihilation. There were two major groups of CPI-ML—PCC CPI-ML and the other of Vinod Mishra whose faction was known as Central Committee, AICCCR All India Coordination Committee of Communist Revolutionaries came in existence in November, 1967 and before formation of CPI-ML in April, 1969, Kunnikal Narayan had formed a Naxalite group separately in 1968 in Kerala. Ajitha was with him then. Parimal Dass Gupta group named itself as coordination Committee in 1972 in West Bengal.

CPI-ML after its formation broke up in Kosal Ram Dass group in 1970, Ch. Tajeshwar Rao group in 1971 in Andhra Pradesh, APUC of Kolla Venkaiha in January 1978 in Kerala, Liberation Party of India in April 1978 in Orissa and Unity Liberation Party of India in April 1978 in Orissa and Unity Committee in 1978 in Andhra and in Orissa under PBM Patnaik.

S.N. Singh group had separated itself in November 1971 from original CPI-ML of April 1969. It also got divided in groups like Provisional Centre in 1978 and Kishan group in 1978, CROC in June, 1978 under Bhola Chakravarti and Keshar Singh, OCCRI in July, 1978 under Ashim Chatterjee and Jangal Santhal and Kanu Sanyal, Central Team of CPI-ML in 1978 (it was known as anti-S.N. Singh group as well. Subhash Mani and D.S. Dosanjh were the leaders of this group. In West Bengal yet another group by name of communist party of Indian Union-ML existed in July, 1977 whose leaders were Sudhanshu Niyogi and Diptimoy Roy Choudhury but their strength of membership was negligible. In J&K there existed a unit by name of Democratic Conference in June, 1964, which was Pro-CPM but in

1967 it turned Naxalite. It also broke into democratic conference (Sethi group) in 1968 and democratic conference (Saraf group) in 1968 which turned into Pro-S.N. Singh group in 1972 and ultimately became Pro-Charu Mazumdar group in 1972. Earlier K.D. Sethi, Gulam Mohammad Malik and R.P. Saraj were together. But later on R.P. Saraf was joined by Abdul Kabir Wani and K.D. Sethi while K.D. Sethi became Pro-S.N. Singh. Ram Piara Saraf group had influence in Haryana and Delhi besides J&K. Far away in Kerala, K.P.R. Gopalan group which came into existence in August 1968 turned itself into Communist Unity Centre in May 1972 and merged with A.V. Angan group which ultimately became communist Bolshevik Party in November 1978. The Unity Centre of Communist Revolutionaries of India (Marxist-Leninist) UCCRI-ML was also formed in April, 1975.

Santosh Rana was the first Naxalite who favoured parliamentary democracy, contested elections and won assembly seat in June, 1977. S.N. Singh was influenced by the fact of his being elected and he chose the course of favouring ballot box. However the movement split and about a dozen faction cropped up in West Bengal in late sixties and early seventies. Encouraged by the success of Santosh Rana, this group set up a number of candidates in January 1980 Lok Sabha elections. Workers of this group even campaigned for Janata Party candidates.

Kanu Sanyal, the hero of 1967 Naxalbari uprising set up an organisation under the name of coordination committee of communist revolutionaries but his close friends Sourin Bose and Ashim Chatterjee chose not to join it and instead maintained friendly relation with the CPM. When Jyoti Basu government came to power in July, 1977 only 8 lakh of 35 lakh sharecroppers (Bargadars) were registered. Between August, 1977 and March, 1978 they registered another eight lakhs. The aim to register the sharecroppers was to make it difficult for the landlords to evict them. In order to hasten the process of registration 'operation BERGA' was launched in June 1978 with the aim to register all Bargadars by June 30, 1979. But because of Floods which swept away over 15000 people and affected another two million, the operation could not be carried on any further. West Bengal government allotted the land to how many SC and Tribals is a question. But one thing is sure that the Jyoti Basu government had good intentions. It had amended the Land Reforms Act which put the onus of proving that a cultivator is not sharecropper on the landlord. Under the law, the landlord was required to issue a receipt for the produce he received from the bargadars. Immediately after Naxalbari uprising (1967-70) about five lakh acre of land was distributed but out of these three lakh acres was taken back by the landlords between 1972 and 1977. In July, 1977 the Left Front government redistributed 1.5 lakh acres and began distributing 2.5 lakh acre of land that were vested with the government. Meanwhile landlords approached the court and the work came to a halt. There have been instance of forceful occupation of land by zealous Left Front supporters in late sixties but Jyoti Basu claimed that the allegation of 'the forceful occupation of land even in the late sixties was essentially the discovery of their political opponents. (Interview by Gautam S.G. Vohra with Jyoti Basu in the *Times of India,* December 3, 1978). In an interview with Ms. Parvathi Menon, Jyoti Basu replied to a question–What has been impact of land reform on the lives of peasanty?—His reply was : Quote "The peasants had been demanding two-thirds of the share of the produce. So a very big movement took place in which we played a major role. Soon after the Panchayats were formed we could not find the land documents. The landlords (Jotedars) had distributed land in various names, even to their cats and dogs! The Kisan Sabha helped us in this big struggle for land distribution. They said if land documents could not be found, it did not matter, as they know which land belonged to whom. By 1978 we had distributed surplus land and enforced the rule of two-thirds of the share. This was operation 'BERGA'. It was a great success. Unquote. *The Hindu* January 18, 2010 article by Parvati Menon.

The trend that appeared on the political scenario of Naxalite movement after its failure during the first phase (1967-72) gave impression that (i) the Naxalites of all hues desired unity among all Naxalite factions after rectifying the past mistakes particularly after 1977 when they re-emerged in order to form genuine communist party of all groups that were part of AICCCR but refused to join CPI-ML should be brought back was the opinion that surfaced. (ii) boycotting of parliamentary democracy i.e., non-participation in elections and (iii) keep all the activities/movements of the party underground and secret and continue with earlier programmes and strategies.

Largest concentration of Naxals of all shades right from their re-emergence in 1977 was in Krishnanagar. Once the emergency clamped by Indira Gandhi was over and the Naxals were released from prisons in 1977, CPI-ML held an open session urging all Naxalite of different groups to unite. Ramen Shah, leader of the Second Central Committee of CPI-ML lead by Azizul Haq and Nishit Bhattacharya, continued to dominate the political scene in Krishnanagar and its neighbouring areas till his (Shah's) arrest in 1982. Ramen Shah, known for his militancy had joined the Second Central Committee in 1978 and taught the anti-social elements of the area and started enjoying mass support. Ramen Shah took over the control of local fisheries, mango orchards etc. that were controlled by local toughs. But his group used the income received from these properties for their own use resulting in bloody clashes with people opposing them and making Krishnanagar a scene. There were murders in quick succession. The situation in the area was so bad that one could not venture out of his house after evening hours were over. Every other day 'Bandhs' were called resulting in tremendous difficulties to the area inhabitants. After 1977 various Naxalite factions realised their mistake in boycotting elections and some of them corrected themselves to participated in parliamentary process stating that the struggle should also be build up even through parliament. They also laid emphasis on mass and democratic movements as well as open activities and encouraged civil liberties movement which gave a wider base to Naxals. Naxalite leader Nagbhushan Patnaik wrote about the Left govt. "The LF has been able to create an illusion among the masses even though it has not brought any radical changes in the state. But through its reforms it has been able to gain the support of a section of the rural poor, who had earlier been neglected by the Congress-I." He points out that for the communist revolutionaries working in WB, it is much more difficult to fight the Left Front than those working against the Congress-I in Bihar. For, he explained, in Bihar the land relations and the exploitation by the feudal lords and rich landlords are much more open and blunt and even if a political party tries to implement the 20 point programme in the state it would seem a revolutionary step. Whereas, in West

Bengal, though, the rich landlords continue to be benefitted by the land reforms of the Left Front government, apparently it seems that a number of the poor and landless peasants have got the benefits of these reforms. Here the explanation is on a much more subtle level and therefore, the task of the communist revolutionaries is much more difficult in West Bengal." (The retreat by Pranay Sharma in Focus.)

However, by the year 1980, around thirty (30) Naxalite group were active all over having membership of about 30000 cadres.

Reasons for Failure of Naxalite Movement (1967-1975)

Dr. Sailen Debnath writes "the Naxalite movement, though continued intensively from 1967 to the middle of 1970 and surfaced after same years, could not go a long way achieving anything commandable because of the following reasons":

1. The Naxalites wanted to surround the towns and cities by the villages i.e., they wanted to encircle the urban centers with organised peasant forces of the villages. If the peasant militia could have occupied the cities, according to Charu Mazumdar, the so called bourgeois government would fall making the passage to the coming of a socialist government; but the Naxalites could not and did not came up to a stage capable of organising the peasants and thereby encircling the towns.
2. Mazumdar gave sole importance to secret organisation and training of its members for the purpose of eliminating the class enemies. As the Naxalites did not have mass level organisation, they lacked mass support. Only with select few armed elements not properly educated in political line no big thing could be done.
3. "Khatam" or the action of eliminating the so called class enemies in villages was a wrong principle of political mobilisation by individual murder of select few people whose political class-character was never adjudged by their socio-economic conditions, and the properties they possessed, but very often only by their political affiliation or by name and colour of the party or parties they directly or indirectly belonged to for a long or a short period of time. As for example, in Jalpaiguri and Alipurduar

they killed some petty jotedars who otherwise could have been comrades in actions against the capitalist or could be friends in a revolution for radical changes.

4. Recruitment in the Naxalite party was never done on proper judgement and scrutiny of the political characters and behaviours of the recruits. It so happened that many people only to feast on their animosities with their personal enemies got recruited in the Naxalite party only to utilize the help of the Naxalites to have their personal enemies in the neighbourhood killed on the basis of pseudo-identification of them as class enemies.
5. In many cases dreaded criminals too enrolled themselves in the Naxalite party with the objective of getting fire arms and to train themselves in the manufacture and use of fire arms. Thus very soon the party turned to be an organisation of professional criminal outfits who soon deserted the party after their training period had been over or the cherished objective of owing armaments had been met or realised. Many of these criminals with fire arms soon turned to be dacoits and in many cases they informed the police all about the hidden training centres of the Naxalites and their main purpose in doing so was to have the original Naxalites arrested or else they themselves might fall victims of the Naxalites target as approvers in favour of the government.
6. The ruling Congress party inserted their supporters inside the unguarded and porous Naxalite organisation for the purpose of knowing and finishing its secret bases and arresting its supporters and in the same way, the personnels of the government intelligence branch and police too in disguise of Naxalite sympathisers got into the party inner organisation and rounded most of its leaders including Charu Mazumdar into the Jail. Thus police had information all about the movements of Charu Mazumdar after he had gone underground in 1970, and he was nabbed in Calcutta in July, 1972. The end of his life came in the Jail in some days after his arrest; and how he had to pass through the gate of death, most probably in the night of 27th or 28th July, 1972, nobody except the police and the government could know properly, of course, it was told from the side of the government that he died of heart attack.

7. Ordinary people in village were terrified at the brutal and gruesome ways they killed the fellow villagers vilifying them as class enemies. As for example, at Bholardabri in Alipurduar they killed Rajan Pandit who was a refugee from East Pakistan and arduously was running a family of 12 dependents. By any means he was no class enemy at all. In another case, they killed a person, chopped his head off the torso and hanged the head and the torso down the branches of trees with ropes in two separate places, the horrible sights of which cast a gloom on the faces of bemoaning villagers. Certainly after that they could count no support from the villagers at all. (Wikipedia, the free encyclopedia : downloaded from http://en.wikipedia. org/ wiki/Naxalite.)

Describing the status of Naxalites before 1975, A.K. Roy former member of parliament from Dhanbad writes in his article under the caption "spring thunder and after" published by the Telegraph of June 2, 1987; "The Naxalites had nothing to do with legislatures. But the parliament and state legislatures had a lot to do with them. There was no Naxalite member in the House, but there were constant references to them. The number of times the Naxalites figured in the press was a record in itself. While plotting the Land Reform Bill in the Bihar Assembly the revenue minister pointed to the 'writing on the wall'. While addressing the Chamber of Commerce, the finance minister referred to the 'danger ahead'. Agitated at not getting files from his subordinates, a secretary to the government shouted that only Naxalites could set his office right. The beleaguered chief minister of Bihar startled his favour-seeking audience by announcing that the Naxalites were correct and the poor could expect nothing from the system. There were whispers among dissidents ruling party members about contacting Naxalites in order to teach the ministerialists a lesson. Panicky armed guards shouted 'Halt' at any person approaching the Patna treasury after some Naxalite slogans appeared on it walls. Ideology could be a material force if it gripped the mind of the people. So said Marx and the Naxalites proved it to be so. Revolution was a festival for the people, so wrote Mao, and the Naxalites demonstrated it to be so. Thousands of young men and women fanned out from cities into villages. The timetable for the revolution was drawn up. The landless peasants were to be organised. A red army was to be formed. A war had to be declared against the bourgeois establishment. And the war had to be won. And everything was to be done within 1975. Even if it was mere dream, those who had cast their lot with the movement believed that it was dream worth living and dying for. And many died not only cadres, but leaders too. And they died unheard unsung and even unaccounted for : on the fields of Naxalbari, the hills of Mushahari and the Jungles of Srikakulam. Nowherc in the world did so many top leaders of so new a party lay down their lives in so short a time to uphold their socio-political convictions. Thousands of others languished in jails until the political order changed in the country. An officer of the Hazaribagh Central Jail, accused of killing 16 Naxalite prisoners in Jail and facing a departmental inquiry on that score, revealed before this, writer (A.K. Roy) that he saw smiles on the lips of the dead Naxalites boys. What was it that taught them to die with a smile, he asked rhetorically. Unquote.

But the end of emergency was followed by lifting of the ban on the extremists groups in 1977 which made the leaders of the Naxal groups re-think their ideological stand, policies and programmes. Almost all the groups laid emphasis of ideological re-education of their respective cadres and launch a well organised and well directed propaganda campaign to popularize their revolutionary ideology among masses of different strata.

Around six major and thirty minor groups existed at the end of the year 1977. There was differences of opinion and no unity among them. Each leader wanted to have his own group. At the same time it prevailed up some same leaders that without forging unity, among Naxal groups, the future of their movement would not be very bright in India. This was precisely the reason that some of the Naxal groups, named their respective groups as 'unity group of CPI-ML' or 'United CPML' adopting moderate stand. It branded the Janata government as 'patriotic and democratic' and in April 1977 rejected any call to overthrow this government as 'sheer madness' and 'left adventurism' and also admitted that its earlier stand of not participating in elections was wrong.

The central committee of the United CP-ML after pinpointing its shortcomings set itself the task of :

(i) participating in civil liberties campaigns at all levels.

(ii) availing of all opportunities of legal remedies to carry on anti-imperialist and anti-feudal struggle.

(iii) build up a single united CPML party.

The shortcomings it appropriated for itself were :

(i) Not to carry on or continue the task of armed struggle for the time being because masses were not revolution-conscious.

(ii) Regularly occurring impediments in Naxal movement.

(iii) Factionalism tendencies among the revolutionaries.

Unity Committee of CPML led by Bhaskar Nandi, Dhruv Chowdhuri and Khokan Mazumdar appreciated the line adopted by S.N. Singh's united CPML and decided to merge into it around 1977.

CPI-ML had appealed on April 22, 1978 on the occasion of the foundation day of the party that all communist revolutionaries should unite under the party's flag.

In February 1979 the total strength of Naxalites of all shades was estimated be around 15,000, publishing 70 periodicals, having 200 front organisations among students and teachers in High School, Colleges, Universities etc. The bases were shifting from rural areas to urban centres. Naxalites were active in West Bengal, Andhra Pradesh, Bihar and Punjab. The position of main Naxalite factions were :

1. Pro Lin of CPI-ML –1300 members, largest following in rural areas of West Bengal, Andhra, Bihar and a small pocket in Delhi.
2. Anti Lin of CPI-ML–3500 members, largest base in Kerala sizeable membership in Bihar, Bengal, small following in UP and Punjab.
3. COC CPI-ML–1500 members. Main concentration in Andhra Pradesh.
4. Original Central Committee — about 4000 members (*The Statesman,* February 4, 1979).

The following major groups of ML existed in West Bengal : during that period :

1. PCC CPI-ML : Kanu Sanyal.
2. PCC CPI ML : Liberation group led by Vinod Mishra – It was more violent than others. It even broke statues in Calcutta.
3. PCC CPI-ML : Sadhan Sarkar.
4. PCC CPI-ML : Led by Santosh Rana and Bhaskar Nandi.
5. Party Unity group of CPI-ML.
6. Second Central Committee of CPI-ML led by Azizul Had and Rehman Shah.
7. Second Central Committee of CPI-ML led by Subir Talukdar.
8. Indian People's Front – an umbrella group.
9. Central Committee led by Mahadev Mukherjee.
10. Communist Revolutionary Legue led by Ashim Chatterjee.
11. Central Team.
12. Marxist Leninist group.

Naxal movement though took its birth in West Bengal but it took roots in Andhra Pradesh swiftly and flourished there. Bihar, Orissa were other states where Naxalism spread rather quickly. By mid-80 at all India level, by and large, the following Marxist Leninist factions were functioning :

1. PCC CPI-ML : S.N. Singh.
2. PCC CPI-ML : Chandra Pulla Reddy.
   (i) CD Reddy group : K. Rajanna Faction in Andhra Pradesh.
   (ii) CD Reddy group : Phani Bagchi Faction in Andhra Pradesh.
3. Pro-Lin Piao : Nishit Bhattacharya and Azizul Haque faction, Mahadev Mukherjee faction, Shanti Pal faction.
4. Anti-Lin Piao : Vinod Mishra.
5. UCCRI-ML : D.V. Rao faction, Shanti Roy faction, Parallel Central Committee, Harbhajan Singh Sahi, Sohan faction, Ranjit Singh Sohan.
6. CRC CP ML : K. Venu.
7. CPI – ML : (People's War Group) K. Seethaaramiah.

8. Democratic Conference (C.P. Reddy) : K.D. Sethi.
9. OCCR : Kanu Sanyal.
10. Maoist Communist Centre : Amulya Sen and Kanai Kamal Chatterjee.
11. CLI-ML : Raj Bahadur Rai, Harsh Vardhan Chaddha.
12. COC CP-ML : Jagjit Singh Sohal.
13. COC CP-ML : Suniti Ghosh.
14. Central Team of CPI–Ml–Sudhir Roy and Harinder Singh.
15. Communist Unity Centre – Sadhan Chakraborty.
16. Unity Organisation of the CPI-Ml – Bhaboni Roy Choudhury.
17. Unity Committee : D.S.M. Patnaik.
18. Coordination Committee of Communist Revolutionaries – Parimal Das Gupta.
19. Democratic Conference – (Pro Charu Group – Ram Piara Saraj).
20. APUC : Kolla Venkaiah.
21. Communist Bolshevik Party : KPR Gopalan.
22. KTUC : K.P. Kosal Ramdas.
23. Kunnikal Narayanan Group : Ms. Ajitha.
24. Communist Ghadar Party of India – Gurdev Singh.
25. Calcutta 24 Pargana – Burdwan Nadia Anchalik Bureau.
26. West Bengal State Committee of CPI-ML – Sudhir Roy.

The ideology, tactics and the cult of violence practised by today's Maoists have been criticised by the three veterans of Naxal movements who were initially responsible for Naxal uprising in late sixties. The three living legends Kanu Sanyal, Santosh Rana and Asim Chatterjee have denounced the present day Naxals. (Kanu Sanyal has also expired). Viewing the violence in Lalgarh, Kanu said "they are indulging in wanton killings of innocent villagers. Communism does not approve of this." Santosh Rana says, "They will not win. They will not be able to achieve their goal." He feels Maoists have damaged the Lalgarh peasant uprising. "Initially the uprising was so strong that the government was forced to withdraw forces. The formation of maoist hit squads, their occupation of villages and declaration of free zones have invited state repression." Asim Chatterjee holds the view "Their struggle is based on underdevelopment, not economic exploitation, as was the case during Naxalbari revolt. The maoists are targeting the state machinery; this is not the way to develop a people's war. Political struggles can not be launched with guns. The way Maoists are killing poor people in the name of fighting CPM is suicidal." (*The Hindustan Times,* February 9, 2010).

Ravi Sharma, a top class Naxalite and a member of the Central Committee of CPI-Maoist, after his arrest on October 10, 2009 along with his wife B. Anuradha told the police "that he did not regret killing of thousands of people. During a revolution one does not care how many are killed, only the goal should be achieved". Ravi Sharma is a agricultural scientist hailing from Andhra Pradesh.

Agricultural land, poverty, oppression etc. may be a few causes that give birth to 'Moaism' but they are not necessarily the main causes. Moaism flourishes because of a handful people who take advantage and exploit these issues to gather strength with the aim of capturing state power. With the help of these poor people, who get incited and led to believe that the whole would be theirs if they join the movement and actively participate, these handful people take on the administrative machinery of the state by way of annihilating the class enemies. But their ultimate aim is to capture state power and then rule — to their own advantage. Poor and innocent tribals are swayed by their false promises. On one side Maoist themselves have been preventing development works and improvement of communication links while on the other they have been systematically destroying school building, preventing school going children from going to schools, preventing road building process and damaging a lot of other facilities meant for these very tribals. They would be doing yeoman service if they prevent injustice to people done by anybody– any state organ or state authority, help poor people, tribals with schools, hospital and other development works. People would automatically choose and nominate them to rule.

2

Various CPI-Marxist-Leninist Outfits (1967-2000)

1. People's War Group (PWG)
2. Maoist Communist Centre (MCC)
3. Central Organising Committee (COC)
4. United CP-ML
5. Pro-Lin Piao group of CPI-ML
6. Anti-Lin Piao
7. CPI-ML (Liberation group)
8. Communist Organisation of India (COI)
9. Organising Committee of Communist Revolutionaries (OCC RI-ML)
10. All India Re-organising Committee of CPI-ML (AIROC)
11. Unity Centre of Communist Revolutionaries (UCC RI-ML)
12. CPI-ML (Party Unity)
13. CPI-ML (Jan Shakti)
14. CPI-ML (Red Flag)
15. CUC/MUC
16. Indian People's Front
17. Split in PCC CPI-ML (S.N. Singh faction)
18. Split in CP Reddy group of CPI-ML

19. The movement in early eightees.
    - (i) Tamil Nadu
    - (ii) Kerala
    - (iii) Bihar
    - (iv) Punjab
    - (v) West Bengal
    - (vi) Andhra Pradesh
20. Frontal Outfits that came to Naxal-aid.

PEOPLE'S WAR GROUP (PWG CPI-ML)

In Andhra Pradesh after the Girijan uprising in Srikakulam that started in the early 60s was suppressed by the police by 1970 and shooting down Naxal leaders like Vempatapu Satyanarayana and Adibhatla Kailasam on July 10, 1970, revolutionaries kept on itching for giving vent to their suppressed feelings by way of starting a movement which ultimately took shape in the form of an association known as Central Organising Committee (COC) formed by Kondapalli Seetharamiah, K.G. Satyamurthy and Suniti Ghosh in December 1972 with the purpose of mass mobilisation. The first armed struggle was launched in Srikakulam on November 25, 1968 with the attack on a house of a landlord in Parvatipuram by Nagbhushan Patnaik etc., alongwith 250 tribals and looted foodgrain, destroyed documents etc., To begin with Kondapalli was with Charu Mazumdar. He encouraged party cadres to loot and snatch money from affluent people and business groups which resulted in his arrest on April 26, 1977 in Nagpur. Police intercated a vehicle carrying arms and traced the source to Kondapalli. The guns were meant to be used for an attack on a police station in Koratla where some party activists were interned. He was released on conditional bail on October 19, 1978. He was later granted bail by Andhra Pradesh High Court. But in February 1980 he jumped bail and started agitating and organising underground activities by himself remaining underground. Thus he broke away from COC and formed Peoples War Group (PWG) of CPI-ML on April 20, 1980 on the bank of Godavari in Karimgunj district Andhra Pradesh State Committee of CPI-ML turned into CPI-ML Peoples War Group. Kondapalli Seetharamaiah himself became the first general secretary of the underground set up which became most violent. PWG had a 13-member Politburo. Muppala Laxman Rao succeeded

Kondapalli Sitaramiah. Differences arose between them that fully surfaced in August 1991 Central Committee meeting which reached point of no-return at the party plenum in October 1991. In fact PWG suffered a major set back in the year 1992 in the sense that six of its front organisations were banned on May 20, 1992. Mupala Laxman Rao @ Ganpathi who became general secretary after ousting Kondapalli was a former teacher. Prasant Bose @ Kishenda, a more militant Naxal became its member. Politburo has a Central Committee, Central Military Commission and a Central Technical Commission. Under it are Zonal and State Committees, District/Division Committees and squad Area Committee. Their plan was to liberate 35% of India by the year 2000.

From the very beginning, Kondapalli, leader of PWG believed in annihilation of class enemy, kidnapping of government officials, adopting violence, destroying public property etc. After police crushed down the Srikakulam uprising (1968-69) in 1970. Naxalites largely took to underground activities mainly confined to Khammam and Srikakulam districts. It gained momentum after Emergency was lifted in 1977 and one of the result was formation of a Naxalite group-PWG. T. Nagi Reddy alongwith a few other Naxal leaders was arrested by police in December 1969. He had earlier formed Andhra co-ordinating committee (an Andhra unit of AICCCR) which was disaffiliated by All India Co-ordination Committee of Communist Revolutionaries. While Naxal struggle in Srikakulam was being carried forward, T. Nagi Reddy led the movement in Warangal, Khamman etc. through Revolutionary Communist Committee of Andhra Pradesh in 1969. After his arrest, the leadership was taken over by Chandra Pulla Reddy. On May 20, 1981, it so happened that police fired on a gathering of Gond tribals at Indravalli in which 13 Gonds were killed and this incident provided ammunition and proved a boon for PWG which exploited it to spread its mass base among tribals after siding with them. Moreover, Kondapalli was a dedicated, devoted and dynamic leader. He was again arrested on January 2, 1982 for a second time at Begampet Railway Station at Hyderabad in a murder case. While undergoing treatment in Osmania Hospital in Hyderabad he escaped on January 4, 1984 from police custody in which he was helped by I.V. Sambasiva Rao, Mukku Subba Reddy and N.C. Shivaji.

Split in PWG emerged in 1987 after which new groups like CPML–Jan Shakti, CPML-Red Flag emerged. Kondapalli formed separate fronts for different sections of society like Ryot Coolie Sangham, Radical Students Union etc., which became very active. He established close links with Andhra Pradesh Civil Liberties Committee (APCLC) to propagate against the state repression. Revolutionary Writers Association (RWA) was yet another important front that became highly successful in propagating its revolutionary ideology. Meanwhile PWG was held responsible for 32 murders, 22 dacoites and 284 offences in 1984 alone. It liquidated three members of rival Chandra Pulla Reddy group. In 1988 (January to May) it had done 55 murders compared to 77 in 1987. Kandapolli re-appeared in December 1990 and addressed PWG central committee and inaugurated a memorial.

In 1979 December, January Myrdal son of Gunnar Myrdal, a noble prize winner of 1974, travelled to forest of Khamman and East Godavari in the Company of Gummadi Narasaiyya, a Naxalite MLA from Pyala Vasudev Rao faction of CP Reddy group of CPI-ML from Illandu, one of the disturbed areas, for 10 days. Place called Illandu, wrote G.S. Radha Krishna, was a relic of the past where the Subedari system of the Nizam was still followed. Nearly 20,000 acres of land in Tekulapalli area alone 'held' by 75 pattedars who were in the Nizam's Army collected fee from their 'tenants' who have been paying the land tax for two generations now.[1]

Kondapally and K.G. Satyamurthy harbored differing views on ideological issues as also the functioning of the party. While the former rejected the move for modification of the concepts put forward by Mao-Tse-Tung including the 3-world theory, Satyamurthy held the view that the theory was of no significance in relation to current times in mid-eightees. He also accrued Kondapalli of flouting the norms of basic tenets of democratic centralism. In return, Kondapalli accused Satyamurty of trying to load the Central Committee with his supporters. Resultantly, Satyamurty was compelled to resign from the party posts. This move of Kondapalli was not liked by many others in the party leadership and ultimately K. Satyamurthy was expelled from the party in 1991 alongwith Satyanarayan Reddy making Muppala Laxmana Rao @ Ganpathi as secretary of the provisional committee.

In 1992 this group was considered by others as an outfit with Charu Mazumdars designs. PWG was active in Telengana region of Andhra. During 1986 in extended its hold and activities in Anantpur, Vishakhapatnam, Nellore, East Godavari etc. It even spread its influence in Tamil Nadu. Its state secretary was arrested in May 1986 with more than 100 weapons, lakhs of rupees in cash and Walkiely Talkie set, ban was imposed on PWG and its front organisation on June 21, 1992 which lapsed in 1995. In 1994 yet another split was caused in Kondapalli's faction by his earlier supporters. After the ban on PWG was allowed to lapse, PWG became more aggressive, militant and violent and the government was compelled to re-impose the ban in July, 1996.

PWG had the following fronts :

1. Raitu Coolie Sangham (RCS)–Peasants, Workers Association.
2. Radical Students Union (RSU)–formed on October 12, 1974.
3. Radical Youth League (RYL)–1978.
4. Jan Natya Mandali (JNM)–formed in 1973.
5. Virasam Viplava Rachay : Thala Sangham – Revolutionary Writers Association.

RCS, RSU, RYL, JNM etc. were in exisience in Adilabad, Warangal and Karimnagar led by Singer-Poet Gaddar.

K.G. Satyamurthy had the following fronts :

1. AP Civil Liberties Committee (APCLC) (formed in March, 1974).
2. Revolutionary Writers Association (RWA).

Satyamurthy surfaced after remaining underground for 10 years.

Since 1980 PWG members visited nearly 500 villages in groups of 8 to 12, began moving south Bastar and ask the villagers whether forest officials like Forest Guard/Rangers and Revenue Officials like Patwari etc. have been troubling them or behaving properly. They, at times, made encounters with the police leaving their literature, weapons and ammunition behind. On the basis of the literature seized, it became clear that People's War Group had divided its sphere of operations into the plains area and the forest area. (Bastar fell under this category). Its aim in the forest area in 1980s was to :

(i) propagate ideology

(ii) make targets who exploit tribals

(iii) deforestation of forest and forcible cultivation on reserve forest

(iv) struggles against forest and government officials

(v) developing organisations to struggle on behalf of tribals and

(vi) forming village cells.

The documents also revealed that in the plains area, group's aim was :

(i) organising labour

(ii) organising students and forming associations of teachers, writers, journalists, lawyers etc.

PWG had two-tier organisation : underground cadres and the legal or overground cadres. This group believes in defensive violence, protective violence and selective violence. It is more interested in expanding its area of influence. Its literature says that it will pursue its plan in the following manner :

(i) phase of organisation

(ii) phase of terrorism

(iii) phase of guerilla warfare

(iv) phase of mobile and traditional warfare

In Gadchiroli district of Maharashtra and Andhra, the Naxals have started the second phase of terrorism. In Madhya Pradesh they were in their first phase. The violence perpetrated against forest employees was to win the favour of the villagers.[2]

From the documents realised in Bastar, it showed that the estimated cadre strength of all Naxalite groups should be 20 to 25000 and those who are not active but do support the movement must be over 3,00,000. These groups had their front organisations among students, farm labourers and industrial workers as well.

Around 1984 Naxalites had about 10 groups functioning in more than one state. Money for them came from the pro-Chinese Canadian Communist Party and the Pro-Albanian Communist Parties in different countries. But gradually they dried up and the Naxals has to develop on money action.[3] In Andhra alone by 1987 the Naxalite strength was estimated at 5000 including 500 hard core cadres. There were about a dozen Naxal groups but four (4) of them were active—most dreaded and most militant among them was Kondapalli's People's War Group. In between 1983 to December 1987 Naxals had murdered 200 people including 35 policemen in Andhra alone. Other groups operating were CPI-ML (C.P. Reddy group), CPI-ML (Pyala Vasudev Rao group), Rawoof group, T. Nagi Reddy group, Revolutionary Communist Party, Pro-Charu Anti-Lin Piao Develapally Venketeshware Rao group and Anti-D.V. Rao group. About 50 'dalams' (armed groups) were operating with bases inside jungles of Nizamabad, Adilabad and East Godavari district and action in ten Naxal-effected areas viz Adilabad, Warangal, Khammam, Karimnagar, Nizamabad and Coastal East and West Godavari, Srikakulam, Vizainagaram and Vishakhapatnam. On July 30, 1987 itself six (6) policemen were killed in an ambush by Naxalites near Doraguda in thick Jungles of East Godavari district. On August 18, ten (10) policemen were shot down inside Alamalli forest in Adilabad and on October 8, a policeman was among three killed in a Naxalite raid on an armoury in Karimnagar district. On October 18, a 'Sarpanch' of a village was shot dead and two Naxalites were gunned down by police the next day in an encounter. PWG was involved in all these killings. They were organised in a military pattern and its men in olive green uniform roam in the Jungles. Meanwhile, Naxalites of different shades started participating in elections also. In 1985, itself in Andhra Pradesh Assembly 45 Naxalites stood as independent candidates with a view to enlarging their political base. When Andhra Pradesh nationalised collection of 'bidi' leaves, Naxalites retaliated by burning down 1280 bags of bidi leaves valued at Rs. 11 lakhs in Bhadrachalam and Nizamabad areas.[4]

PWG had been very alert about its rights. It had made Bangalore (Karnataka) its Headquarter as a safe House which was stumbled upon by chance in may 1986 when police arrested some of the PWG workers or information extracted from arrested persons. PWG sent a telegram to the Supreme Court stating that the police arrested a party official on May 2, 1986 but were holding him without producing him before a Magistrate.[5]

PWG was extorting Rs. 3 crore a year. Seetharamaiah saw no wrong in extorting money from contractors, landlords and other people who loot the people. After police unearthed in May 1987 several dens, captured a huge cache of arms and arrested PWG's state secretary Mr. Nalla Adi Reddy–PWG tightened its security system. PWG, in fact, was running a parallel government in Andhra Pradesh. Its cadres there had gone on the rampage over the week end (May 17, 1988) in the northern Telengana district in reprisals to the killing of one of their front-rank leaders in charge of Field operations in a police encounter last week.[6]

A 430-page judgement on February 27, 1989 by Second Additional Metropolitan Sessions Judge of Hyderabad on a 14 and a half year Secunderabad conspiracy case in which Kondapalli Seetaraimaiah, K.G. Satyamurthy, Pendyala Vara Vara Rao etc. were charged for conspiring to overthrow the union government by violent means, declared 'a group of people holding a particular ideology resorting to annihilation of their class enemies is not war against the state'.[7]

Kidnapping became very handy for PWG. In a daring action it kidnapped seven (7) IAS officers including the principal secretary to the government of Andhra Pradesh Mr. Sankaran on December 27, 1987 at Pulimatu in East Godavari district. It brought a wide publicity for PWG. On January 12, 1990 PWG kidnapped one Mr. Vasat Cashier of Grameen Bank at Utnoor in Nizamabad district to demand release of Naxalite Gangbabu from prison. Government had to exchange the PWG man with the cashier on January 13, itself. But on the part of Andhra Pradesh state it has also acquired notoriety for encounter killing and disappearances. Blackmail through kidnap became strategy of PWG to which they frequently adhered to. On January 27, 1993 the kidnapping of Nalaraju MLA (took place) was disliked. The Chief Minister of Andhra Pradesh N.T. Rama Rao bowed to the pressure of PWG leaders who demanded release of four (4) named Naxalites from government's custody to enable PWG to release IAS officers. The government relented and released named Naxalites. It encouraged PWG to adopt this tactics in future as well. But once when the Telugu Desam government refused to buckle down, PGW killed their captive Malhar Rao, a Mandal Praja Parishad President in Karimnagar district. The abduction and killing of Malhar Rao brought sharp criticism of Telugu Desam government. When Congress-I government returned to power led by Chenna Reddy in

November 1989, he continued the appeasement policy towards PWG and other Naxal groups which gave them ample opportunity to widen their base and influence. Reddy even freed 200 undertrial Naxalites.[8]

Ideological differences always persisted among all the groups and accordingly they directed their actions. PWG continued its opposition to parliamentary process. Violence was their main weapon. Eighteen cops were killed in two incidents in 1987 and 1989. By 1989 PWG was believed to be acquiring AK-47 from LTTE contacts. It was also estimated that PGW had 50 to 60 AK-47.[9] PWG had even given a call–given by PWG state committee secretary Ganpathi–for AP Bandh on October 10, 1990 to protest against the stay order granted by the Supreme Court on the implementation of Mandal Commission Report. The Naxalite movement though born in Bengal, flourished in Andhra Pradesh which had a history of resolute fights against the then administration e.g., Srikakulam tribals revolted under the leadership of Alluri Sitaramartaju against the British. As already said kidnapping became a handy tool to PWG. Sudhir Kumar, Congress MLA S/o P. Shiv Shankar former union minister was kidnapped by PWG on May 11, 1991 was released on May 13 after the state government released four arrested PWG Naxalites namely Bhaskara Rao, G. Sami Reddy Purushottam and his wife Jaya Lakshami.[10] Killing of Donthe Markandeya, Secretary North Telangana Regional Committee and Gundaboyina Anjaiah, Secretary Warangal District Committee infuriated PWG which, in retaliation, killed K.S. Vyas DIG police on January 27, 1993. In the year 1995 there was increased militarisation of PWG.

CPI-ML (Party Unity) and Peoples War Group merged to form a new outfit by name of Peoples War i.e., CPI-ML PW in September 1998. Comrade Kanai Chatterjee had been endeavouring for unity talks with com. Kondapalli Seetaramaiah right from 1981 but the talks finally failed in 1995. In February 2003 the unity talks between these Naxal outfits were restarted on political and organisational issues.

Strictly speaking, none of the CPI-ML outfits sincerely believe that the parliamentary system could improve the lot of the poor, though some of them participating in election process. Most of them have taken this recourse simply to expose the futility of the system and to show the masses that it does not bring the desired results of social upliftment and justice to poor and downtrodden. But PWG strictly followed the poll-boycott call. Participation in the electoral process was mainly utilised to help consolidate and expand mass movement, expose the character of ruling class parties and focus attention on the problems of the people. Towards the end of the decade of eightees, Naxalites of PWG shifted to Chandrapur and Bhandara districts in Maharashtra.

On December 2, 1999 Andhra Police killed three top members of the central committee of PWG namely Nalla Adi Reddy, E. Santosh Reddy and Seelam Naresh in Koyyuru Forest Area. PWG termed it as fake encounter. In March 2000 a Panchayat Raj Minister and TDP leader A Madhav Reddy was killed in a landmine blast. On June 4, 2003 PWG looted cash and nine (9) kilo of gold from State Bank of Hyderabad branch at Dondapadu village in Nalgonda district. On October 1, 2003 PW militants blasted the car of Chief Minister N. Chandrababu Naidu at Alipiri near Tirumala. The CM escaped unhurt.

Violence started in Orissa in 2001 when PWG formed Andhra, Orissa Border Special Zone Committee with Sabyasachi Panda as its chief in Orissa. Panda scripted a sensational attack wherein over 80 armed Naxalites attacked a sub-jail and a police station in R. Udaygiri town of Gajpati district on March 24, 2006. The rebels freed the prisoners, killed two policemen and took hostage officer-in-charge of the local police station., Rajan Kumar Mallick and Jailor Rabinarayana Sethi before releasing them a few days later.[11]

Promode Mishra, a politburo member of CPI-ML who was arrested in Dhanbad on May 11, 2008 said during his interrogation that "the Maoists on Nepal had sent their delegates under the leadership of one Gaurav to attend the 9th party congress of erstwhile PWG in March 2001 held in the Jungle of Bastar in Chhattisgarh. He further disclosed that the Nepal Maoists and PW had also formed an India-Nepal Border Region Committee to co-ordinate their activities in North Bihar and other border areas.[12]

In Tamil Nadu PWG had the support of A.M. Kothandaraman, Youth activist Tamizharasan and others. C.P. Reddy faction was led by Raghavan. The ban on PWG enforced by Andhra Pradesh was allowed to lapse in July 2004. It has been outlined under public security Act 2002 in Andhra. In order to facilitate talks between PWG and the AP government. The ban was not extended. But Tamil

Nadu banned the group on September 10, 2004 to guard the state from any possible infiltration by PWG cadres under criminal Law Amendment Act 1908 after declaring it an unlawful organisation.

On September 21, 2004 CPI-ML-PW and Maoist Communist Centre of India (MCCCI) merged to form CPI (Maoist) and Mupalla Luxman Rao @ Ganpathy was elected its general secretary. A little prior to this development, People's War Group had taken steps to facilitate and hold peace talks with the Andhra Pradesh government then led by Y.S. Rajashekhara Reddy and a 'cease-fire' was agreed upon by both sides on June 16, 2004. Cherukeri Rajkumar @ Prakash, an M. Tech from Andhra University was one of the seven (7) members of the polit bureau in the central committee of PWG. Sakhamuri Appa Rao was Andhra Pradesh secretariat member then. Prakash was categorical in stating that "leaving the line of armed revolution is out of the question." While the talks with the Andhra government were being processed to stop violence, the Frontline managed to get a charter of demands of PWG much before it was made public by them. The demand list was as follows under 10 categories :

1. A democratic atmosphere should be created in the state. The government should respect peoples right to fight for their democratic demands.
    - The government should not prevent agitations, peaceful demonstrations and meetings.
    - Lift the ban on the Communist Party of India (Maoist-Leninist) PW and other organisations.
    - Scrap the system of rewards on workers of PW, people's Guerilla Army and other mass organisations.
    - Scrap Grey Hounds, Special Security Forces and the Special Intelligence Branch (SIB) and withdraw the central paramilitary forces.
    - Release all political prisoners.
    - Scrap the system of giving acceleratory promotions and unofficial incentives to police officers who kill Naxalites in fake encounters.
    - Scrap the informant network in villages. The government

should end the practice of winning over PW workers and using them as cover agents.

- Control 'lumpen' gangs such as Green Tigers, Kranti Sena, Palnadu Tigers, Tirumala Tigers and Nayeem Gang.
- Order a judicial probe into all take encounters and punish the police officers responsible.
- Left all cases registered against workers of mass organisations and other revolutionary parties.

2. Implement reforms in the agricultural sector
   - Implement land reform. Handover to the occupants the endowment, government, and forest land and land belonging to landlords already occupied by people.
   - Implement the land ceiling act.
   - Complete all pending irrigation projects. Farmers should be given irrigation facilities and supplied adequate power.
   - Waive all private loans taken by the farming community to stop suicides by farmers.
   - Prepare a permanent and integrated plan for tackling the drought situation.
   - Scrap corporate agriculture.
3. Implement policies of industrialisation and other schemes based on local resources in place of the liberalisation, privatisation and globalisation policies being followed now.
   - Withdraw all world bank projects and schemes supported by imperialists.
   - Stop the retrenchment of workers and the privatisation of public sector enterprises (PSEs)
   - Protect small and medium-scale industries from competition by multinational companies (MNCs) and revive co-operative and other PSEs.
   - Withdraw user charges on drinking water, education and health services.
   - Scrap all agreements with the World Bank, MNCs and other countries.

4. Recognise the tribal people's rights on forest.
   - Announce autonomy for the tribal people.
   - ❖ Implement the "1/70 Act" which provides protection against the alienation of land held by tribal people in scheduled areas to non-tribal people. Stop settling of non-tribal people in scheduled areas to non-tribal people. Stop settling of non-tribal people in areas inhabited by tribal people.
   - Initiate steps to develop and support tribal languages.
5. Form a separate Telangana State.
6. Formulate an integrated plan for the development of backward regions of north coastal and Rayalaseema areas.
7. Punish those who belittle the self-respect of Dalits. Take action against police officers and upper-cast members responsible for attacks on Dalits in Karamchedu, Tsundur, Neerukonda and Vempenta.
   - Provide job reservation for dalits in the private sector.
8. Equal property rights for women.
   - Reservation for women in the private sector.
   - Stringent punishment for those who commit atrocities on women.
9. Implement total prohibition.
10. Order a probe into the illegal amassing of wealth by officials, politicians and capitalists, corruption scandals by officials and politicians.
    - Recover money from the affluent who evade tax.

(Frontier, August 13, 2004)

Kondapalli Seetharamaiah of People's War Group had been very keen on his unification efforts with other Naxal groups and Maoist parties of other countries. PGW, MCC and the party unity had jointly met towards the end of 1993 and declared that "the Mao-Tse-Tungs' thought is the Marxism-Leninism of the Present day". It also forged links with Communist Party of Nepal (Maoist) and issued a press statement on July 8, 2000 appealing 'to the people of both Nepal and

Indian to rise unitedly to oppose the fascist and genocidal policies of the Indian ruling classes and their lackeys, including the Nepali ruling classes, and fight for the freedom of both countries from the imperialists' onslaught and against the strategies on Indian expansionism, and for the total liberation of the masses from the clutches of domestic reaction.'

In a self-critical revicw, People's War (PW) brought out a document "Summing up the past let us advance victoriously along the path of armed struggle" listing following shortcomings on their part :

1. **An incorrect understanding of the area :** Concrete assessment of the relative strength and weakness of the opposing sides of the revolutionary forces and the enemy was wanting. "What should have been done instead" is to base (tactics) on a concrete assessment of the relative strength and "weaknesses of opposing sides of the contradiction, in a revolution."

2. **A wrong estimation of the International and National Situation :** 8th Party Congress had assessed that the US intervention in Kampuchea was the beginning of World War III which was strongly assessed by the party as the situation in the country and therefore the party called the people to start armed struggle everywhere.

3. **A disregard for the subjective factor :** There was no proper estimate of the strength of the revolutionary forces vis-a-vis that of the enemy. Tendency to get carried away by immediate success of the struggles.

4. **Giving immature slogans :** The over-assessment of the objective factors of revolution led to many immature slogans and calls.

5. **The line of Annihilation :** "All forms of struggles are subordinate to, and are guided by the concrete political line. If the concrete political line deviates from the mass line, the forms of struggle cannot but be otherwise .... So in order to negate the line of annihilation, we have to negate the wrong ideology which is alien to Marxism and its consequential political and organisational manifestations . . . The problem is not whether the class enemy will be annihilated or not . . . . Rather the

problem is whether the party should adopt the mass line or not .. . Every Marxist-Leninist Party must propagate revolutionary violence which may express itself in various forms of struggle; one of which may be annihilation of class enemies." The party had earlier assessed that the annihilation of the landlords was the only means of arousing the landless and poor peasants.

6. **The rejection of other forms of struggle and organisation :** "In order to combat the long-standing revisionist practice of conducting mass struggles on the lines of economism and adopting legal and open forms of organisation as the only from of organisation, our party arrived at a one-sided and wrong formulation that the armed form of struggle is the only form of struggle and armed form of organisation is the only form of organisation."
7. **A wrong approach to the United Front :** The document in its assessment of the earlier position said "The United Front will be formed in the course of struggle only ... to work for it right from the inception of the struggle is the bounden duty of the working class. To say instead, that it will not be possible to form a United Front until one or a ten liberated base areas are established... amounts to rejecting in practice the truth, that a United Front is essential for the victory of revolution."
8. **Guerilla struggles in the cities :** PW confessed that it was wrong in their part to have started urban Guerilla warfare in Calcutta which led to enormous losses.
9. **Wrong bureaucratic tendencies in organisation :** Bureaucratic methods, a lack of self criticism, a lack of committee functioning, sectarian methods of solving differences and finally the assertion of Com. CM's individual authority above the party... did much to damage the movement. The document also added that this was a major reason why the party could not correct errors in time.[13]

During June 1991 and end of 1992, over 300 comrades had been killed in AP alone by police. PWG responded by forming Guerilla Zone and outlined the following tasks for itself in North Telangana and Dandakaranya Zone. A Guerellia Zone in an area where both the revolutionaries and the ruling classes contend for power :

1. To build two or three local Guerilla squads under the central Guerilla squad functioning at present, to gradually develop them into platoons.
2. To separate political and military tasks in the squad area committee and to develop political and military leadership.
3. To develop a military command from bottom to top.
4. To consolidate the party organisation at the village level.
5. To establish the United Front of revolutionary classes at the village level with the aim of establishing their political power through building the 'Gram Rajya Committees' and to destroy the state power of the comprador bourgeoisie and landlord classes.
6. To establish people's power by building village development committees, village defence squads, Panchayat Committees etc. under the leadership of the Gram Rajya Committee.[14]

People's Guerrilla Army, Left Wing Extremists

The military wing of the People's War Group (PWG), the People's Guerrilla Army (PGA) was reportedly founded on December 2, 2000 in Bihar and Jharkhand and a month later, on January 2, 2001, in Andhra Pradesh, somewhere in dense Dandakaranya forests in the North Telengana Region, by reorganising its guerilla force. The formation of the PGA coincided with the first anniversary of three top PWG leaders, including Central Committee members, killed in an encounter in the Koyyur forests, Karimnagar district, Andhra Pradesh. It is styled on the pattern of similar guerrilla forces in Turkey, the Philippines and Peru, the PWG said in a statement at the founding of PGA.

The formation of the PGA was apparently in response to a government decision to launch coordinated action against the Naxalites by police forces of the various Indian States affected by Naxal violence. The PGA functions under a single operational command, the Central Military Commission. In the Indian State where the PGA has a presence, there is a State Military Commission and in special guerrilla zones there is a Zonal Military Commission. A Regional Military Commission supervises a group of State Military Commissions or Zonal Military Commissions. Each Regional Military Commission reports to the Central Military Commission. All armed cadre of the PWG are organised under the PGA.

The PWG announced that the PGA would consist of a main force, a secondary force and a people's militia. The PWG seeks to steer the PGA as a village militia and a regular army force to capture state power. Village militias are, indeed, in existence at some places. In the PGA, there are military platoons at the district or division level, sometimes a special guerrilla squad (SGS) in districts that do not have a military platoon, and local guerrilla squads (LGS) that have limited operational jurisdiction stretching across a cluster of villages. Further, there are also action teams and special action teams to undertake activities such as reconnaissance of a target, which could be a person or a location; killings; abductions; or damage and destruction of property. During meetings of cadres in large numbers, protection platoons are formed from amongst the existing men and women to provide cover and are subsequently disbanded. While cadres are not simultaneously represented in more than one arm, it is also likely that all the arms may not be present in all the districts.

Reportedly, the strength of a platoon varies between 25 and 30 at whose head are a commander and deputy commander. In turn, each platoon is divided into sections led by a section commander and a deputy section commander. The strength of a guerrilla squad varies between five and eight, while an action team consists of two to three cadres.

THE REDIFF INTERVIEW/ GANAPATHY

'A voluntary federation of nationalities with the right to secede is what we want'

The People's War has today come to be identified as another militant outfit, another sore on India's troubled landscape. You are being equated with the insurgents of the North-East and Jammu and Kashmir. How is your fight different from theirs?

The movements of NE and JK have a very restricted aim. They are nationalist movements. They are fighting to protect their nationality interests. The PW, on the other hand, is leading a protracted people's war. Our aim is to dislodge the imperialists with the gun. The party, which is based on communist ideology, is building a movement that

will bring forth the rule of the proletariat. Proletariat dictatorship. In that sense we have a wider, all-encompassing view.

Why have you chosen the path of violence? Why not democratic means to achieve your aim?

Because the rule of the masses cannot be achieved through normal political methods. The Indian people have only one way to usher in modern democracy: armed struggle. You cannot get anything for the poor from the existing democratic system. Despite millions taking up armed struggle in various forms, despite the so-called democratic methods, the so-called parliamentary procedures, the people are not able to enjoy even basic rights, leave alone political power. Such is the state of the State, the Establishment, the System.

The feudal system is still continuing here. Indirectly, the rule of imperialists is on. They are ruling through proxies, brokers. In this kind of system, it is not at all possible for people to empower themselves politically through conventional means.

We are leading what is basically an armed people's struggle. It has been launched by the people. It is natural that the ruling classes have to be overthrown for the downtrodden to come to power. Be it in America, Britain, Germany or Russia, the same thing applies, the same thing holds true. And this will be so in the future also. Even a small country with a tiny population of a few hundred thousands cannot escape this truism.

The Establishment has been labelling us revolutionaries variously as anti-social elements, extremists, terrorists etc. in its bid to isolate/distance/sever us from the people. We shall counter such propaganda politically.

The land should belong to the one who tills it, not the landlord. They (*the landlords*) have kept vast tracts of land in their vice-like grip. They have been living off, pestering and frustrating the peasantry for ages. Will they give up land if normal methods are used? No. This problem has never been solved by any commissions constituted by Parliament. Nowhere in the world has this problem been appropriately resolved. So why should we lay our faith in such a system?

Another point is imperialist investments. These are sucking the Indians dry. Reducing them to pulp. The imperialists are looting the natural resources, riches and skilled human resources of this country. The middle-classes and even the bourgeoisie are being looted. All the development and production now happening in India are variously described as state-of-the-art, ultra-modern, wonderful, fantastic etc. But the fact is that these are nothing but characteristics of a neo-colony. All this so-called development is not happening for the good of the natives; it is certainly not happening with an intention to harness people's skills. I mean, the resources are ours, the labour is ours, but the capital is not ours. And the production is not for our people.

In such circumstances, will the imperialists go away if asked to leave, leaving behind their shops? It is on these very issues that the CPI and CPI-M fought elections for the last 50 years. But what is the result? The imperialists' investments have only risen, not dropped. Prior to 1947, it was only the British that were in power in India. After August 15, 1947, every imperialist country in the world has barged into India and looted it, just like that, to their heart's content. Why will they leave now like gentlemen if asked to?

How then can we fight by laying our faith in this parliamentary system?

Likewise, the big bourgeois. These guys have mortgaged our nation's interests to the imperialists. They are making their pot of gold in the process. The Tatas, the Birlas, the Dalmias, the Singhanias and several other capitalists with other names, companies — these people are looting the country by suppressing the small and the middle-classes and the downtrodden. They are keeping their cut and passing on the major cut to their imperialist bosses. If we, the victims merely request an end to their rule, will it end? Is it possible to do it using parliamentary methods? If yes, why have not the CPI and the CPI-M been able to do it in the last 50 years? So, it is clear that solutions are not possible through ordinary means.

Both the State and your party are using violence. And caught in the crossfire are innocent Indians. Innocent proletariat Indians. Are you being fair to them?

Terming our activities as violence is not correct. Ours is counter-violence. Ours is a resistance struggle. We are resisting the violence unleashed by the State on the proletariat. Again, I would like to remind you that it is not the PW who is fighting the imperialists. It is the masses against the State. The PW is only leading them. So it is the people against the repression. It's the people's war. And who else will be killed in a people's war but people? Over 1,300 people have been killed in the crossfire. Of this, only a very small number were guerrillas. The rest were all prey to the violence unleashed by the State. The State is responsible for their deaths.

How have you changed the landscape—social, economic and political—of your areas of operation?

The PW adopts reformist ways to create awareness among the masses. On the political level, the PW has created awareness among the masses by exposing the selfish aspects of the so-called democratic political parties.

On the economic level, we believe in adopting self-sustenance methods. We mobilised people for several struggles. When the crops failed recently, we collected and distributed Rs. 3.6 million among the farmers. In North Telangana, we had captured a lot of land from landlords. Due to repression, these lands were uncultivated. This year, we organised the peasants to cultivate on 2,000 acres of captured land. In Dandakaranya, due to our struggle, the *tendu* leaf pickers and bamboo workers are earning a decent living.

Our developmental committees took up several struggles demanding schools, teachers, buildings etc. All these struggles were taken up in areas where the people faced severe repression. Still we achieved remarkable success through sacrifices and blood.

Yet, 30 years after the Naxal movement started, your organisation is still confined to only a few pockets in Andhra, Orissa, Madhya Pradesh and Maharashtra. Isn't your movement dying down?

This question was posed to us in 1980, in 1985, in 1991, in 1995 and now again in 1998. Our mass base has been expanding all these years. We are spreading to several areas. Simply alleging that the PW is limited to this part or that part without considering the spread of our mass base is not fair. It is a fact that we are not growing fast. But it is also a fact that we are a growing force. We are spreading. When we started, we were a few individuals in Telangana. Now we have a full-fledged organisation. With this merger, our party is spreading further.

Students, an integral part of any revolution, are not with your party today. Why is this so?

It is true that the student movement has decreased in AP. But if you consider the situation in the country as a whole, their movement is gaining strength. It is growing in Tamil Nadu, Karnataka, Delhi, Bihar, Bengal etc. The revolution is rejuvenating its forces. The trouble is that the party is not in a position to consolidate the entire movement and transform it into a unified struggle. This is because of the severe repression we are facing now.

The major reason for the students to be at a low ebb in AP is that we lost around 100 student comrades in the last 10 years. The students faced as severe a repression as that faced by the peasants. For the peasants, the terrain and the movement are conducive to survival. In the case of students, this is not true. Their area of operation is limited, as they are all concentrated in urban areas. The middle-class also contributed to this. The upper middle-class is now more secure, more affluent. But sections in the middle-class are facing more problems. After the new economic policies and privatisation, the lower and middle-class are feeling insecure. I will give you an example.

In AP, there are 300,000 government teachers. There are about 200,000 qualified teachers. These people, many of whom are postgraduates, are now working as casual labourers. This situation is leading to great dissatisfaction and frustration among them. Such happenings are growing day by day. This will ultimately lead to anti-government movements again. The wave will come in the near future. The teachers are now almost ready to lead the students into struggle.

Another point: Earlier, the student movements of our organisation were concentrated in urban areas. Today, these have taken roots in rural areas too. We expect a rapid growth.

Which are these rural areas?

Areas of North Telangana, South Telangana and certain places in DK.

The middle-class intellectuals who once formed the backbone of your party have grown apart from you. Today they label you as 'romantic fools.' They say you are chasing mirages. Can you explain this transformation?

First, the middle-class and middle-class intellectuals are not our backbone, never have been our backbone, and never will be our backbone. Our party's backbone is always the proletariat, the agricultural labourers and the poor peasants. Not the middle-class and middle-class intellectuals — not in the past, in the present or in the future. We agree they played an important role in our movement. In future also, they will play an important role as an alley of the revolution.

What happened in the past was that some sections of the middle-class and upper middle-class came in a wave into the revolution with a lot of romantic thoughts. And then they went back. That happened. But now the lower and middle middle-class and intellectuals are coming closer to the movement. The number of such people who have relation with the party is growing day by day. We have several all-India level mass organisations. All these organisations are mainly manned and led by the middle-class. These exist even in AP, where we are facing severe repression — not openly as our front organisations. We are building many such organisations. This shows that the intellectual and middle-class base of the party is not decreasing but increasing.

If that's the case, why is the trend not visible?

You can't see this trend because we are not in a position to reveal it. We are organising them under different covers. It is not the objective conditions alone that are making the middle-class come back to the party. The party is consciously putting effort into this. We have started many organisations for this. This effort is in its beginning.

So we can't reveal details now. But we are certain that in the near future you will be convinced of the truth about this.

Near future is a relative term. Can you specify a time frame?

We can't give dates at this point.

Are you claiming that there is no alienation of the middle-class from your movement? That they are still with you as they were in the 1980s?

No doubt, a section of the upper middle-class and the middle-class intellectuals have moved away from the revolution. This is due to the penetration of the imperialist policies into the country. On the other hand, there is the lower middle-class and middle-class. The distance between these sections and the revolutionary movement is closing day by day. This positive action more than makes up for the alienation of the upper middle-class sections.

The upper middle-class and the upper middle-class intelligentsia — and here I include the NRIs, who form the majority of your readers — do not at present have a good opinion of our party. But we believe their opinion can be changed. We are sure that the ongoing crisis in the world will bring about a change in their view. They will be disillusioned with the existing system of imperialist government. Already in Germany, movements against the Turks have started. And in America and other capitalist countries, fascist and racist forces are growing. Soon the people, the NRIs, will become the targets of fascist and racist movements. This will make them recognise the real nature of imperialism. They are bound to become pro-people and pro-democratic.

If the NRIs are not enemies of the revolution, why is it that the PW opposes investments from them?

We do not consider all NRIs who invest in India as allies of imperialists. We do not oppose the NRIs as a whole. A section of them colludes with imperialists. It is the capital coming in from this section that we oppose. We welcome capital from NRIs who are not imperialist agents.

A recent PW document says you are planning to target banks for funds and would tax the traders operating in your areas. Is that justifiable? The banks, after all, have the deposits of the poor and the middle-class. And how do you expect small traders to pay tax to you as well as the government?

It is true the PW released a document saying we would target the banks for funds. But the State-controlled press highlighted only this point, to defame the party. They only gave details regarding this sensational aspect. They completely neglected the other aspects like how we would collect funds from other enemies, and how these funds would be used for the people's cause.

The banks are supposed to repay the money to the people. They can't say the PW looted the bank, so we will not pay you back. If we find that they are not repaying their depositors, then we may reconsider this decision.

Regarding the taxation of small traders, the party will tax only those traders who are above middle-class. We will not touch the poor and the middle-class. We will impose tax only on those who can afford it — namely the higher middle-class and rich traders.

The authorities allege that the PW has relations with many anti-Indian groups like the ISI and LTTE.

(*Laughs*) We deny the ISI part. We do not have *any* relation with them. That's State propaganda to discredit us.

What about the LTTE?

We have had no relations with the LTTE till now. But we are not against having relations with them. We will certainly have links with them if an opportunity arises. We feel that such a relation would be conducive to the revolutionary movement.

Are you exploring the possibility? Have you sent any feelers?

No, we haven't.

The LTTE is not a revolutionary party. Why, then, should you be interested in them? How will they be able to help your cause?

We support all parties/organisations in the world that are suffering due to the exploitation of the imperialists and the comprador bourgeoisie. In Sri Lanka, the Sinhalese are oppressing Tamilians with the help of the Indian ruling classes and other imperialists. As communists, we support all genuine national movements. So we are supporting the Tamil national movement. The LTTE is the leader of that struggle. However, that does not imply that we support all the tactics and politics of the LTTE. Our support is basically to the Tamilian nationalist cause.

You said you haven't had any relations with the LTTE. Are you denying that LTTE instructors conducted training camps for your squads?

They were not LTTE. They were ex-LTTE. What happened was that these people came to India after leaving their organisation and formed communist groups. The PW had relations with these groups. As part of that, they held training camps for us.

You said links with the LTTE would be good for your cause. How?

We will know the advantages only after we have relations. Without having relations, how will we be able to say?

What are you expecting out of the relationship?

Such a relation would bring solidarity between the masses of the two countries. It will also prove a major morale booster for all nationalist fighters.

If that is the case, why are you not actively pursing the possibility?

There are many organisations in South East Asia that the PW would like to have links with. But our resources are limited. We would not be able to maintain relations with all these movements at this stage. Once the revolution progresses, we will certainly try to have relations with such movements, including the LTTE. It is part of our policy to have relations with all communists and nationality struggles.

What kind of international relations do you have?

All communist parties will try to have relations with other parties having similar ideology. The PW too has developed relations at different levels with different militant communist organisations across the world, which follow the ML thought. We are now developing primary level relations with some other parties.

What are the parties with which you have relations? In which countries?

All I can say about this is that we have good relations with some strong parties that are following the correct line.

What kind of aid do you receive from these parties?

That's a technical point. I don't want to answer it.

Coming back to insurgent groups, what is the PW's basic criteria for having links with them?

Let me make one thing clear: Our support to any nationalist movement does not mean that we support all the activities of that organisation. We will support an organisation only if they support the ongoing revolutionary movement. We support only those struggles that we know are genuine nationalist struggles. There are struggles in Jammu and Kashmir, the struggles of the Nagas in the NE. We assure all of them the right of self-determination. On this basis alone we would hold relations with these people.

Wouldn't the right to self-determination lead to the disintegration of the country?

No. That's an untruth preached by parties with narrow nationalism, like the BJP. When nations are forced into a political system, there will always arise fresh national movements. You cannot hold on to nations that do not want to be part of your set-up. Force will always lead to division.

On the other hand, a voluntary federation of nationalities with the right to secede will lead to unity. That's what we want. The kind of federalism advocated by the ruling classes is not the right kind. Our federalism is based on equality, not bargains like the one that Chandrababu Naidu is talking about. That is why we support the Telangana movement. That's why we put forth the slogan of democratic Telangana.

MAOIST COMMUNIST CENTRE (MCC)

'Dakshin Desh' formed in Calcutta on October 20, 1969 changed its name and formed Maoist Communist Centre (MCC) in 1975.

MCC became Maoist Communist Centre of India (MCCI) after Revolutionary Communist Centre of India (RCCI) merged in it in the year 2003. Kanai Chatterjee @ KC and Amulya Sen @ Master Moshai, two main founders of this group led it by remaining underground from the very inception of the outfit in 1969. MCC surfaced in Bihar hilly tracks of Aurangabad district in Bihar (till then it was mainly operating in Jangal Mahal area of Burdwan district of West Bengal) for the first time in 1972. Dakshin Desh did not join CPI-ML in 1969 though supportive of Naxalbari struggle. In fact it was the only CPI-ML outfit that retained its independent identity. Dakshin Desh was named since India was south (Dakshin) of the Himalayas. In Sundarban area of the 24-Pargana district this group became active and carried out annihilation of top class enemies. The emphasised on forcible occupation of agricultural land through the help of landless labourers and small and marginal farmers. Kanai Chatterjee did not join Charu Mazumdar when the latter staged Naxal uprising. In fact, they were opposed to each other on the issue of formation of communist party and revolutionary struggle. Kanai considered Charu Mazumdar's line as "left adventurist and terrorist". After the death of Amulya Sen in March 1981 and that of Kanai Chatterjee in July 1982, Shivenji and Ramadhar Singh took over the leadership of the party but soon Shivenji developed differences with his deputy Ramadhar Singh on the questions of individual annihilation. Ramadhar left MCC and joined Kanu Sanyals's CPI-ML. Later on Promod Mishra and Sanjay Dushanjh took over the leadership and built up a number of front organisations on students, agriculture etc. particularly in Bihar. MCC became faction-ridden after Kanai's death. It was active is West Bengal and Bihar. Before his death Kanai had formed Bihar-Bengal Special Area Committee. In West Bengal it was active in Jangal Mahal area till 1976 but during Emergency about 100-150 activists of the group were arrested. MCC was opposed to parliamentary process and believed in carrying out clandestine activities by remaining underground and forming armed squads to carry on militant activities but later on it started functioning through front organisations like Jan Surkshya Sangharsh Morcha (JSSM) and Jan Adalats (People's Courts). JSSM was banned in April 1991 but the party was prompt in replacing it with a new named front Jan Pratirodh Sangharsh Manch (JPSM). Kannai Chatterjee formed the committee of Bengal-Bihar Special Area which was the group renamed as MCC in 1975.

On May 29, 1987 MCC had killed 43 Rajputs at Dalachak and Baghaura (Aurangabad district) which forced the government to impose ban on the party. Police also blamed MCC for the ambush on a police party in the Chatra Forest of Hazaribagh on December 29, 1987. MCC document nearly two months after the massacre claimed that the primary reason that led to this incident were land, absentee landlordism and anti-peasant action taken from time to time by powerful landlords of the area and referred to Ram Naresh Singh, a former MLA of Aurangabad in this connection. On May 29, 1987 MCC while annihilating Rajputs, had slit throats of 28 of them out of 43 killed, 13 others were thrown into the bonfire created out of the thatched roofs. The operation was over by 10 pm and the 'action squads' melted away after shouting slogans. "Maoist Communist Centre Zindabad" leaving behind several leaflets in which MCC justified 'reprisals' on the ground that the government and the police were in league with upper casts.[15]

Earlier in October 7, 1986 MCC killed 11 Rajputs at Darmia village in Aurangabad district raising the slogan "He who tills the land, sows the seeds and harvests the crop is the real owner of the land." In yet another horrific action, 37 members of Bhumihar families were killed on February 12, 1992 in Bara village of Gaya district.

MCC was said to have fraternal relations with the Revolutionary Communist Party of India in Punjab, the People's War Groups in Andhra Pradesh and with the Azizul Haq faction of the Naxalites.[16] In the year 2004 it merged with people's war after merging with Punjab based Revolutionary Communists centre of India (Maoist) and the naming the new outfit as MCCI as announced on January 15, 2003. MCC is opposed to anti-Lin Piao faction of CPI-ML which in its assessment is 'revisionist'.

MCC relied more in armed action. Its fronts were :

1. Krantikari Kisan Committee (KKC) backed by Red Defence Corps.
2. Red Defence Corps i.e., Lal Raksha Dal.
3. Youth and Women Front.

4. Krantikari Buddhijivi Sangh.
5. Jan Suraksha Sangharsh Manch.
6. Chatra Sangh.
7. Communist Youth League.
8. Janwadi Mazdoor Sanghthan Samiti.

MCC has spread its wings in UP also. Bitni a Nirmala, a member of Maoist Communist Centre and Women Wing Commander was arrested on September 2, 2000 in Sonebhadra district of UP. Her husband Ram Virksha Kol is an Area Commander of his outfit. MCC is active in Mirzapur and Chandauli districts of UP.

In the year 1992 MCC joined hands with PWG and party unity to give a philip to the Naxal movement in various states like Andhra, Bihar, Maharashtra etc. and chose on appex body by name of All India People's Resistance Forum (AIPRE) to build and develop a powerful anti-feudal and anti-imperialist struggles.

In January 2003 MCC and the Revolutionary Communist Centre of India (Maoist) united and the new outfit was named as Maoist Communist Centre of India (MCCI). Subir Talukdar group of CPI-ML and Revolutionary Communist Centre (Marxist) also merged with MCCI soon aster.

Why PW and MCC were close to each other was because both of the outfits were totally opposed to any participation in the parliamentary elections. Incidently, other CPI-ML outfits which campaigned for boycott of polls were CPIML (Jan Shakti), CPML (Naxalbari) Shanti Pal group of CPML, Ajit Chakravarti group of CPI-ML, Tamil Nadu State Organising Committee (ML) Tamil Nadu Marxist-Leninist Party and Kothandaraman group of PWG in general elections held in 2004.

MAOIST ORGANISATIONS UNITE IN INDIA

Revolutionary Worker #1200, May 25, 2003, posted at rwor.org

We received the following article from A World to Win News Service.

On January 15, the Maoist Communist Center and the Revolutionary Communist Center India (Maoist), issued a communiqué "wholeheartedly declaring before the toiling people of India" that they have united to form a single group. "Our united organisation will be based on Marxism-Leninism-Maoism and remain firmly committed to the long-cherished need of the great Indian people to carry forward and complete the New Democratic revolution," the statement said.

The united party, now called Maoist Communist Center (India), is a participant in the Revolutionary Internationalist Movement (RIM). The MCC was a 'participant' before; the RCCI (M) was a 'candidate participant'. The two formerly separate groups had been conducting struggles in different Indian states. The MCC had strongholds in Bihar, Jharkhand and West Bengal in the northeast part of the country, and the RCCI (Maoist) in Punjab in the northwest. The people in all these states have a long history of heroic struggle going back to the armed peasant uprising that began in Naxalbari and spread throughout India in the 1960s and '70s, giving birth to India's Maoist movement. Forged in 1969, the MCC had a long history of struggle on the ideological and political fronts, even before its formation. Its founders had taken Maoist China's side in the debate against the revisionists led by Khrushchev, who restored capitalism in the USSR and tried to impose their betrayal of Marx and Lenin on the international communist movement. It upheld the path of protracted People's War and New Democratic Revolution in India and carried out armed struggle. Having undergone twists and turns in its political life and significant line struggles within the Party, it became a participating organisation of RIM in 2002.

The MCC has united vast sections of the poor peasants of Bihar and Jharkhand. Bihar is a state in India where classical feudalism still exists. The feudal landlords have their own armies under the protection of the Indian government, which they used to suppress the peasants in their own interests. Under the reactionary Hindu Branashram system, people are divided into several castes. The brutality of the upper-cast feudals reduces the masses to the level of slavery. Destroying the strongholds of these landlords bit by bit, the MCC has been confiscating land from the feudals and distributing this land to the poor people in the areas where it has sufficient power. On December 19, 2002, in the Singhabhumi district of western Jharkhand, the MCC led a military action against the reactionary armed police who had been carrying out brutal repression of the masses. Eighteen armed police were killed and 38 others wounded. All their weapons and ammunition were seized.

Similarly, the reactionary state of India has left the people of Jharkhand in very backward conditions. The MCC has turned Jharkhand, the hilly area formerly part of Bihar and now a separate state, to Lalkhand (Lal means red) by uniting these tribal (indigenous) people against feudals and Indian occupiers. The revolutionary armed struggle has been transforming the life of the oppressed people, for example, by doing away with child marriage and other backward practices. A large percentage of the indigenous people of Jharkhand are no longer mere downtrodden but are becoming free men and women.

Punjab, too, has been a hotbed of revolutionary struggle, from the time of General Dyaras's Jaliawala Bagh massacre of Punjabi peasants fighting against British imperialism before India's so-called independence up to today. Although it has a different character to the most backward areas of India, these have been heroic struggles by the people against the reactionary system. When a misguided movement broke out for an independent Sikh state (Khalistan), the RCCI stood firm on the orientation of New Democratic Revolution in India to overthrow foreign imperialism, feudalism and bureaucrat capitalism linked to both of the former.

The MCC(I) communiqué highlighted the importance of this goal and of advancing in this direction. It declared, "A pressing need at this time is unity among all the genuine Maoist forces operating in India. Possibilities and strong aspirations for turning this need into an actuality are also coming into view."

In particular, the unity of the Maoist forces in India means uniting forces who come from the Communist Party of India (Marxist-Leninist) as well as MCC(I) and others. The CPI (ML) founded under the leadership of Charu Mazumdar in 1971 splintered into many pieces following his death in 1972. After the death of Mao Tsetung in 1976 and the coup d'état carried out against his successors by Deng Xiaoping, the world communist movement fell into a great crisis. The Indian movement, too, was divided into many trends. The Maoist parties and organisations had to defend Mao and Maoism (then known as Mao Tsetung Thought), and oppose Deng and also the dogmatic attacks on Mao launched by Enver Hoxha of Albania.

One of the parties descended from the original CPI (ML) which continues to uphold the banners of Mazumdar and Maoism is the CPI(ML) (Naxalbari), like the MCC a participating party of RIM, which is continuing to work for the unity of the Maoist revolutionaries in a single center in India. The CPI(ML) (Naxalbari) has been advancing especially in the states of Kerala, Maharastra and Karnataka. Of particular importance among the other parties in this same category is the CPI(ML) (People's War), which has a long history of leading the masses in waging armed struggle. The CPI(ML)(PW) has strongholds in broad rural areas in the states of Andhra, Maharashtra, and Orisha, as well as Bengal, Bihar and elsewhere. The CPI(ML) (PW), along with the above-mentioned RIM participating parties and organisations, are members of CCOMPOSA (the Co-ordinating Committee of Maoist Parties and Organisations of South Asia).

A united revolutionary Maoist party has been a strong desire of a great many Indian masses since the setbacks suffered by the Naxalbari uprising and the splintering of the Maoist forces. Conditions in vast areas of the Indian countryside are ripe for waging a People's War to make a New Democratic Revolution and march ahead toward socialism and world communism. India, reeling under semi-colonial and semi-feudal production relations, has also seen many revolutionary explosions throughout the country that have taken the form of armed national liberation movements, such as in Kashmir and Bodoland, in addition to the Maoist-guided armed revolutionary movements that involve millions of peasants and others, such as those led by MCC(I) and CPI(ML)(PW) in Andhra Pradesh, Bihar, Jharkhand and Dandakarnya. Because of the lack of a united Maoist party, a people's army and revolutionary united front, the full revolutionary potential of the situation in India has not been fully realised.

The Maoist movement in India already is having a worldwide impact, and a successful revolution in the world's second-largest country would help change the face of the earth. The oppressed masses the world over are looking forward to greater victories and advances by the Indian Maoists.

CENTRAL ORGANISING COMMITTEE (COC CPI-ML)

Charu Mazumdar's faction in Telengana was known as COC whose leader was K. Seetharamiah. Formed in December 1972 by Kondapalli, K.G. Satyamurthy and Suniti Kumar Ghosh, COC followed the line adopted by UCCRI-ML though differences among leaders existed on the role of violence. The party felt isolated and could not form an all India base. The first priority the leaders accorded to COC, of course, was to build a mass base if it wanted success in its future struggles. Its leader Kandapalli Seetharamiah went even to the extent to come overground if Janata Party was willing to grant general amnesty to all the communist revolutionaries. One of its central committee members Mani Di Appalasuri wanted to participate in the elections process also thereafter. But the views of its Punjab unit were different and they never wanted to give up armed struggle. COC CPI-ML comprised of state committees from Punjab, West Bengal, Andhra Pradesh and Bihar.

In Andhra, as already said, an All Indian Unit of Central Organising Committee (COC) led by Kondapalli Seetharamiah already existed. In August 1974, three member committee Kwataramaih, Appalasuri and Mahadevan was formed. During emergency, Mamadi Appalasuri, K Seetharamaih, K.S. Mahadevan etc. had gone underground and kept on guiding the party even shifted its base from Andhra Pradesh to a nearly state and made Nagpur its seat of activities. K.S. Mahadevan died in August 1976. Kondapalli himself was arrested in March 1977 and Mamidi Appalasuri was arrested in August 1977 which brought down the party activities in Andhra. After the Emergency was over Naxal leaders like S.N. Singh of CPI-ML, Sumiti Kumar Ghosh of COC CPI-ML and Khokan Mazumdar of the Unity Committee sent a signed letter to the then PM Morarji Desai asking him to release all party worker and withdrawal of cases against them and repeal of laws like MISA and DIR. On May 3, 1977 the PM announced at Ahmedabad that the centre has instructed states to release the Naxalites. Party also did a sole-searching exercise soon and came to the conclusion that the policy of annihilation was counter-productive and as such should be abandoned and instead the party should concentrate on massline and building a mass base. This was the conclusion of both Kondapalli and Satyamurty, but again as in other parties, more radical and aggressive party colleagues defected to Pro-Lin Piao faction. The existing COC was formally dissolved in May 1977. Since it could not really get off ground. A new state committee was set up in May 1977 with Mukku Suba Reddy as its state secretary having two six-member regional committees for Nalgonda and Karimnagar. Since the party had no mass base, it gave up armed struggle and took the task of building it first and fast. Pro-Lin faction of CPI-ML in fact, won over COC CP-ML cadres in Nalgonda and Warangal district. It made an unsuccessful attempt to loot the Kothagudem Branch of IOB in Khamman district on September 20, 1977. In West Bengal, a petty Jotedar was killed in Bankura district on September 28, 1977.

COC directly owed its allegiance to Charu Mazumdar. Its leader in Punjab was Jagjit Singh Sol who played a leading role in Bhojpur Movement under the name of Sharma. COC's policy was to send revolutionary guards to rural as well as to urban areas, especially to union industrial undertakings and creating guerrilla squads to protect such bases. Party activities were done clandestinely. COC became almost non-functional because of preoccupation of Jagjit Singh in Bhojpur movement. In Telengana COC was known as central committee of CPI-ML.

After COC became defunct in 1977, the APCC State Committee did not made any further attempts to unite other CPI-ML outfits cadres.

In Punjab Gurdayal Singh was state committee secretary who was pursuing struggle in the state and was opposed to the parliamentary process. He was also opposed to the S.N. Singh's line. State Committee member Samarjit Singh exhorted party cadres to build up guerrilla squads to carry on the struggle and for the purpose of procuring arms, he suggested, that is should be procured from the Indian Army through 'friendly sources' and prepare masses for an armed struggle. It had opened up fronts like Naujawan Kissan Sabha, Naujawan Bharat Sabha, Punjab Student's Union etc. The activities were at a low key-level. The party had about 350 members in Punjab.

In Bihar, during Emergency it was almost defunct. But after Emergency was lifted Surjit Kumar Das Gupta a member of the Bihar–Eastern UP State Organising Committee of the party asked the party to continue both underground as well as overground activities through its front organisations.

The Naxal movement kept on growing even in early year of eighty which engulfed almost 18 states of the country, registering considerable increase in the Naxal cadres, their frontal organisations. But they remained divided inspite of hankering for unity among themselves. Violence continued to increase. About 30 Marxist-Leninist groups including small ones like Communist Ghadar Party of India with its negligible following in Delhi, Punjab and Maharashtra existed. All the Naxal groups agree :

(i) To use violence leading to annihilation of class enemies. Here Pro-Lin was more blunt and violent. Anti-Lin favoured exercising caution and selected class enemies for annihilation. At that stage of Naxal movement, they did not wish to annoy the rich peasants.

(ii) Struggle involving masses and forming united fronts to mobilize peasants, students, industrial workers to carry on armed agrarian struggle.

(iii) Building up PLA for guerilla struggles, preparation of revolutionary warfare.

(iv) Setting up "Base areas" in rural area at liberated zones then carry on the struggle to urban areas.

(v) To carry the struggle after going underground i.e., do it covertly.

(vi) Taking inspiration mainly from China.

Though the COC contained the best elements of CPI-ML, yet it obliterated literally in 1977.

UNITED CP-ML

Formed by S.N. Singh and Chandra Pulla Reddy in 1975, it merged with united CP-ML of Bhaskar Nandi and Khokan Mazumdar group in December 1977 and it was named as provincial committee of CPI-ML. In a significant departure from the set line, S.N. Singh announced its desire to participate in Parliamentary elections in 1977 post Emergency era and to offer the government a critical support. Both Bhaskar Nandi and Khokan Mazumdar did not like the idea and withdrew their support accusing S.N. Singh of adopting "Counter

Revolutionary Methods". It had fielded seven (7) candidates out of which only Santosh Rana got elected. Khokan Mazumdar and Bhaskar Nandi who had left the party rejoined them, and the party was renamed as provisional central committee ML (PCC CPI-ML). S.N. Singh formed mass based front organisations. He floated IFTU with a view to control labour union, Krishak Mukti Sangh in West Bengal to highlight Kisan's issues, student front Progressive Democratic Students Union (PDSU) and democratic students front. A section of its cadre rejected the conciliatory approach of S.N. Singh and formed a dissident faction under the banner of West Bengal spate organisating committee of CPI-ML but it did not assert itself.

The new ML outfit had its following in Andhra Pradesh, Punjab, Bihar and West Bengal etc. One of the important leaders in Andhra was V. Venkataramaiah who was arrested in a police encounter in April 1976 while the other two Neelam Ramachandrayya died in November 1975. All this resulted in having adverse effect on the party set-up in Andhra. During 1975 Emergency days a number of its cadres were arrested. The Forest Regional Committee (it was so named since it was operating from forest region) headed by Chandra Pulla Reddy and Plains Regional Committee headed by Neelam Ramchandrayya were compelled to stop their activities and the 'Dalam' members were directed to lie low and seek safe shelters outside their dalams. Though the 'Dalam' themselves were depleted by the end of 1975, soon after the Emergency was clamped, yet the violence conducted by united CP-ML did not stop. Murders, dacoity and extortion of money from forest contractors continued. After the Emergency was over, United CP-ML supported the party line as propounded by S.N. Singh. But those 'dalam commanders' who were busy making money through extortion were not in favour of laying down arms and tread the path of parliamentary democracy. Dalam Commanders like Sama Anthi Reddy and Gaddam Venkatramayya were of this view. So much so in 77 one of the important dalam commander, Rayala Subhash Chandra Bose defected to Pro-Lin-Piao faction alongwith his followers. But later on it demanded release of political prisoners, withdrawal of cases and warrants of arrests against its leaders as also police enquiries etc. by way of joining the platform of civil liberties forums. In July, 1977 the Andhra State Committee brought a Telugu mouthpiece of the party 'Praja Panth' (Mass line) edited by Madala Narayanswami.

In Punjab because a group revolted against S.N. Singh's line of participating in election and giving up of violence, there became a distinct group of united CP-ML known as Punjab, Himachal State Unity Committee whose convenor in 1976 was Darshan Singh Dosanjh. Surjit Singh Bhatti, Tari Singh Chalaki etc., over other participation. Police arrested Bikkar Singh Aishi General Secretary Ravinder Singh President of United CP-ML during Emergency. It had on estimated strength of about 450 members. Punjab and Himachal state committee of the party was headed by Baldev Singh Sanghol who was also a central committee member besides being state committee secretary. It was divided in three (3) zones. Party had DOABA Zone. Majha Zone and Malwa Zone. It had stormy front bodies among Kisan (Kirti Kisan Sabha) students (Punjab Student's Union) which had staged 'Dharna' and hunger strikes in May/June 1977. On civil Liberties front it had Punjab civil Liberties Union, on cultural front it had Natak Kala Kendra.

In West Bengal the united CP ML had good following. Santosh Rana had successfully contested Assembly poll in 1977. Yet Calcutta district committee opposed the revised tactical line and thus two state committee members were expelled who formed a parallel state committee. Rana encouraged party cadres to set up a Kishan Mukti Samiti of which he became president. It threatened the local landlord to distribute the land to landless peasant otherwise violence would be imposed on them.

In Bihar its strength was around 450 members. Party had set up a state committee with Gurbux Singh, CCM as secretary at Jamshedpur. A state committee for Chotanagpur was also formed. They formed trade unions in the industrial belt particularly in Heavy Engineering Corporation Ranchi. Santosh Rana and S.N. Singh paid frequent visits to them to guide the party. Gurbux Singh advocated ideological propaganda among the masses and even started publishing a journal 'KRANTI' edited by himself.

PRO LIN PIAO

When Lin Piao was disgraced in China at the 10th congress of communist party of China in August 1973. A section of the CPI-ML stood for him and another rose against him making the outfit Pro-Lin and Anti-Lin. Pro-Lin group was led by Mahadev Mukherjee. It held its 2nd party congress in December 1973.

One of the most militant, violent and extremist group later on led by Azizul Haq and Nishit Bhattacharya, had unflinching faith in Mao Ise Tung's thoughts and its tactical line based on guerilla tactics propounded by Lin-Piao. Large member of its 'action squads' were engaged in annihilation of landlords, in attacking police and snatching arms and ammunition from them. Creating 'Liberated Zones', looting fire arms from licence holders and building up PLA operating under overall command of North Bengal–Assam Border Regional Committee which later on split into Tarai Dooars Regional Committee and North Bengal–Assam Border Regional Committee were its main objectives. This faction of Marxist Leninist party was opposed to participating in elections. It was active in Malda Dinajpur in North-West Bengal and Katihar and Purnia in Bihar beside having cadres in Mungher and Bhagalpur. A committee by name of Purnia-Katihar Area Committee and Mungher–Bhagalpur Regional Committee was formed in these area, of course, under the supervision of North Bengal North-East Frontier Zonal Committee. Activities of these sub committee were confined to posturing and leafletting. But later on, in a daredevil attempt this group snatched 5 rifles when it attacked a police camp in August 1980 in Bhagalpur district. Towards the end of 1980 the group carried out Naxal activities in the name of Revolutionary Government which it claimed to have established in these areas. In February 1981 guerilla squads were involved is the murder of a land owner in Mungher district, looted 65 to 70 fire arms from Licence holders. Yet no harm was suffered by the Naxals.

Azizul-Nishit group was also known as second central committee group.

The revolutionary government had under it guerilla squads led by Jayant Das Commanding a Brigade by name of Shyam Brigade which had about 75 cadres divided into three groups. The party had carried out about 8 murders to punish opponents of the revolutionary government.

This Naxal group also stepped up its activities in urban areas in industrial belt by forming Industrial Area Committee in Calcutta in March 1981. Its party cadres 'Red Guards' carried party activities vigorously e.g. infiltrating among students, industrial workers distributing and circulating party literature win over the unemployed youth etc., organising mass fronts, forming revolutionary committee in all villages. The central committee of Pro-Lin, Piao faction of CPI-ML claimed in its party organ 'Deshbrati' that the party have revived Srikakulam days in North Bengal and that the party has chalked out 6-point programme as under :

1. Activating the revolutionary committees in all villages in collaboration with the party and the armed forces of the revolutionary government.
2. Adoption of democratic methods in implementing party programmes.
3. Organisation of mass fronts of the peasants, women and the youth.
4. Emphasising the economic demands of different cross sections of the people to attract participation.
5. Formation of guerilla squads, and
6. Village resistance groups equipped with arms.

Pro-Lin fraction of CPI-ML split into 4 factions :

1. Subir Talukdar Group–also known as 2nd Central Committee in 1973 led by Nishit Bhattacharya and Azizul Haq, Ramesh Shah etc. This underground group split in February 1986 into two (2) Sub-splinters ...
   (i) Dilip Bannerjee group
   (ii) Subir Talikadar group of (West Bengal State Secretary). They split on the issue of participation in mass organisation and smothening of Charu's Theory. But later on, they tried for unity.
2. Mahadev Mukherjee Group
3. Shanti Pal Group

   Anti-Shanti Pal Group

4. Central Organising Bureau.

CPI-ML Pro-Charu Mazumdar group of Pro-Lin Piao faction of Mahadev Mukherjee group was most violent group in early seventies but 1975 it god blunted because of arrest of all of its leaders. Because of liberal attitude of the government both at central and state levels after emergency almost all Naxalites were set tree. Once it was done, all the released leaders joined this Naxal group back. Mahadev Mukherjee himself came out of Jail on bail on December 27, 1977 but kept a low profile. He developed differences with other prominent leaders of his group i.e., Azizul Haq and Prof. Nishit Bhattacharya on the point of forming revolutionary committee at the village level, a resolution which already stood passed by the central committee Mahadev Mukherjee wanted to accord top priority to the formation of revolutionary committee at village level as the principle task of the party whereas others wanted continuation of violent activities. They even ridiculed Mahadev Mukherjee for organising flood relief and processions over release of political prisoners. Mahadev resigned from the central committee on August 24, 1978.

Shanti Pal group of CPI-ML Pro-Mazumdar faction was earlier operating under the name of North Bengal Bihar Border Regional Committee having its bases in that area through not a firm and strictly organisational one. Both Pro-Lin and Anti-Lin were exhorted to attack security forces deployed to perform election duty and also scare away voters.

The 10th party congress of CPC denounced Lin Piao and ignored Charu Mazumdar's line of action of mass annihilation, anti-Lin faction of CPI-ML was formed in December 1973. Vinod Mishra—a Pro-Chinese extremist group most militant and violent, dangerously left extremist group operating in West Bengal endorsing the ideology of formation of People's Liberation Army organising base areas and killing class enemies took up the leadership of anti-Lin group. It created a very strong organisational base in Naxalbari belt of Darjeeling district and in some rural areas of Bankura district. The group had a following of about 3000 in WB, Bihar, UP, Delhi, TN, Tripura, Assam and Kerala. It subsided later on and settled for adopting a moderate line with mass line and united front tactics. The armed struggle since it was successful was relegated to the pages of Naxalite history.

Though it set up fronts but rejected participation in elections even for limited and tactical purposes.

In Andhra, the leader of Lin Piao was Intha Ramana Reddy. It had maintained its militant and violent activities in Andhra but the death of same of its important leaders like Ratnam Surya Verma, Attaluri Mallikarjuna Rao, Desari Kottayya, Badugu Jaye Rao, Intha Krishna Reddy, M. Basavaraju and Vanga Satyanarayana in police encounters forced it to cool down. Besides, many important cadres were arrested. Intha Ramana Reddy was sentenced for life and put in Vizag Jail in 1977. In May 1975, it carried out an attack on the Cherukupalli police station in Guntur district and made an unsuccessful bid on September 20, 1976 to loot the Indian Overseas Bank in Khamman district. It used to conduct raids in the houses of rich landlords and businessmen to loot money.

In West Bengal, inspite of the arrest of Mahadev Mukherjee secretary Central Committee Satyabrata Dutta, Azizul Haq, Prof. Nishit Bhattacharjee, Kancha Dalvi @ Haru and a number of activists during emergency, this group remained active and carried on with the line of violent militant activities like dacoity, murder and attack on police as propounded by Charu Mazumdar. It broke the Calcutta Presidency Jail in February 1976 and made escape of 40-45 extremist of this group possible. The party faced organisational crisis and slowly tried to revive itself. It also revived it party organ, 'Deshbrati' in August 1977 and desired unity even with Anti-Lin group. It committed a gruesome murder of a 'Jotedar' on August 28, 1977 in Phansidena (Darjeeling).

Anti-Lin Piao faction (led by Vinod Mishra), Pro-Lin factions of Mahadev Mukherjee and Azizul Haq and another faction led by Shanti Pal of North Bengal) of CPI-ML firmly believed and adhered to violence in the form of annihilation of class enemies. Snatching of arms from police etc. was also their one of the main aims. Vinod Mishra faction had in 1978, been involved, in all probabilities in desecrating the statues of Vidyasagar, Netaji Subhash Chandra and that of Raja Ram Mohan Roy.

ANTI LIN PIAO / LIBERATION

Because of K. Venu and K.N. Ramchandran, this group functioned almost independently in Kerala. Kunnikal Narayanan's group and Kosal Ramdos group were also functioning. In early 1975 K. Venu reorganised Anti-Lin group after he was released from Jail and set up a state Committee designating himself as secretary and making K.N. Ramchandran as chief ideologue and Kutti Krishnan @ Dass, K.P. Amir Ali, Natesan and T.N. Joy as members. It brought out Mass Line in English and comrade in Malyalam. District committees were set up and nearly 250 party units and 700 study groups were set up all over the state of Kerala but everything was done with utmost secrecy. Effective party's underground apparatus was also built which provided shelter for cadres, effective courier system. So much so it established contact with Hindustan Ghadar Party in Canada after building up a clandestine channel of communication from whom it received all its regular financial help. Perfect secrecy used to maintained in all its operations. Over enthusiasm in carrying out violent activities in North Waywand area of Cannore district in August 1975 where it carried out 'money action' and an annihilation of Ernakulam district in September 1975 led the police to probe its (Anti Lin Group) activities further resulting in startling findings. Meanwhile, it carried out further violent acts in early 1976 which included an attack on police party in Mallapuram district during which one police officer died and another attack on police station in Kayanna in Calicut district. Nearly 300 prominent activitists were arrested by police, its underground apparatus was uncovered and the party was dealt with a heavy hand by police. After 1977 the party slowly tried to rebuild itself, formed ad-hoc state committee and districts committee in Calicut and Cannore. From, Cannore it launched a journal under the name of 'Samasya'.

In Bihar, Anti Lio Piao was able to engage low caste Hindus and Harijan (particularly in Bhojpur and Patna districts) to involve them in violence. It had created a state committee and 9 Area Committees besides 55 cells in Bhojpur-Patna belt. On declaration of Emergency about 550 extremists of this party were arrested. Prominent leaders like Subrata Datta @ Johar CCM, Dr. Nirmal Kumar, Narayan Kavi, Sudhir Kumar @ Ravi CCM and Srinaryan Thakur (Secretary Darbhanga Area Committee) were killed in police encounters which slowed down the extremist violence in Bihar. The party cadres annihilated 50 persons including 6 policemen during 1975 and 31 including 3 policemen in 1976. It snatched a number of firearms from victims. Anti-Lin always aspired to avenge the death of their leaders at the hands of police. Post-emergency, they established base areas and liberated zone in Bhojpur and Rohtas. Party all through maintained militant posture and indulged in leafletting renewing their resolve to bring in violent revolution and glorifying annihilation programme / attacks on police. In 1977 they carried 12 murders and 3 attacks on police. It has about 1100 members. Though most violent group, it went on to became one of the largest CPML group after working both ways i.e., overt as well as covert. Overtly it participated in mass issues. Overtly it, carried on violence and countered the threat passed by private 'Senas' and rival CP ML groups.

Whatever be the Marxist-Leninist group, they always had differences on participation in elections and carrying on violent activities to achieve revolution. Yet all of them were desirous of unity among themselves. This urge led MCC, PWG and CPML-DU to form an All India People's Resistance Forum (AIRPF) in 1992 of which an international seminar was held in New Delhi in February 1996.

INDIAN PEOPLE'S FRONT (IPF)
(CPI-ML Anti-Lin Piao)

IPF, a political front of Anti-Lin Piao group of CPI-ML in April 1, 1982 formed by Subrata Dutt as a cover for Vinod Mishra led CPI-ML (liberation) based in Bihar under the chairmanship of Nagbhushan Patnaik. The Ist convention of IPF was held in Delhi from 24th to 26th April 1982. Dutt was killed in Police encounter and the command of liberation Group was taken over by Vinod Mishra. It created public opinion against state terrorism and Black laws like NSA and the Terrorist and Disruptive Activities Act 1985 in Bihar in 1986. On August 21, 1986 it gave a call for 'Gherao' of Bihar Assembly. Nagbhushan Patnaik toured Punjab and incited public for not resolving Punjab problem. Thus it entrenched itself in Punjab and formed a State Committee in 1985 itself. IPF was formed by Liberation Group simply to make their entry into politics. It was a conglomeration of about 200 mass organisation and political formation all over the country.

IPF fielded candidates for State Assembly elections and Parliamentary elections but it failed to get a single seat in either of them. But it did keep the front to enlarge the base among masses and consolidate its hold.

After 4th Party Congress at Jahanabad in January 1988, it was projected as a full-fledged party to enable the party congress to participate in elections and provide a platform to other ML and democratic forces to come together and then participated in 1989 parliamentary elections and won one MP and six MLA seats in Bihar. It floated front organisations among students, labour, women folk etc. success in these elections encouraged them to come out in open and function as an over ground organisation and contest elections under the party CPI-ML which already stood registered with Election Commission as a political party. In 1995 it won 6 seats in Bihar Assembly elections.

Whenever there were judgements against the police, Anti-Lin, all Naxals became happy. Nishat Qaiser a JNU student in late 70s was happy over the judgement holding Arwal police guilty of deliberate firing on a peaceful gathering of villagers on April 19, 1986. IPF Calcutta unit was looked after by Sapan Mukherjee state General Secretary of IPF Calcutta.

IPF spearheaded an agitation in Delhi for removal of PM Rajiv Gandhi. Purushottam Sharma, convenor of Delhi Unit of IPF issued an appeal on 27.8.1987 in this effect and exhorted people to participate in the campaign in increased number. In a handout issued by him, he stated that a meeting on September 23, 1987 was arranged to be addressed by chairman Nagbhushan Patnaik Bihar State Committee of IPF had organised such a Rally on October 15, 1987 for removal of Rajiv Gandhi. A 'Rajiv Hatao Morcha' was held in Lucknow on October 14, 1987 and a Rally held in Delhi on October 15. IPF Delhi was indulged in wall-postering, Gate meetings, Group meetings in Factories, corner meetings etc.

IPF had a 3-tier structure of leadership : a 12-member Central Executive (CEC) comprising the national President and 11 national general secretaries, a 40-member Central Working Committees (CWC). 11 National vice-President and Presidents of all state units. IPF had fielded one Virendra Vidrohi of IPF against Chief Minister Jagannath Mishra from Jhanjharpur in Bihar Assembly elections in February 1990 as a symbol of protest since he was languishing in

Jahanabad Jail for blackening former Chief Minister Bhagwat Jha Azad's face in 1988. IPF held a massive rally in Delhi on Oct 8, 1990 aimed at fighting communalism branding Congress for "Satisfying vested interest" and Janata Dal for trying "to capitalise on the minority vote bank".

In December 1992 after CPI-ML liberation group had the party Congress in Calcutta, it decided to start functioning openly as a political party and IPF was proposed to be disbanded. On February 26, 27, 1994 at a meeting in Patna, IPF dissolved its all India Committee individual annihilation theory of Kola Vankaiah (Unity Committee group) was criticised by IPF. IPF in defunct now.

CPI-ML contested Lok Sabha and Assembly elections under the banner of IPF. It consolidated its position in Bihar. In 1990 it had secured 5.5 lakh votes, it secured 7.5 lakh votes in 1995 Assembly elections. In Lok Sabha polls it secured 1,16,000 votes in Arrah Constituency in 1991, the party candidates polled 1,46,000 votes in the election in 1996. Besides the party improved its position in Jehanabad, where it polled 1,30,000 as compared to 1,13,000 in 1991. It also improved its influence in Siwan and Buxar where it polled more than 1 lakh vote in each of these constituencies in 1996 as compared to about 20,000 in 1991.

SPLIT IN PCC CPI-ML (S.N. SINGH FACTION) IN 1984

Personality cult and clashes, ideological differences and irrelevant issues dogged the Marxist-Leninist movement in India, though S.N. Singh orientation was one of the largest group but a vertical split developed simply because of personality clashes and internal differences. It became S.N. Singh V/s Baskar Nandi and Santosh Rana combine. The crisis was simmering since 1983 which culminated in August 1984 both the groups accusing each other, S.N. Singh who was itching to exit took the side of Sadhan Sarkar (PCC member and staunch supporter of S.N. Singh) whereas Santosh Rana and Co. which dominated the PCC took disciplinary action against him which ultimately culminated in the vertical split.

Besides, they differed on the issues like importance of Stalin's role in International Communist Movement, acceptance of foreign financial assistance and appropriate and ripe time and conditions for launching armed struggle. Baskar Nandi and Santosh Rana combine opined that revolutionary situation existed in the country for organising militant struggle, S.N. Singh refuted it and accused them of denegrading Stalin and minimising his importance as a leader of the working classes of the world. S.N. Singh also accused his rival group of accepting foreign financial assistance without prior approval of the party. Bhaskar Nandi, in turn, accused S.N. Singh of breaking the party after formenting groupism and creating cliques. But when West Bengal state conference of the party was held on August 9-13, 1994 at Beliatore (Bankura), sharp differences appeared among the rivals in same party conference. PCC held a meeting on August 16, at Calcutta and suspended Sadhan Sankar for disobeying its instructions. S.N. Singh, in retaliation, also called a separate national conference of the party which was held on August 27-28, 1984 in Birbhum district and accused Bhaskar Nandi and Santosh Rana of conniving with imperialist forces and bringing a split in the party. The National Conference called by S.N. Singh was attended by about 35 delegates from HP, Punjab, UP, Bihar, Delhi and WB besides fraternal delegates like Ashim Chatterjee of Communist Revolutionary League of India, Kanu Sanyal of OCCR, D.V. Rao group of UCCRI-ML, Marxist-Leninist group of Calcutta and West Bengal State Organising Committee of CPI-ML. On the conference the split was ratified and S.N. Singh was elected general secretary of his faction. Party operational HQ were located in Calcutta and official HQ in Patna. A 9-member Provisional Central Committee was elected. His faction demanded to intensify efforts for mass fronts and condemned both the Superpowers and as far as Republic of China was concerned, it would decide its stand on issue-basis. However, it desired unity of all communist revolutionary in the country.

On the other hand, Bhaskar Nandi also held party conference in Jalpaiguri, North Bengal from August 29, 1984 where S.N. Singh was expelled for deserting the Naxalite path. Santosh Rana exhorted the Party Cadres to resort to armed struggle and fight against authoritarianism of present establishment and make all out efforts to dislodge Mrs. Gandhi from power. Ad hoc Central Committee was formed and Santosh Rana was elected Secretary.

But on July 17, 1985 both the faction owing allegiance to late

S.N. Singh and late Chandra Pula Reddy signed an accord to merge into one party under the banner of PCC CPI-ML which would bank on agrarian revolution and recognised the Marxism-Leninism-Mao Tse Tung thoughts as ideological guides. Bhaskar Nandi group was more active at state level in Assam. Its ultimate object was to bring about armed revolution by way of adjusted to the ground realities and utilising parliamentary process to acquire broad mass base. After 1977 it utilised the political situation to build its organisation and underground base, mobilised rural poor, agricultural workers under the banner 'Khetak Santhas' and organised Peoples' court to give relief to agriculture labour against harassment by landlord, grabbing their land, forcible harvesting etc. It also tried to bring womenfolk under its fold by way of floating a Pragatisheel Narisangh' and infiltrated industrial and semi-industrial areas and spreading their net to tea-workers, Rikshaw pullers etc. Like other ML groups, student were their main targets. To take them under party's influence was top priority and it was done under "United Students' Federation" and attract more and more students.

Incidently, S.N. Singh bade good bye to the world on October 21, 1984 at the age of 65. He died of a heart attack in King George Hospital in Vishakhapatnam on Sunday October 21, 1984. His body was brought by Saifuddin, who was with S.N. Singh at the time of his death, to Calcutta to be cremated at Keoratala Burning Ghat.

SPLIT IN C.P. REDDY GROUP OF CPI-ML

CPI-ML (C.P. Reddy group) that came into existence in May 1980 further split in the CPI-ML group of CP Reddy in 1984 on ideological grounds when its state Committee defied the Central leadership and formed Pyala Vasudeva Rao group. Pyala said "Rao often acted whimsically'. The rival faction in the State was called Nirmala group led by widow of Chandra Pulla Reddy. CP Reddy ruled his party for almost 10 years in a dictatorial way till his death in early 1985. His wife Nirmala had also behaved like power into herself instigating party worker against provisional committee. Nirmala group had influence in Warangal and Karimnagar while Pyala group was active in the plains and forests of Khammam and West Godavari district and good following in parts of Adilabad, Nalgonda, West

Godavari and Guntur districts. Pyala group had little support from intellectuals.

Pyala Vasudev Rao, leader of the largest group in Andhra Pradesh was drawn to the Communist ideology as a student in 1953. He became full time party worker in 1962. In 1982 following the encounter-death of Naxal leader Vempatapu Satyanarayana and Adibhatla Kailasam, the Srikakulam Committee of CPI-ML came to be under the leadership of Pyala in 1976. On the death of P. Ramanarasaih in 1976 in an encounter, Pyala became the Secretary of AP state committee of C.P. Reddy group. In 1984 most of the members of State Committee deserted Pulla Reddy group and formed Pyala Vasudev Rao group.

C.P. Reddy faction had suffered on other fronts also. Baldev Singh Mann State committee member of his faction of CPI-ML was killed on September 26, 1986. CPI-MLA Darshan Singh Candian was also killed on September 25, 1986. which resulted in the formation of a new platform 'Inquilabi Ekta Kendra' by Dr. Gursharan Singh. Some other left extremist groups also sided with Gurshan Singh on the agitation for Punjab issue.

In Andhra C.P. Reddy group (K. Rajanna faction) had contested nine (9) Assembly seats and was victorious in Sircilla in Karimnagar district from where M.V. Krishnaiah was elected as an MLA. The issues Rajanna faction took up were :

(i) Land to the tiller.

(ii) Withdrawal of all draconian laws atrocities on Dalits, increasing taxes, price rise and growing unemployment.

C.P. Reddy group considered Russia as main threat to peace i.e. Soviet Union's "Social imperialism" was the chief source of threat of war–more than American Imperialism. It had held its special congress 9th Congress from October 1 to 4, 1980 in Punjab where C.P. Reddy was elected general Secretary and it adopted three documents relating to Party's programme, Constitution and its tasks in the present situation.

C.P. Reddy's wife Mrs. Nirmala @ Radakka (45) of Andhra Pradesh was arrested on May 29, 1982 in connection with 10 cases of violence, attempt to murder and dacoities etc. She carried a reward of Rs. 15,000 on her head.

To begin with C.P. Reddy was with Andhra Pradesh coordination Committee of Communist Revolutionaries (APCCCR) when CPI-ML took birth. At that point of time Dakshin Desh which later became MCC and APCCCR did not join the party led by Kanu Sanyal/Charu Mazumdar. The APCCCR later split into T Nagi Reddy and DV Rao faction on one side and CP Reddy faction on the other. But CP Reddy faction later on merged with SN faction of CPI-ML in 1975 and again separated from it after developing differences with S.N. Singh.

References

1. *The Week*, July 20-26, 1986.
2. *The Statesman,* April 18, 1984.
3. *Ibid.*
4. *The Times of India,* December 29, 1987.
5. *The Times of India,* May 17, 1986.
6. *The Times of India,* May 18, 1988.
7. *The Indian Express*, February 28, 1989.
8. *The Indian Express*, December 10, 1990 Naxalites on the Rampage by T. Lakshmi Pati from Hyderabad.
9. *The Times of India*, January 5, 1990. "The Peoples War Group – A Formidable Force by C. Lokeshwar Rao.
10. *The Times of India*, May 13, 1991.
11. *The Indian Express*, October 7, 2008, report by Debabrata Mohanty.
12. *The Pioneer*, May 12, 2009, article by Amarnath Tiwari "Arrested Maoists leaders Belies Prachanda's Claims".
13. 30 years of Nanalbari : An Epic of Heroic Struggle and Sacrifice.
14. *Ibid.*
15. *The Telegraph,* Sunday, June 8, 1987.
16. *Ibid.*

[illegible]

[illegible]

References

[illegible]

The Times of India, May [illegible], 1986.

[illegible]

The [illegible], [illegible] 1986.

[illegible]

[illegible]

[illegible]

3

The Movement in Early Eightees

TAMIL NADU

Naxalbari uprising of 1967 had its repercussions in Tamil Nadu also. In CPM itself which was created in 1964 a distinct Maoist group existed even in 1965 in its state unit - a faction led by militant trade unionist and Kisan Sabha activists in Coimbatore. The group formed TAMIZHGA MILL THOZHILALIGAL SANGHAM. Militant trade unionist and Kisan Sabha activist L. Appu became President who later on represented Tamil Nadu in Charu Mazumdar's All India Coordination Committee of Communist Revolutionaries. Tamil Nadu coordination Committee metamorphosed on April 22, 1969 into CPI-ML. The new party's line of action initially was to organise, agricultural labour, confiscate landlords crops and expropriation of landlords properties. But this mass action was abandoned in favour of annihilation policy advocated by Charu Mazumdar. In Tamilnadu, a large number of revolutionaries opposed annihilation and quit the party. First annihilation planned for May 1, 1969 ended in failure when the target landlord from Nellithurai in Nilgiri district was away from home. This was followed by annihilation of Ramaswamy founder, a landlord and moneylender. Lot of annihilation followed eliminating class enemies. Perianna Chetty, a rich money lender in Nagarasampathi in Dharampuri district who lent money charging 300% interest and obtaining signature on blank papers, Gopalkrishna Naidu, a feudal landlord in Thanjavur had allegedly set fire a barn in which 40 Harijans were locked and roasted them alive. (He was acquitted by the Supreme Court). Naxalites infiltrated his workforce and stabbed him to death.

By 1970 most of ML leaders were arrested by Police. L. Appu vanished. A.M. Kothandaraman and Kaliaperumal were arrested. By 1971-end the Naxalites were almost done away with in Tamil Nadu. But post-1977 several groups re-emerged.

Charu Mazumdar had secretly visited the state in 1970 to recruit followers for his extremist philosophy. His supporters from Tamil Nadu had also visited West Bengal for training the same year. A civil rights organisation formed by doctors, lawyers etc. by name of 'Makkal Urumai Kazhagam' and another organisation "Makkal Nala Urumai Manram" (People's Welfare and rights association) were considered to be front organisations by the Police. About 800 was the strength of Naxalites in the state. They lived and worked with the villagers in order to win their confidence emulating the example of Chinese Communists of thirtees and fortees.

Mr. Kannamani, called 'the leader' by his followers, who belonged to the dominant "annihilationist" group in Tamil Nadu was killed in December 1980 in a police encounter. His position was taken over by his brother-in-law Mr. R. Dhanpal. In Tamil Nadu Naxalites have been most active. They organised the peasants in Thirupattur area of North Arcot district to revolt against the oppression of landlords. The Nawab of Thirupattur had assigned tax collection responsibility to contractors who in turn behaved ruthlessly with peasants and used to extract much higher rent and this had led to revolt by peasants. Thereafter E.V. Ramaswami Naicker took up peasant's cause and they became conscious of their rights. Peasants' group was led by one Sivalingam who came in contact with CPI-ML in early seventies and they organised agricultural workers in Poooneri village to enforce the agricultural minimum wages act in 1975. Ever since the landlords in connivance with the police, have systematically been annihilating peasant activists. Chettiars are the major landowners who had been suppressing Vanniyar agriculturists.

At national level, the 'real CPI-ML' was known an Vinod Mishra group of CPI-ML which was having support in Tamil Nadu from P.V. Srinivasan faction which had rejected democratic institutions outright. It also split in State Organising Committee (SOC) and the Tamil Nadu Organising Committee (TNOC). PWG enjoyed the support of A.M. Kothandaranan etc. K. Venu, S.N. Nagrajan and K.N.

Ramchandran etc. had their own party-Communist Revolutionary Committee (CRC). Yet another group was led by Kanamani which police liquidated. Kaliaperumal, on his release from prison, made an attempt to unite various CPI-ML groups by way of holding a state level conference at Pennadam with the active help of Thamizharasan who still supported annihilation. Incidently a call was made for an independent Tamil State for which Perunchitranar was mainly responsible and became friendly with Kaliaperumal who was won over to separatist view point. Thamizharsan was full of regional and linguistic ferver as well as a supporter of Tamil Nadu Liberation Front (TNLF) demanding a separate Tamil homeland. He was also responsible for floating Radical Youth League and Radical student's Union – both owning allegiance to Kondapalli's People's War Group. But after reorganisation of Pennadam, both of these outfits/ceased to exist. (*The Illustrated Weekly of India,* July 10, 1988).

In late eightees, say around 1989, the following five major Naxal groups existed :

1. **Anti Lin Piao :** Its front organisations were :
   (a) Indian People's Front
   (b) The Tamil Nadu Youth Movement.
2. **People's War Group :** led by Kondapalli Seetharamaiah : Its front
   (a) Radical Youth League
   (b) Radical Student's Union.
   (c) The Revolutionary Cultural Movement
   (d) People's Democratic Rights Association
3. **The Tamil Nadu Organising Committee (Marxist-Leninist):** The front organisation were :
   (a) The Organisation for Civil and Democratic Rights
   (b) People's Cultural Association.
4. **Tamil Nadu State Organising Committee :** Its fronts were:
   (a) People Art and Literary Association
   (b) The Agriculturist Liberation Front
   (c) Radical Students Youth Front.

5. **The Tamil Nadu Communist Party (ML) (Kaliaperumal Group):** It had two front organisations :
   (a) The Tamil Nadu Revolutionary Students Youth Forum
   (b) Aruna Sugarcane Farmers Association (*Frontline*, September 2-15, 1989 issue).

KERALA

In order to make efforts to form a United Party to lead a national struggle on the non-parliamentary path, Naxalites representatives of 13 revolutionary organisations held a secret conference from January 30 to February 2, 1981 in Patna. MCC participated in the conference. Four groups i.e. Central team of CPI-ML, the Indian Communist Party (a breakaway group of CPM in Karnataka), UCCRI-MLDV Rao group and Bolshevik Party expressed themselves in favour of unity but desired concrete results. They opined that unity could not be achieved by mere talks. The Lin-Piao faction of Nishit Bhattacharya and Azizul Haq which were primarily responsible for the series of gun snatching incidents in West Bengal in 1980-81 was not invited since it did not believe in mass movements. Since Kanu Sanyal, Ashim Chatterjee, Gurbux Singh were Pro-CPM, they were also not invited (*The Times of India*, March 27, 1981).

In early 1981, 13 CPI-ML factions met in Trichur district under the guise of Janakiya Samskar Vedi (People's Cultural Forum). The naxalites have been engaging in the politics of Intimidation. The re-grouped Naxalites brought out a clandestine publication "Inqulab" which said that their objects was to topple the rule of "Feudalism, bureaucratic over lordism and imperialism" in India through guerilla warfare and to institute "People's power" in a new democratic revolutionary set-up.

In eightees, four important factions of CPI-ML existed in Kerala, most prominent of which was anti-Lin Piao group – an ultra militant faction of COC CPI-ML led by Rauf which itself was a faction of the group led by Kondapalli Seetaramaiah. Other factions that existed were the provisional Central Committee of CPI-ML (SN Singh) led by Dilip Kumar, Communist Bolshevik Party led by A.V. Aryan and the Kausal Ramdoss group.

The leader of the Anti-Lin group was K. Venugopal an accused in Kummil – Nagarur murder case of 1968. Other leaders were K.N. Ramchandran, Murali Kannambally (son of Ambassador Kamambally), Alleppey Ravindran and T.N. Joy @Benny. This group had been emphasising in building mass line/base through cultural and political propaganda but simultaneously, adhering to the objectives of violent revolution and 'action' and claimed credit for the murder of class enemy Madhathil, Thomas of Kenichira, a Wynad landlord on January 16, 1980. (*The Hindustan Times,* May 5, 1980– "splits shatter Naxalite dream of capturing power) It also did not deny when the murder of Sonarajan, an industrialist of Allepy on March 29, 1980 was attributed to it.

The movement grew in the year 1982. More members came into extremist's fold, more fronts were started, organisational strengthening was done by almost all the extremist groups. Central Reorganising Committee (CRC) was formed in January 1982. People's War Group (PWG) also flourished by spreading its influence in Orissa, Tamil Nadu, MP and Maharashtra. Pro-Lin Piao faction suffered in the sense that a number of its top leaders including Prof. Nishit Bhattacharjee (CCS) and Azizul Haq (CCM) of West Bengal Central Committee Secy were arrested. Another significant step was that a part of independent faction of COC-CPI-ML led by Appalasuri of AP and Unity Organisation of CPI-ML led by Bhabani Roy Chowdhuri of West Bengal merged and formed a CPI-ML (Party Unity). IPF was formed in 1982 by Anti Lin Piao faction which was spread over 15 states. PCC CPI ML formed on All India Students' body called Indian Students Association. Other group like CRC CPI ML and PWG also made similar attempts class-oriented activities and organisational activities were taken up by all groups. Parallel Central Committee of UCCRI-ML Pro-Lin Piao faction, CRC CPI-ML, PWG, CPI-ML (CP Reddy group) joined in Anti-CPC stand, branded it as revisionist and accused it of abandoning Maoism and not adhering to the tenets of Marxism-Leninism. Even S.N. Singh had criticised CPC in its polit bureau meeting in Calcutta in December 1982.

Naxals, during initial years, of course, opposed to the parliamentary system and were hell bent to bring armed revolution to overthrow the states and central government through violent means. But gradually after say 1977, some of their groups like PCC, CPI-ML (CP Reddy), Anti-Lin, Piao faction of CPI-ML, OCCR, COCCPI-M (Umadhar Singh) UCCRI-ML (both DV and Anti D.V. Rao groups) participated in elections with ulterior motives of reaching out to masses through participating in elections to bring about revolutionary ideology. However, Pro-Lin Piao faction (Subir Talukdar group), Peoples War Group, CRC CPI-ML, Marxist-Leninist study centre (dissident CRC) etc. opposed elections and propagated for boycott of polls. The participation of certain CPI-ML groups in the 1980 parliamentary elections drew a blank in Lok Sabha but in State Assembly four (4) candidates - 2 each from S.N. Singh and C.P. Reddy group were elected in 1980.

The Communist Party of India (Marxist-Leninist) split on August 17, 1987 with a faction opposed to the policies of K. Venu, Secretary of the party central reorganisation committee (CRC) appointing a 'provisional committee' replacing the existing leadership. K Venu's group CRCCPI ML had given up the theory that feudalism was the only hurdle to socialism. His group redefined India in 1983-84 as a "neo-colony" exploited by different important powers and that India was a multi-racial country, each nationality must have the right to self-determination, including the right to secede. He even supported the demand of 'Khalistan' starting that it is based on the "new democratic Punjab" i.e. state under the leadership of working class. This line of thinking resulted in split and K.N. Ramchandran walked away to form another splinter group.

BIHAR

Marxist-Leninist movement was ushered in Bihar in the year 1967 by Jagdish Mahto and Rameshwar Ahir of Bhojpur district who were actively helped by Charu Mazumdar. In 1967 itself Satyanarayan Singh, Tufan Chandra Josh and Umadhar Prasad Singh formed Bihar State Co-ordination Committee at Mushahari in Muzaffarfur district. Under this committee, the seeds of agrarian movement and bloodshed were sown by oppressed landless and marginal farmers who launched armed retaliation against upper caste landlords. The Naxalite movement, thereafter, developed passing through four stages:

(i) The peasants fought against social and caste exploitation in which they were led by Naxalites.

(ii) Thereafter they questioned the economic exploitation and demanded minimum wages as fixed by the governments.

(iii) Then they switched over to land disputes and entered into direct confrontation with landlords demanding occupancy rights over surplus land.

(iv) And landless peasants started grabbing land. Today they are trying to retrain what they had seized.

By mid-1968 the movement spread to Muzaffarpur district where peasants harvested Zamindar's crop and also seized the crop resulting in clashes with the police and Zamindars. Many a Naxalite factions had started their movement in Bihar, clashed with police and continued their attacks on class enemies.

In Bihar, Maoist Communist Centre and Santosh Rana's CPI-ML party unity, Vinod Mishra's Liberation Group which functioned under the mass front-Indian People's Front were active. Umadhar Singh, a member of Bihar State Assembly was also heading a CPI-ML small faction in late eightees. There had been frequent clashes between Liberation Group and Party Unity.

During Emergency (1975-77) in Bihar 50,000 acres of surplus land were acquired in marked contrast to the acquision of a mere 9700 acres under the ceiling laws over the years prior to the Emergency. The state Govt. also received 20,431 acres under the voluntary surrender schemes which called upon the big landlords to see the writing on the wall and disclose their surplus holdings. About 10,000 acres of acquired land were re-distributed. (*The Illustrated Weekly of India,* July 20,1986).

Land reforms could not be implemented effectively on account of legislative muddles. But in 1987 this movement could not count much on this factor, for the large states have been liquidated on account of growth in the numbers of landlords and rich peasants families,there is not much land above the ceiling in the districts in which the movement was active and also there is not much land vested with the government to be distributed among the landless labourers. Even if the surplus land is considerable, the number of landless labourers is too large to perceptibly benefit by its redistribution. *(The Indian Express, July 24, 1987).*

During the years 1987 to 1997 the Naxal Movement MCC, PWG, party unity, Vinod Mishra group of CPI-ML – were very active in Bihar, in fact not only in the Bihar but in the country itself. All of them together were responsible for 90% of Naxal violence in the country, violence included destruction of government property, looting of arms from security forces and annihilation of class enemy, applying intimidation so that people do not dare vote in elections. Attacking voters to lower their moral was also yet another form of Naxal violence. A new trend was also noticed during this period. Naxalites insisted on the strategy of giving calls of 'Bandh', enriched their armoury by sophisticated weapons like AK-47 to match with that of the states. 'Bandh' was mainly used to highlight the state repression among masses.

Middle classes and professional groups accepted the ideology of Marxism-Leninism which had about 20 groups. Of course, 3-world theory did have its effects but simultaneously groups emerged who questioned the attitude of Chinese leadership and disassociated themselves.

People got fascinated towards the revolution and revolutionary ideas and propagated extremist views and ideas. Many fronts, clubs, associations were floated and seminars, street-corner skits were enacted, extremist literature, journals, magazines were prepared and circulated propagating extremist views. Violence remained the basic weapons of all the extremist groups albeit its application on class enemies was different by different ML groups. Some were more violent, some postponed it for the present, some did it selectively. But on the question of annihilation there were sharp differences.

At all India level, PCC CPI ML (S.N. Singh) groups and C.P. Reddy group had their followers. S N Singh group had adopted more moderate approach in the sense that it did not believe in Charu Mazumdar's theory of annihilation as essential part of revolutionary tactics but carried on armed struggle and violence to achieve its goals. Besides, it did not reject its participation in parliamentary process and in mass and open activities which proved very helpful to the party. Santosh Rana became a sitting MLA in West Bengal Assembly. S.N. Singh groups desired a broad United Front to oppose the expansionist designs of Soviet Union. It identified Cong-I as the main agent of Soviet Social Imperialism. It opted for open political activities, making to build fronts organisations among labourers, mine workers, students, medicos etc., formed a Trade Union at All India Level under the name of Indian Federation of Trade Union (IFTU). It believed in both open as well underground activities involving legal or illegal methods to gain wide acceptance. United CP-ML led by S.N. Singh was indeed moderate whose stand was that the Janata Party was "Patriotic and Democratic" though they also hail from the same bourgeois classes and that they had granted a number of civil liberties which were helpful for the growth of their party. The party never wanted to go for left adverturism that entailed sheer madness and realised their mistake in boycotting armed agrarian revolution. Resultantly it had spread it. influence in about almost 12 states in India where its membership could be estimated to be some where between 5 to 6 thousands.

CPI-ML (Chandrapulla Reddy group)- Ideological differences with S.N. Singh led to the birth of this splinter group in May 1980 of desired revolutionary unity or unification of the revolutionary parties, supported Chinese leadership by endorsing its views on the international situations. Armed struggle programmes cleverly preserving the gains of earlier armed struggle, participating in elections as a matter of technical move and using mass line tactics for building up its influence among youth, students, industrial labour were the policies it adhered to. It had influence among 4000 members in Andhra, Punjab, Maharashtra, Bihar and J&K.

A major group of CPI-ML headed by Vinod Mishra was operating in and from Bihar. Is had it base in Bengal and Tripura. He had formed Anti-Lin Piao faction of CPI-ML in Bhojpur in December 1973.

The leaders of 13 Naxalite groups from all over India met at a secret conclave from January 30 to February 2, 1981 to discuss the then situation in the country. It was believed that the Naxalite movement was bidding good bye to the policy of individual liquidation of "class enemies" like policeman and switching to a nation wide mass agitation. (*The Times of India,* March 5, 1981 news by V G Prasad Rao: Naxalites give up Liquidation policy).

On May 2, 1982 two of the 13 splinter groups of CPI-ML Central Organising Committee of CPI-ML of Andhra Pradesh and unity Organisation of CPI-ML West Bengal merged with a pledge to make sincere efforts for the unity of all the factions of CPI-ML. Its name was chosen as Central Organising Committee CPI-ML Indian People's Front (IPF) was also formed in 1982.

Between 1976 and 2008 Naxals killed 842 people in Bihar. MCC alone was responsible for 100 incidents in 1988 as against 43 in 1987. Anti-Lin Piao faction accounted for 92 incidents in 1988 as against 61 in 1987.

Incidently, when a Sikh youth Amarjeet Singh Sohi, a resident of Gurdaspur (Punjab) was arrested at Azadbigha village in Jehanabad district on November 15, 1988, the police discovered links between a Canada-based organisation IPANA and Naxalites in Bihar. He was described as a "Canada-trained terrorist" by Bihar Police.

Mazdoor Kisan Sangram Samiti (MKSS), formed in 1981 by Dr. Vinayaan became a force to reckon with particularly in Central Bihar. On April 19, 1986 police killed 23 of its workers at Arwal (Jehanabad district). Dr. Vinayan announced severing of its 'fraternal ties' with CPI-ML Party Unity Group because armed squards were very-cunningly and craftily indulging in senseless killing under the cover of MKSS. Party Unity used MKSS as a cover to keep its armed actions secret and the blame came on MKSS. Resultantly, MKSS was banned for violent actions of the Party Unity Group in October 1987. On June 20, 1987 party split and MKSS weakened. Dr. Vinayan himself was arrested on December 21, 1988 at Gaya Railway Station.

A typical situation had developed in Bihar. There were four major "Private Armies" to protect landlords of different castes. Lorik Sena raised after Lorik Yadav was of Yadavs. Lorik had fought against British. Bhoomi Sena, best armed private army - renamed in 1980 as such was Pro-Kurmi. It was earlier known as Kisan Surksha Samiti. The Kunwar Sena set up in 1969 by Rajput landlords named after 1857 hero Vir Kunwar Singh. The Brahmarshi Sena which was formed to counter Naxalite menace in Gaya District. The landless peasants, agricultural labour, backward castes etc. had raised Lal Sena. All indulged in violence. Eight Harijan and three 'sonars' were killed in

Belchi in May 1977. Fourteen Harijan peasants were killed in Pipra on February 25, 1980, thirteen Harijan and backward caste peasants were shot dead or burnt at Parasbigha on February 6, 1980. Nine children and two others were killed in Pipra in January 1984. Thus there were many incidents including Aurangabad done by MCC in May 1987.

In 1972 a splinter group of CPI-ML launched itself under the name of Maoist Communist Centre (MCC) in Aurangabad. With the passage of time, MCC became stronger and stronger with the active support of small peasantry and landless labourers who fought landlords. MCC had formed Krantikari Kisan Samiti and Lal Sena. It forcibly took about 5000 acres of land from landlords and distributed it among its followers. MCC itself was banned by the Bihar Government on June 1, 1987.

PUNJAB

Lal Singh Sekhon, a member of CPI-ML (S.N. Singh faction) asked for the implementation of the Anandpur Sahib resolution which demanded autonomy for the states. He made this appeal on March 22, 1982 asking for support to the Anandpur Sahib resolution which was to be organised on April 13, 1982, Dev Nathan a central committee member of CPI-ML stated (October 6, 1982) that his party supported Anandpur Resolution demanding greater autonomy for states. Naxalism in Punjab surfaced around mid-1967 with late comrade Bhija Singh who ran a school in Chandigarh which propagated Maoism among youths. He formed a state coordination committee in 1986 taking the charge of state secretary of the committee which owed allegiance to the All India Coordination Committee of Communist Revolutionaries. The following year i.e. in 1969 its cadres let loose a reign of terror making it reach to the top by 1970-71 consequently police came into action and party cadres got killed in encounters. Meanwhile in Mid-1971 original CPI-ML split and a strong parallel extremist movement in Andhra took its roots. Punjab Naxalites faced fragmentation. In early eighties three main groups of Naxals existed in Punjab:

(1) Bhatinda group - which was an important component of unity centre for communist revolutionaries (UCCRI-ML).

(2) Central Organising Committee (COC) led by Jagjit Singh Sol @ Sharma. He played a leading role in Bhojpur movement.

(3) SN Singh/Chandra Pulla Reddy combine group which came in existence n 1974 led by Baldev Singh Sanghol. This group was main propagator of Charu Mazumdar.

Three splinters groups also emerged :

(1) Revolutionary view point led by R.P. Saraf. He claimed to be true inheritors of Charu Mazumdar's line.

(2) S.N. Singh faction led by Tara Singh Chalaki in Punjab.

(3) A breakaway faction of central team led by Darshan Singh Dosanj and Surjit Singh Batti: It repudiated the path of Parliamentary democracy. Later on Bhatti expelled Darshan Singh Dosanj and he formed his own and central team on February 25, 1987.

Three party organs were in circulation in Punjab. Nagi Reddy line was followed by 'JAIKARA'. R.P. Saraf group following the line of Charu Mazumdar brought out "PRACHAND" and Central Team circulated 'SURKH REKHA'. CPI-ML programme in May 1970 declared that the basic task of Indian revolution is to throw away the rule of feudalism, comprador bureaucrat capitalism, imperialism and social imperialism.

Prithavi Pal Singh Randhawa (since dead). Malwinder Singh Mali were the militant minds in Punjab. Punjab Students Union (PSU) was the most effective front organisation of Naxalites. It was re-started in 1971 by Randhawa. (It was earlier a CPM outfit and was disbanded). In 1974 a faction of PSU led by Bikr Singh walked out of PSU and formed a rival group which in, turn, further split in 1977 in two splinter groups. PSU had 3 factions in Punjab in early eighties (1) PSU (Mali group), (2) PSU (Ajaib group) and (3) PSU (Kama group). PSU carried out successful bus agitation and military gained an upper hand. They used 'bandh' to bring the state government to a grinding halt. Naujawan Bharat Sabha and the PSU clashed with the police on January 22, 1981 when Labh Singh was killed.

WEST BENGAL

The birth place and epi-centre of Naxals, the movement started with a bang having an element of surprise. Nobody at least no land lord or police had till then ever thought that the sharecroppers would rise in revolt and behave in a militant way. Issues like tenancy rights and wages were taken up by landless labourers and their leaders. In 1969 first attack was made in Dubraj Pur 'thana' and the guerilla squads eliminated about 70 class enemies in the area of about 20 police station (thana). Struggle spread and many students / youths joined the movement. Secret Revolutionary Peasants Committees were established and priority was accorded to seize weapons (guns) from police and landlords. Police and Government acted tough by mid-1971 and movement was suppressed albeit temporarily. The Naxal movement had by then spread to the area of Birbhum, Debra Gopiballabhur in Midnapur district.

During early eighties at least following three CPI-ML groups were very active.

(1) Azizul-Nishit or alternately known as second central committee

(2) Maoist Communist Centre (MCC) and

(3) CPI-ML (Satya Narain Singh)

In February 1981 Azizul Haq-Nishit Bhattacharya group was involved in the looting of 67 guns from three police stations in Raiganj sub division of West Dinajpur district. This group and MCC maintained an underground existence. CPI-ML (S.N. Singh group) had both underground as well as overground set up. (*The Times of India*, August 29, 1981. Extremist groups jolt Bengal Govt. 8 to 10 groups were operating in Bengal)

Ever since the death of Charu Mazumdar in July 1972 most of the groups of CPI-ML began stressing mass activities and renounced the tactics of liquidation of class enemies. With the victory of Santosh Rana in the West Bengal Assembly elections in June 1977, his group led by S.N. Singh opted to gain power through the ballot box.

Land Reforms were carried out in Bengal and the most of the available land was distributed to the tillers after the Naxalite movement. Legislation passed by the Bengal government prevented 'bargadars' Operation Barga proved very helpful and Naxal movement in Bengal remained confined.

About 20 Naxalite factions active in various states decided to form a new party. A Secret 3-days conclave of Naxalites from various states held in a Birbhum village towards the end of March 1985 for holding a larger conference to be held in May end in Naxalbari. Among the participants were Kanu Sanyal member of the organising committee of communist revolutionaries, Mr. Umadhar Singh a Bihar MLA belonging to central organising committee of CPI-ML, Mr. M.H. Krishnappa of the Indian Communist Party, Mr. Ravi Shankar of CPI-ML in U.P. Mr. Shafiq Chowdhury of united committee of communist revolutionaries-ML, Mr Kolavenkayya, a former member of Parliament from Andhra Pradesh and Mr. K.P.P Gopalan from Kerala. The conclave decided on adhering to Parliamentary democracy and shunning the policy of annihilation of class enemies. (*The Hindustan Times*, April 19, 1985).

People's War Group, the Maoist Communist Centre and CPI (ML) Party unity decided to come together to intensify the Naxals movement and constituted a body called All India People's Resistance Forum (AIPRF) in 1992 to build and develop powerful antifeudul and anti-imperialist struggle. AIPRF held its first conference in Kolkata at Shahid Minar Maidan on March 21, 1994.

MCC and Revolutionary Communist Centre of India (Maoist) merged to form MCCI in January 2003. Soon after Revolutionary Communist Centre (Marxist) and CPML (Subir Talukdar group) also decided to merge in to MCCI.

CDML (K.N. Ramchandran faction) and CPI (Marxist-Leninist) also merged and formed a United CPI-ML, announcement of which was made at a Press Conference in Kolkata on September 13, 2004. Thus West Bengal had been playing a good host to all Naxal groups.

ANDHRA PRADESH

The Naxal movement of the present day Andhra Pradesh has its roots in Telengana armed - peasant's struggle or better known as Telengana Armed struggle of 1946-1951 which was ruthlessly and swifly crushed by Andhra government. In this Struggle About 4000 communist and militant farmers were killed and more than 10,000 activits were arrested and jailed for three to four years. Another 50,000 people rounded up were administered good thrashing and tortured for weeks and months together. Around 30 lakh inhabitants from about 3000 villages and 16000 Gram Panchayats revolted and formed 'Gram Rajya' which ultimately has been accorded high priority by the present day Maoists in establishing them in each village. This is the basic village governing body of Naxalites belonging to CPI (Maoists).

Medical Students of Guntur Medical College were the Torch-bearer of Naxal movement in Andhra. They formed Naxalbari Solidarity Committee. Students like Chaganti Bhaskar Rao and D. Mallikarjunudu later joined as Guerrilla fighters in Srikakulam giving up their career in medicine. The uprising could be attributed to an incident on October 31, 1967 when Com. Koranna and Com. Manganna were shot dead by landlords while they were heading to a meeting of Girijan Sangam Conference. Enraged, Girijans of the village Levidi opposed the ways of landlords in a violent and fearful way weilding bows, arrows and other traditional weapons. Government dealt with this uprising by March 1968 and Girijans retreated only to confront the police in a systematic way later on. On November 25, 1968 in an armed struggle, about 260 tribals raided house of a landlord, looted foodgrains and documents. On December 20, about 500 villagers of Ballerugudu village made a guerilla attack on police in which one Circle Inspector and two constables were killed. By early seventy most of the prominent comrade leaders were eliminated by the police.

After initial re-grouping, Telengana Regional conference surfaced, a cultural resurgence and the students' movement took place. A go-to-village campaign was launched and peasants' movement and civil liberties movement emerged.

Naxalites movement spread fast in Andhra Pradesh since 1969 though it had its ups and downs. In early eighties five groups (main) believed to have existed :

1. CPI-ML Chandra Pulla Reddy group.
2. CPI-ML People's War Group of Kondapalli Seetharamiah.
3. Unity Centre of Communist Revolutionaries of India - Marxist Leninist (UCCRI-ML) which functional in two mutually hostile groups led by Devulapalli Venkateshwar Rao and Challapalli Sreemittee (ML).

4. ROC CPI-ML led by S.A. Rawoof.
5. Pro-Lin Piao group led by Myla Narsaiah.

Three move smaller groups also existed :

1. Anti-Lin Piao group led by Intha Ramana Reddy
2. CPI-ML Unity Committee of Kola Venkaiah
3. CPI-ML group led by Manidi Appalasuri.

Districts of Warangal, Karimnagar, Adilabad and Khamman were most disturbed because of Naxal activities. A change in trend of Naxal tactics was believed to have emerged. Earlier, they adopted the path of "annihilation of class enemies" which included Police but now they laid emphasis on "mass action" adopting even legitimate means of agitation. Trade Unions, students and cultural organisations etc. were set up towards this end.

Rawoof and Narsaiah groups of CPI-ML created "liberated zoneds" with the help of "Red Army" and went for an immediate armed struggle and annihilation programme. About 8100 including 800 women were engaged in armed struggle. Pro-Lin groups strength in eighties were estimated to be 320 including 70 women (*The Times of India*, March 2, 1982 "Naxalism rears its head again in AP" by V.G. Prasad Rao.)

People's War Group of Kondapalli Seetharamiah took maximum advantage of post-emergency era and built up its cadres and penetrated students organisations, government employees, youth and workers. Most of the offences in Andhra were committed by this group and took advantage of economic disparities and social backwardness etc.

Chandrapulla Reddy group paid attention to labour, tribals and students laying primary emphasis on "mass base" so that it could even participate in parliamentary elections. The strength of front organisations of these CPI-ML factions was reported to be :

(i) Ryot Coolie Sangham (RCS) 2,00,000 farm labourers as members

(ii) The Progressive Democratic Students Union (PDSU) of CP Reddy group – 25000 members.

(iii) Indian Federation of Trade Unions (IFTU) – 6000 members.

(iv) Progressive Democratic Youth League (PDYL) – 2000 members.

(v) Progressive Organisation of Women (POW) – 450 members.

(vi) Revolutionary Writers Association – 25 members. (*(ibid).*

People's War Group had encouraged 'Gonds' tribals of Andhra, Maharashtra belt not only to occupy forest land but also cut the crops of landlords in the scheduled areas. A few militants of PWG surrendered to the government on receipt of a call of Andhra Chief Minister N.T. Rama Rao. Mukku Subba Reddy, one time lieutenant of Kondapalli Seetaramaiah, Peddola Narasa Reddy @ Ravi, PWG's Nizamabad district committee member and Merugu Satyanarayana. In fact Mukku had surrendered earlier to N.T. Rama Rao's call but Ravi surrendered alongwith his wife Varalaxmi. Government had come out of a scheme to rehabilitate the surrendered Naxalities. There were flaws in the policy of N.T. Rama Rao government in dealing with Naxal problem in Andhra Pradesh. On one hand it launched a package of tribal welfare measures in the Naxalite area to wean the tribals away from extremist influence, the state cabinet, on the other hand, proposed to the centre to scrap a special regulation brought out earlier to protect the tribal lands. In December 1988 the state Cabinet adopted a resolution urging the Centre to repeal the Andhra Pradesh Regulation 1 of 1978 of the Land Transfer Regulation Act which prohibited the sale or transfer of all tribal lands in the agency area to non-tribals. The intention of the government was to legalise the occupation of tribal lands by the non-tribals (*The Indian Express,* August 2, 1989. "Flaws in Policy on Naxalites" by T. Lakshamipathi from Hyderabad.)

Incidently, Kolla Venkaiah (Chilakaruripeta, Guntur district of Andhra Pradesh in a letter to editor (March 26,1990) had demanded, Land Reform first).

Orissa : The Orissa Land Reforms Act 1960 was designed to reform the law relating to land tenures, agrarian reforms and abolition of intermediary interest, conferring better rights on agriculturists to ensure increased in food production and permanent, heritable, transferable rights on land for the tiller. The provision was there that if land is cultivated continuously for 12 years or more by a person other than its owner, the rights to the land shall pass to the cultivator. But there have been no initiatives in the recent past by the Government to record the land in the name of share-croppers. There is further provision of rent not to exceed one-fourth of the gross produce of the land, but in practice owners claim almost half of the produce and farmers' have little option to protest (*The Pioneer,* December 3, 2009 article by Bidyut Mohanty and K. Anuradha).

Madhya Pradesh : A song of Naxals is sung in presence of all the tribals when a Peoples' Court is in progress in deep forests.

"O revenue Patwari, O Police Inspector, O forest Ranger and Khaki-clad tools/Chamchas of the Congress/the Adivasis have awakened/They are out for your blood/you are fat from eating free chicken and goats/you are bloated with free liquor/The Adivasis are coming to cut your throats ......"

In MP the Naxals concentration was mostly in Bastar tribal area where they had their Headquarters also. It gradually spread to Durg, Bhilai, Raipur, Bilaspur and Surguja. Naxal movement gathered momentum in MP in 1977 only after the tribals were displaced again and again from their ancestral forest homes for making way to developmental programmes etc. Naxals of MP worked in close coordination with Andhra Naxals.

4

Frontal Outfits to Aid Naxals of all Hues (Civil Liberty Organisations)

1. Citizens for Democracy (CFD)

Formed in April 1974 in New Delhi. Ist inaugural conference was presided by Jaiprakash Narayan. It started as a non-political organisation to highlight issues of freedom of press, individual freedom, role of police in oppressing the poor people etc. CFD chose Justice V.N. Tarkunde as its President. It played an active role during Emergency, highlighting police excess. B.G. Verghese the famous journalist was President of Delhi Unit of CFD. It had a National Executive Council having 42 members. Delhi Executive Council members were 18 in number.

2. People's Union for Civil Liberties (PUCL)

Formed in October 1976 under the guidance of Jay Prakash Narayan as PUCL and Democratic Rights. On November 22-23, 1988 it renamed itself as the PUCL and adopted a constitution. Former Chief Justice of Delhi High Court Rajendra Sachhar became its President. It opposed actions against left wing extremists, defended human rights by opposing preventive detention and restrictions on freedom of speech. It made a fact finding team in 1973 to study the Assam problem on the spot and criticised the Government for its inept handling of Assam issue. It criticised Army action in Punjab in 1984 and condemned army action in the Golden Temple. It welcomed the apex courts' verdict in Shah Bano case and impressed upon the central government to withdraw the Muslim women's (Protection of Rights and Divorce) Bill.

3. All India Federation of Organisation for Democratic Rights (AIFOFDR)

Formed by UCCRI-ML Anti D.V. Rao group in May 1982 after a decision of Organisation for Protection of Democratic Rights (OPDR) Andhra Pradesh, Orissa, Punjab, Kerala and Maharashtra. PUCR&DR of Rajasthan also okey the formation of an apex body to strengthen the democratic rights of people. The convener was Smt. Rajni Desai. AIFOFDR was opposed to the move for the rocket-testing range at Baliapal (Balasore) in Orissa.

4. Organisation for Protection of Democratic Rights (OPDR-UCCRI-ML/T. Nagi Reddy Group)

In May 1981 UCCRI-ML DV Rao group split in Andhra Pradesh because of ideological differences. It split in D.V. Rao group and another one became T. Nagi Reddy group. It started Civil Liberties group in all the states and campaigned against government adopting repressive and anti-people policies, condemned lock-up deaths.

OPDR (D.V. Rao group) was formed during 1975 with the objective of protecting democratic rights of people.

5. Association for Protection of Democratic Rights (APDR)

Left wing extremists formed APDR, on June 25, 1972. It was mainly active in West Bengal. In 1973 it agitated against awarding capital punishment to Nagbhushan Patnaik and even went on hunger strike demanding withdrawal of capital punishment against him. It formed fact finding committees from time to time. E.g. in December 1983 it engaged a fact finding committee to enquire into the murder of 7 Naxalites at Gopalpur (Nadia district) on December 21, 1983; in January 1984. It enquired about human rights conditions in Bihar, in March 1985, three deaths in a Groase factory in Calcutta on March 15, 1985 was enquired into. In April 1986 it enquired into the a police firing in Arawal in Bihar and in August 1986 police firing at Panighata, Khurseong and Kalimpong (district Darjeeling) was enquired into by its fact finding committees.

5

Communist Party of India (Maoist) CPI (Maoist)

After carrying out deliberations for more than two long years under the supervision of Revolutionary International Movement (RIM) – formed on March 12, 1984 – and coordination Committee of Maoist Parties and Organisations of South Asia (CCOMPOSA)– formed in June 2001 —, two Naxal groups Maoist Communist Centre of India (MCCI) led by Prasant Bose alias Kishenda, general secretary and Peoples' War (DW) led by Mupalla Laxman Rao alias Ganpathy general secretary merged to form a new party by the name of Communist Party of India (Maoist) on September 21, 2004 whose general secretary became Mupalla Laxman Rao. The party's aim was to overthrow the state and establish Communism in India.

A press statement issued after it was jointly signed by Ganapathy, erstwhile secretary CPI ML People's War and Kishan, erstwhile secretary MCCI dated October 14, 2004 on behalf of the Communist Party of India (Maoist) was as follows :

"The New Communist Party of India (Maoist) will continue to act as a consolidated political Vanguard of the Indian Proletariat. Marxism-Leninism-Maoism will be the ideological basis guiding its thinking in all the spheres of its activities. It will continue its struggle against right and left deviations, particularly against revisionism, by taking this as the main danger for the communist movement as a whole. It will still seek to unite all genuine Maoist groups and individuals that remain outside this unified party. The immediate aim and programme of the

Maoist party is to carry on and complete the already ongoing and advancing New Democratic Revolution in India as the part of the world proletarian revolution by overthrowing the semi-colonial, semi-feudal system under the neo-colonial form of indirect rule, exploitation and control. This revolution will remain directed against imperialism, feudalism and comprador bureaucratic capitalism. This revolution will be carried out and completed through armed agrarian revolutionary war i.e. protracted peoples' war, with the seizure of power by armed force remaining as its central and principal task, encircling the cities from the countryside and thereby finally capturing them".

In 2008 an expert group appointed by the Planning Commission submitted a report called "Development challenges in Extremist-Affected Areas". It said "the Naxalites (Maoists) movement has to be reorganised as a political movement with a strong base among the landless and poor peasantry and adivasis. Its emergence and growth need to be contextualised in the social conditions and experience of people who form a part of it. The huge gap between state policy and performance is a feature of these conditions. Though its professed long-term ideology is capturing state power by force, in its day-to-day manifestations, it is to be looked upon basically a fight for social justice, equality protection, security and local development. (*Outlook,* November 9, 2009 issue "Mr. Chidambaram's War" article by Arundhati Roy).

It is the strongest militant outfit of the present day and has shaped into a largest underground Communist party in the world causing global threat by playing a crucial role in unifying Communist rebels all over the globe. It is the most active and dangerous militant Naxal outfit of today.

Peoples' War (PW) had a 13-member politburo whose general secretary was Mupalla Laxman Rao who was a former teacher and headed PW when it decided to merge with MCCI. Maoist Communist Centre of India (MCCI) was led by Prasant Bose alias Kishenda. The new party CPI (Maoist) has a battle cadre strength of 15 to 20,000 with another 50,000 overground cadre. Its weaponary includes AK series Assault Rifles, LMGs, Rifles, Grenades and mortars. It has peoples Liberation Guerilla Army, Central Military Commission and Central Technical Commission. PLGA was formed on December

2,2000 though its formation was announced on April 22, 2003. CPI (Maoist) was banned for the second time on August 17, 2005 by Andhra Government.

In January 2007, the first unity congress of the party was held inside a forest where all the differences of the past 37 years were almost solved. A statement issued after the meeting in February 2007 stated that the unity congress has resolved to advance the peoples' war throughout the country and wage a mass movement against the neo-liberal policies of globalisation, liberalisation and privatisation perused by the reactionary ruling classes under the dictatorship of imperialism. They also decided to expand the armed struggle from Guerrilla war to urban and mobile warfare focussing on Industrial areas. An annual report of the Central Military Commission of the CPI (Maoist) seized by security forces lists several upcoming projects in Bihar, Chhatisgarh, Jharkhand and Andhra Pradesh like the projects of Tata Essar and Jindal groups in Chhattisgarh, the Polvaram irrigation project in Andhra Pradesh as targets.[1]

After holding first 'Unity Congress' it was decided that the reverses in the Gadchiroli –Gondia belt should be overcome. Towards the end of the year 2007 Gopanna alias Kosa, a senior Maoist leader from Andhra was assigned the duty of re-building the political and military organisation of CPI (Maoist) in the region. His report submitted by Mid-2008 gave a dismal picture of the outfit on the recruitment front stating that the party failed to recruit new cadres as also it failed to hold any grip over Gadchiroli division. Thereafter tactical jungle training on military front was imparted to its cadres and a separate military command for North and South Gadchiroli region as part of Dandakaranya sub-zonal committee was formed. Nearly 5000 fire arms were accumulated leading to fresh assaults on the security forces. The assault on police force led by 300 maoist cadres on October 8, 2009 in which 17 policemen were killed was most lethal.

Sudeep Chakravarti in his book *Red Sun : Travels in Naxalite Country* writes : Quote. A 'Unity Congress' of CPI (Maoist) in the last week of January 2007 in the forests of Jharkhand, after electing a new Central Committee and re-electing Ganpathy as the general secretary of the party, passed several resolutions. Among other things, these focused on combining rural, worker and urban issues and mentioned '......massive attacks on the working class and vicious attempts to bind labour's hand and foot, which has facilitated a massive loot by big business..... Wage freeze, VRS, dismissals, curbs on recruitment, anti-labour Court Judgements, de-facto ban on strikes, etc. are leading to greater and greater impovirisation (sic) of the entire working class.

The party's suggestion : militant workers movements. This plays on the vulnerability that results from the state acquiring land – often through pressure and by offering rates below market on behalf of big projects. When the process should, ideally be a direct transaction between business and those who wish to sell land, with the state intervening only to protect the interests of those who sell and also those who choose not to.

'The 300 planned SEZs are all set to create de-facto foreign enclaves within our country by grabbing lakhs of acres of prime agricultural land by the foreign and local sharks. Together with this, to turn urban centres into elite enclaves and pave the way for big business retail chains, ruthless demolitions and eviction of lakhs of people are taking place, demolishing slums and even permanent housing. The unity Congress of CPI (Maoist) calls on the people to resist the seizure of their lands and houses and beat back the demolition hordes by whatever means possible'. Unquote. (Page 186 of the book *Red Sun*).

To counter the Naxal menace, government created Greyhounds in 1989. A senior police officer K.S. Vyas was responsible for raising this force. He was later on shot at by Naxals and killed on January 27, 1993. (*India Today,* February 11, 2008 issue article by Amarnath K. Menon).

Security forces killed three Central Committee members of CPI (Maoists) on December 2, 1999 in an encounter in Koyyuru but it boomranged later on. Maoists formed a 3-layered People's Liberation Guerrilla Army on December 2, 2000, exactly a year later to observe the first death anniversary of Koyyuru martyrs, which improved their military capabilities spectacularly PLGA has main, secondary and base forces. The main force consists of platoons, companies and Battalions while the secondary force comprised local guerilla squads (LGS) and special guerilla squads (SGS). The base force consists of people militia which could form themselves into Gram Rakshak Dal a.k.a. Dalams (GRD) or Self Defence Squads (SDS). They have come a long way from the days of hit and run tactics to encirclement of security forces. (*The Hindu,* December 5, 2010 article by K. Srinivas Reddy from Hyderabad).

One of the major attacks by Naxals (MCC) was on May 29, 1987 when Naxals killed 42 upper caste villagers in Baghaura and Dalchak (Aurangabad) in retaliation for the murder of seven OBC men at Chukti-Chechani. (*The Indian Express*, June 20, 2008.

Organisational Structure of CPI (Maoist)

A few Naxal groups having influence in Andhra Pradesh, Maharashtra, Orissa, Madhya Pradesh and Chhattisgarh decided to unite to give a new impetus to the movement. Talks went on for almost two years and ultimately a party named CPI (Maoist) was formed on September 21, 2004 after CPI-ML People's war (formed in September 1998) and Maoist Communist Centre of India (MCCI) (formed in May 2003) decided to merge in a single outfit. They were also joined by CPI-ML 2nd Central Committee which was formed in 1976 in Bihar. In fact this 2nd Central Committee had already joined MCCI in May 2003. CPI-ML People's War Group-PWG) formed in 1980 and CPI-ML (Party unity (formed in 1976) merged in CPI-ML (PW) (formed in 1998). In 2000, Maoist Communist Centre (MCC) (formed in 1976) and Revolutionary Communist Centre of India (Maoist) in Punjab which later on became Revolutionary Communist Centre of India Marxist-Leninist-Maoist (RCCI-MLM) in January 2003 in Punjab had merged to form MCCI in the year 2003. Ultimately MCCI and PW merged to form the new outfit known by name of CPI (Maoist).

CPI (Maoist) has an important component under the name of People's Liberation Guerilla Army (PLGA) which is headed by Central Military Commission (CMC) under it comes Regional Military Command and under that state Military Commission (SMC). Sub-zonal Military Commands (SZMC) works under SMC and Divisional Commands (DVC) work under SZMC. Under DVC three of forces work i.e. Main Force there are Battalions, Companies, Platoons, Special Action Teams and Intelligence units. Secondary force has Local Guerilla squads, Local Revolutionary Guerilla squad, Local Organisation squad and Local Revolutionary Organisation squad. Basic Force has People's Militia, Gram Raksha Dalam and Area Raksha Dalam under it.

Another important organ is Central Committee. Provisional Bureau and Central Military Commission function side by side with Central Committee. Under it came Regional bureaus, then State/Special zonal, special area and state Organising Committee. Regional Committee functions under state/Special Zonal Committee. Then comes Divisional Committee or district Committee or Zonal Committee. Under their command come sub-District Committee or Sub-Divisional Committee or Sub-zonal Committee. Below them come Area Committees.

Yet another very important part of CPI (Maoist) is Central Military Commissions which has Central Regional Military Command and Eastern Regional Military Command. Dandakaranya, North Telangana Special Zonal Command, Andhra Orissa Border and Andhra Pradesh come under Central Regional Military Command. It has two Battalion Commands – One and two which in turn commands 3 companies i.e. Company 1, Company 2 and Company 3. Battalion Command two has Coy 1 and Coy 2 under it. Eastern Regional Military Command takes care of Bihar, Jharkhand, West Bengal, Assam and North Orissa. It has Battalion Command 1 and Coy 1 and Coy 2 under it.

Budget/Finances

Francois Gautier in one of his brilliant articles (*The Pioneer*, July 9, 2008) under the heading "Red banner of Terrorism" says "The Maoist have a budget of 60 crores of rupees for carrying out its armed struggle during 2007-09. This amount has been raised by NGO's abroad".

On November 29, 2009 Chhattisgarh Director General of Police Shri Vishwa Ranjan stated that Maoist annually extorted upto Rs. 20 billion across India mostly targeting iron and local mining corporations.

Maoist state secretary of West Bengal unit Sudip Chongdar alias Kanchan who was arrested by police on December 3, 2010, during his interrogation told the police that the red ultras have amassed a huge amount of money-nearly 10 crore over the past 20 months, a large chunk of which was used for research and development, purchasing transport and weaponry. A major portion of this amount,

Kanchan said, came from extortion while the rest was raised as donations from sympathizers residing in the cities.

Maoist's Aim

1. To deter voters by disrupting polls – but they hardly succeeded in Maharashtra. In all 288 Assembly Constituencies 61 to 62% people cast their votes out of 7.58 lakh voters. In 2004 Assembly polls the percentage was 48.81.
2. To continue with blasts and bombs and simultaneously giving a call for 'Bandh' e.g. unleashing terror, about 150 Maoist stormed Banshipur Railway station in the Patna-Kiul-Jhajha sector under Danapur division on October 12, 2009 and torched a Railway panel room and destroyed traffic control system.
3. Siphone Panchayat Funds at gun point. e.g. they would compel the villagers to construct ponds and road and themselves take away all the money from Panchayat officials. The officials are hand-in-glove with the Maoists and they also get their cuts. (*Pioneer,* October 15, 2009). Loot village schools, Ganja smuggling are other sources of funds. They impose 3% tax on every construction work (*ibid*).
4. Inert Judiciary strengthens Naxals.
5. Where District Administration fails to reach poor villages at the time of their need, Maoist reach there – which gives rise to Maoist activities.
6. Maoist have emerged the biggest enemy of the development. Naxalites do not want any development work in backward districts e.g. in Gadchiroli district of Maharashtra, they shot dead an engineer-contractor Mr. Nagi Reddy on November 19, 2009 who was laying down a 3-km long road connecting Mahawda and Dudhnaha village after having obtained a contract from Maharashtra Government. In Gadchiroli, Naxals killed a number of road contractors in the last few months of the year 2009.
7. Naxals of CPI (Maoists) do not want elections – They called 'Jharkhand Bandh' or November 29 -30, 2009 in protest against Assembly elections in the state on December 2. They had

announced poll boycott and blew up school building in Girdih, Palamau and Latehar districts. They also killed 4 CRPF personnel in a landmine blast in Gumla district.

8. Announce 'loan waiver' for farmers and warn the lender that if anybody tries to squeez money out of the farmers, he will be branded a people's enemy ...., tried in People's court, according to Polit buro member 'Kishenji'. They announced it in West Midnapore district of West Bengal. (*The Hindustan Times,* December 17, 2009).

International and National Linkages

CPI (Maoist) has links with the organisation known as Revolutionary International Movement (RIM) which has membership of various other Maoist parties like :

1. Communist Party of Bangladesh (ML)
2. Revolutionary Communist Party of USA
3. Communist Party of Peru
4. Communist Party of Nepal (Maoist)
5. Communist Party of Iran (Marxist-Leninist-Maoist)
6. Communist Party of Afghanistan
7. Cylone Communist Party (Maoist), Sri Lanka
8. Communist Party of Turkey (ML)
9. Maoist Communist Party, Italy (Maoist-Leninist)
10. Communist Organisation of Tunisia
11. Revolutionary Communist Group, Columbia.
12. Proletarian Party of Purbabanga, Bangladesh.

Other affiliate organisations are known as International League of Peoples Struggles (ILPS) and World People's Resistance Movement (WPRM). They participate under the name of World Social Forum (WSF).

CPI (Maoist) is also member of Coordination Committee of Maoist Parties and Organisation of South Asia (CCOMPOSA) :

1. Bangladesh Samyawadi Dal (ML)

2. Ceylon Communist Party (Maoist) Sri Lanka
3. Communist Party of East Bengal (ML) Bangladesh
4. Communist Party of Nepal (Maoist)
5. Maobadi Punorgathan Kendra, Bangladesh
6. Purb Banglar Sarbohara, Bangladesh.

Maoists were extended some sort of support by Nepal Maoists. C.P. Gajurel, a senior standing committee member of UCPN-M stated "We have extended our full support and co-operation to the Indian Maoists." (*The Hindustan Times*, November 4, 2009). An article in Nepalese local daily read "Maoist Politburo member Indramohal Sigdel 'Basanta' held meetings with Indian Maoist leaders including Kisenji from October 8 to 11, 2009. A couple of years ago, Nepalese Maoist leader Mohan Karan Vaidya was arrested near Siliguri (West Bengal) with documents that later revealed that he had spent to the tune of one crore rupees purchasing explosives in Siliguri (*The Pioneer*, November 9, 2009).

Maoists also looked to build links with separatists in various parts of India particularly in Northeast and J&K. Among the groups the Maoists support are United Liberation Front of Asom, National Socialist Council of Nagaland, Tripura National volunteers and many J&K separatist outfits. The Maoist also support statehood demands in Vidharva (Maharashtra), Telangana (AP), Coorg (Karnataka) and Gorkhaland (Bengal). Koteshwar Rao @Kisenji, Politburo member of CPI (Maoist) said a coordination Committee comprising members from each of the separatist groups will be set-up. The organisation was in touch with North-east rebel groups to achieve "sovereignty for the people of Asom, Nagaland, Manipur, Mizoram and surrounding area." (*The Hindustan Times*, December 14, 2009).

In an interview that took place in deep interiors of a forest in West Midnapore district of West Bengal, Koteshwar Rao alias Kishenji stated that Maoists (CPI Maoists) had joined forces with separatist groups such as ULFA in Assam, NSCN and the PLA in Manipur – that they support all outfits fighting state-sponsored oppression – the likes of ULFA, NSCN and PLA – because our enemy is common. We have recently signed an MoU with NSCN, ULFA and PLA for helping each other in our fight against the state. (MINT : Exclusive partner of the *Wall Street Journal*, dt. May 29, 2009. Interview by Romita Datta and Aveek Datta "Mainstream politico not for us").

Elsewhere, Kishenji confessed that they got arms from Trinamool Congress for fight in Nandigram (West Bengal). (*The Times of India*, April 27, 2009).

Ganpathy, also known as Mupala Laxman Rao General Secretary of CPI (Maoist) once admitted that the Maoists had once tried to establish relations with the Liberation Tigers of Tamil Ealem but were turned away. (*The Hindustan Times*, October 16, 2009).

CPI (Maoist) Politburo Members (as on February 18, 2008)

A 14-member CPI (Maoist) politburo is the main decision-making body of the ultras. Seven out of 14 top leaders were from Andhra Pradesh – four of them from Karimnagar district. The names of these top leaders were revealed by a politburo member Misir Besra @Bhaskar @Sunirmal after his arrest in Jharkhand.

Politburo members

1. Muppala Laxman Rao (15 aliases including Ganapathi, Ramana, Srinivas and Malanna) was party chief. The 58 year old science graduate from Karimnagar district (AP).
2. Prashanth Bose (aliases Nirbhay, Mahesh, Kajal) is number 2 in the politburo, belongs to West Bengal. Represents the outfits at meetings with international and Indian revolutionary organisations.
3. Cherukuri Raj Kumar (aliases Uday, Parimal, Arad) aged 55 years. Belongs to Krishna district (AP).
4. Mallojula Koteshwara Rao (aliases Prahalad, Baswaraj Ramji, Kishenji) aged 55 years. Belongs to Karimnagar district (AP). Responsible for merger of PWG with MCC. Currently looks after Bengal.
5. Nambala Keshavarao (aliases Ganganna, Basavraj) aged 53 years. Belongs to Srikakulam district (AP).
6. Kobbad Gandhi (aliases Saleem, Rajan, Kishore) In-charge of Central propaganda bureau looking after party documentation.
7. Promod Mishra (aliases Ban Bihari, Janardhan) Belongs to

Aurangabad, Bihar. In-charge of Delhi, Punjab, Haryana and J&K.

8. Sumanand Singh (aliases Sujith Da, Suman) aged 55 years. Native of Bihar. In-charge of 'military' activities in West Bengal. Considered very good in planning armed operations.
9. Malla Raji Reddy (aliases Meesalanna, Sayanna, Sathenna) aged 55 years. Belongs to Karimnagar (AP).
10. Mallajula Venugopal (aliases Bhupathi, Sonu) belongs to Karimnagar (AP).
11. Katakam Sudershan (aliases Anand, Mohan, Birendar) aged 50 years. Belongs to Adilabad district (AP).
12. Akhilesh Yadav (aliases Ramanji, Prabodh, Bhupesh) aged 65 years. Former school teacher and eldest politburo member. Belongs to Gaya (Bihar). His son too is a Maoist.
13. Balraj (aliases BR) aged 50 years. Looks after publication, In-charge of north Bihar.
14. Ashuthosh (aliases Bipul, Ashok) 45 years. Belongs to Jharkhand. Elevated to the top groups after Besra's arrest.

(*The Times of India*, February 18, 2008)

Besra is Misir Besra also known as Sunirmala Vivekand Bhaskar. A politburo member, he was arrested in September 2007 near Khuti, Bhagnadih village in Jharkhand and forcibly freed on June 23, 2006.

"CPI (Maoist) had a budget of no less than 60 crores for carrying out its armed struggle during 2007-09. And of that Rs. 42 crore was earmarked for arms, ammunition and explosives, Rs. 2 crore for intelligence gathering. The remaining amount was allocated for transportation, computer training, propaganda and documentation." Shri Vishwa Mohan correspondent writers in the *Times of India* of February 18, 2008 that he obtained this report from Misir Besra. He also made the following revelations in an interview with the *Hindustan Times* as he awaited his court hearing in Ranchi. He said Naxal organisation has spread to atleast 15 states – though armed fighters were present in fewer states. There would be between 15000 and 20000 armed guerrillas in the Naxalite movement – with upto 40% of them women. (*The Hindustan Times,* March 12, 2008 "Guerilla days over, Naxals ready for new war" report by Neelesh Mishra).

As per record of District Administration, the total strength of armed cadres of CPI (Maoist) in Chhattisgarh state is 8900. CPI (Maoist) has a 21-member Central Committee. One of its CC member Motilal Soreng @ Asutosh Tudu @ Ashok was arrested on March 2, 2009 for murder of VHP leader Swami Laxmanananda Saraswati. He was arrested under Brahmanitarang police station area of Rourkela. (*The Indian Express*, March 3, 2009).

Central Committee Members of CPI (Maoist)

1. Mupala Laxman Rao @ Ganpathi (Secretary)
2. Prashanth Bose @ Kishanda
3. Namballa Keshava Rao @ Baswaraj
4. Misir Besra @ Sunirmal
5. Mallojula Venugopal @ Abhay
6. Katakam Sudershan @ Anand
7. Malla Raji Reddy @ Sathenna
8. Tippiri Tirupati @ Deoji
9. Dev Kumar Singh @ Nishanth
10. Jiniugu Narshimha Reddy @ Jampana
11. Akkiraju Hargopal @ Ramakrishna
12. Kuppuswamy Devaraj @ Ramesh
13. Kadari Satnarayana Reddy @ Kosa
14. Gajanand @ Parush
15. Chanderi Yadav @ Payag
16. Mohan @ Mahesh
17. Ranjith Bose @ Kanchan
18. Manoj @ Rajesh
19. Pulluri Prasad Rao @ Chandranna
20. Ramchandra Redy Pratap Reddy @ Chalapathi
21. Moden Balakrishna @ Bhaskar

(*The Hindu*, November 26, 2011)

CPI (Maoist) was banned by the Central government on June 22, 2009.

Misir Besra was freed by Maoists after gunning down a policeman and hurling bombs to scare away people. He was freed on June 23,

2009 after a daredevil attack on police team on a court premises in Lakhisarai district of Bihar. Besra, a native of Madunadi village in Giridi district of Jharkhand. He joined Maoist Communist Centre of India (MCCI) in 1985 while was dong his graduation and by 2003 he was co-opted into the central committee. After the merger of the MCCI with CPI-ML. People's War (PW) he continued to be in the politburo and the Central Military Commission (CMC) in addition to being a member of Eastern Regional Bureau (ERB) which co-ordinates the Maoist movement in Assam, West Bengal, Bihar, Jharkhand, Orissa and Chhatisgarh. (*The Hindu,* June 24, 2009, "Maoists attach police, free top leader from Court premises", Report by K. Srinivas Reddy).

Ganapathi : Also known as Mupala Laxman Rao, Ramanna, Shrinivas, Chandrasekhar and GP, Ganapathi is the general secretary of the Communist Party of India (Maoists). He was general secretary of the People's War Group (PWG) until its merger with the Maoists Coordination Centre (MCC) to create the CPI (Maoists) in 2004. Aged between 40 and 50 years, Ganapathi is a native of Karimnagar district in Andhra Pradesh and used to be a school-teacher. He was a close associate of Kondapalli Seetharamaiah, whom he replaced as the leader of the PWG in 1992. Ganapathi is believed to be spending his time in the Ambujgarh area of Bastar, which the Maoists consider their 'capital' and impenetrable by the police. Andhra Pradesh police have closed in on him twice – once in Kerala and once in Rourkela in Orissa. (*The Hindustan Times*, Sunday, April 19, 2009).

Kishenda : Alias Prashant Bose, was general secretary of the MCC. When it merged with the PWG, he became the second most powerful man in the new Maoists party. Very little is known about him, apart from the fact that he is in his late 50s. (*The Hindustan Times*, Sunday April 19, 2009).

Mallojula Kateswar Rao alias Kishanji, born in a village in Karimnagar in Andhra Pradesh has spent 34 years (out of his 53 years of age) of his life in hiding, waging a relentless, bloody war against the state. In an interview to the *Times of India*, he claimed to have killed 93 people till 2009 beginning. During Emergency he went underground and came in contact with, CPI-ML leaders. In 1980 he co-founded Peoples War in Andhra Pradesh. In early ninetees he moved to Bihar, then a stronghold of Maoist Communist Centre of

India (MCCI). He tried and succeeded in unifying PW and MCC in the year 2004. He sidelined many senior leaders who fell out with him. He is No. 2 behind Ganpati. Once he assaulted Manik Da, a Maoist state secretary during a Conference. He is a media friendly guerrilla. (*The Times of India*, February 17, 2010, Cruel Killer? Not me, says Maoist leader Kishanji).

Kishanji's Biodata

Date of Birth	: July 25, 1956
Date of Marriage	: August 8, 1984
Wife's name	: Myna
Favourite weapon	: AK 47
Biggest regret	: Never meeting Charu Mazumdar (*The Hindustan Times,* February 19, 2010).

He became full time member of CPI-ML (People's War) in the year 1974. While he studying for B.Sc (Mathematics) degree in Karimnagar (Andhra Pradesh), he was drawn towards revolutionary movement.

Koteswar Rao @ Kishanji, CPI (Maoist)'s second-in-command appealed to the Air Force "not to strike at the sons and daughters of the soil" when the Air Force Chief declared that air force be allowed to fire in self defence whenever its helicopters or aircrew come under attack and that they have already put up a case before the Defence Ministry. Koteswar Rao also issue a threat "And if you dare to be adventurous, be prepared for a befitting retribution" Koteshwar Rao further said from his hideout in West Bengal that "Chidambaram (Home Minister) is acting on the directives of the FBI" "We will teach centre a lesson that no other revolutionary has taught them : "Think twice or thrice before going in for an air strike against the revolutionaries. Should the raids take place, this would polarize the nation as the civil society won't watch silently (*The Hindustan Times*, October 3, 2009). Kishenji was killed on November 25, 2011 in a police encounter in forest area of Jangal Mahal region of Paschimi Medinipur district of West Bengal.

Kobad Ghandy, one of the Politburo member, was arrested by Delhi Police on September 20, 2009 from Bhikaiji Cama area. Kobad, hailing from a wealthy Parsi family, joined Naxal movement in Seventies. While studying in England a course for Chartered Accountancy, he got involved in left-wing politics but was soon arrested and deported. By 1982 he had left Mumbai along with wife Anuradha, a sociology professor and fellow Maoist who died last year (2008) of cerebral malaria. In the CPI (Maoist) Ghandy was entrusted with responsibilities of propaganda, agitation and publicity and played a privotal role in the urban spread of the organisation. He was inspired by Kondapalli Seetharmaiah to join the then CPI-ML – People's War Group in Andhra Pradesh. Seethaamaiah's vision was to spread the movement in Maharashtra and Tamil Nadu. Ghandy's preference to work in urban areas had triggered a clash between him and Seetaramaiah. He drifted towards T. Nagi Reddy's UCCRI-CP ML in the later part of the 80s. In 1994 Ghandy was instrumental in bringing Naxal factional groups like CPI-ML (Party Unity) and People's War Group to form All India Peoples Resistance Forum. (*The Times of India*, September 23, 2009. News item by Nauzer Bharucha and Soumittra S. Bose captioned "was deported from Britain for Left-wing Politics.")

CPI (Maoist) spokesperson Azad stated (September 29, 2009) that Kobad Ghandy is a role model. The country should unite to fight against attempts by the State to persecute revolutionary intellectuals and Maoist leaders like Ghandy. They (government) churn out numbers to show how thousands have become victims of Maoist violence. But the fact is that while Maoists had punished only the repressive forces of the state, the anti-people feudal forces and the police agents, police, para-military and armed vigilante gangs like Salwa Judum are continuously carrying out a mass murders campaign. (*The Times of India*, September 30, 2009).

Not only Kobad Ghandy, but politburo members Promod Mishra, Narayan Sanyal, Sushil Roy and Amitabh Bagchi have also been taken into custody earlier from cities like Ranchi, Patna, Kolkata and Raipur (*The Hindustan Times*, September 25, 2009).

Cherukuri : Raj Kumar @ Azad, @ spoke person of CPI (Maoist) central committee released a press statement giving a call for Bharat Bandh on October 3, 2009 to protest Kobad Ghandy's arrest. Further CPI (Maoist) abducted Jharkhand Police inspector Francis Induwar and subsequently killed him on October 5 (*The Pioneer* October 9, 2009) in order to seek release of Kobad Ghandy.

The chargesheet put up by Delhi Police before the court on February 19, 2010 contained Ghandy's claim to have met Nepal's Maoist leader Prachanda to discuss the defferences that had arisen with the organisation. The charge sheet also, stated that Kobad used 13 aliases and new of centers Anti Maoist plans. (*The Times of India,* February 20, 2010) Nepal Maoists denied Ghandy met Prachanda.

Kobad Ghandy's accomplice Arvind Joshi,. said to be a member of the central committee of CPI (Maoist) and also secretary of northern regional committee who was doing his M. Com from Delhi University was arrested from Kanpur (UP) on February 8, 2010 along with seven other ultras. He was alleged to have fled from Badarpur in Delhi along with hard discs and other documents after the arrest of Kobad Ghandy on September 20, 2009.

Cherukuri Raj Kumar alias Azad was killed in an encounter on July 2, 2010 in Adilabad district of Andhra Pradesh. He was third in CPI (Maoist) hierarchy, next only to chief Ganpathi and Prasanta Bose in the politburo. He carried a reward of rupees 12 lakh on his head and had 16 cases pending against him. He hailed from Pedasanagallu village in Krishna district. His wife Seetakka is also an underground cadre leader.

Mouthpiece of the banned Communist Party of India (Maoist) is "Peoples March" which was proscribed in February 2008. But was allowed to print again from August 7, 2009. The first issue came out in November 2009 edited by P. Govinda Kutty who worked from his residence in Ernakulam (Kerala). Later on Swapan Dasgupta became its editor. He was arrested by police in October 2009. He became the first person to be arrested under Unlawful Activities (Prevention) Act for helping Maoists. While in police custody, he was admitted to SSKM Hospital on December 17, 2009 where he died on February 2, 2010 SSKM-Seth Sukhlal Karnani Memorial Hospital, Kolkata).

A document which, in fact, was a Maoist Balance Sheet of the period between July 2008 and September 2009 was circulated among membes of the CPI (Maoist) and its military wing, the people's

Liberation Guerilla Army in December 2010 to mark the 9th in anniversary of the army. The Maoist balance sheet claimed that the rebels killed 270 security personnel during above said period. The document prepared by the central military commission of the outlawed Communist Party of India (Maoist) also claimed that the outfit snatched 200 guns during this period. Treating the strategy employed to take control of Lalgarh in West Bengal as a model, the document further said "the class hatred and anger of the people against the enemy should be enhanced............ We have to carefully develop such methods by which the enemy will not be able to get any support from the masses."

Among the leaders the party lost are central committee members Sudhakar Patel, (Chief of intelligence wing of CPI-Mao killed on May, 24, 2009 and Cherukuri Raj Kumar @ Azad killed on July 2, 2010) two Andhra Pradesh state committee members, 11 members, of the divisional zonal commands and 20 members of sub-zonal committees. But the report card said the setbacks seemed of have been compensated by the triumph in Lalgarh, which first attracted national attention on November 2, 2008 when the Maoist exploded a landmine, that hit Bengal Chief Minister Buddhadeb Bhattacharjees convoy. The alleged highhandedness of state police after the attack led to the formation of the People's Committee Against Police Atrocities which has functioned as a front of the Maoist. (*The Hindustan Times,* January 2, 2010. Report by Debdutta Ghosh).

Maoist opened their account in 2010 in West Bengal by killing a zilla parishad member. Bhagabat singh, Who was also a secretary of CPI (Marxist) local committee in Gopiballavpur in Bengal's West Midnapore District. (*The Hindustan Times*, January 3, 2010).

The politburo of CPI (Maoist) had brought out a 14-page document on "post election situation - Our tasks" on June 12, 2009 giving an insight into how Naxalites try to motivate their cadre. The document not only carries the ultra's counter-plan to take on security forces but also appeals to its sympathiser to utilise 'the worst ever economic crisis' to build up their cadre. Interestingly it drew its inspiration not only from Maoists in Nepal and China but also from Hamas in Gaza, Hizbollah in Lebanon and Taliban in Afghanistan and Pakistan's Swat Valley and FATA. (*The Times of India*, dt. August

18, 2009), News item by Vishwa Mohan captioned "Naxal letter helps PC drive home point").

Under the sub -title "Post Election Situation - our Tasks", Kobad Ghandy of CPI (Maoist) who drafted this 14 - page document of June 12 it says "We have to keep in mind that the results have given scope for the UPA Government to enact more draconian Legislation and implement more Fascist measures and suppression of the People's struggles...."...'the US Imperialist have been excerting pressure on Pakistan to concentrate all its forces on the western border to finish off the Taliban. The US can not think of loosing Afghanistan which is the gateway to the oil - rich Central Asian region. It is also essential for the US to keep South Asia under its thumb as part of its designs for global hegemony and its rivalry with China, the newly emerging global competitor to the US. It (US) is trying to mediate between India and Pakistan to reduce the tensions between the two countries so that both can free their forces from the borders and concentrates on what the US imperialists think are the real threats the Taliban and other Islamic fundamentalist forces, Maoist revolutionaries, Anti-American movements and other people's movements. If the Americans succeed and most likely they would, then the Indian ruling classes will have some flexibility on the western front and in Kashmir. It (India) can relieve some of the Central forces from Kashmir and re-deploy them in out guerilla zones and other areas of armed struggle" assessed the politburo in June.

Under the subhead 'immediate Tasks' the document exhorted its cadre 'to take initiative to unite with other struggling organisations' and enthuse other insurgent outfits with daring counter-offensives' carried out by the Maoists and prepare them to undertake similar operations and enhance the involvement of the 'masses' infighting and defeating the 'superior enemy force'. The so called people's mañdate for stability and neo-liberal reforms is meant to legitimise the brutal state terror and economic oppression of the people! Prepare the Party (CPI-Maoist), PLGA (People's Liberation Guerilla Army) and the people for the new brutal offensive being unleashed by the UPA government. "Election-2009 has earned the distinction of being the most discredited election held so far in the Country. More people stayed away from the polling booths than those who went to cast their votes. And even among those voted the majority had little trust in the candidates or the party who can change loyalties after the votes are cast", says the document. (*The Pioneer*, September 25, 2009).

People's Liberation Guerrilla observes December 4 as its Foundation Day.

Because of inflation, Maoists also hiked its 'Protection Money' from two to five percent of project costs to five to ten percent in mineral-rich belt. Almost every business house or contractor pays this extortion money. Accordingly to a rate chart seized for Maoists in December 2009 the new 'Taxes' were as follows :

1. Annual exortion business said to be worth Rs. 2000 crore.
2. Rate for construction/maintenance works of Pakka roads doubled from 5 to 10%.
3. For Kaccha road under block development schemes hiked from 5 to 7%.
4. Charges for construction of bridges and dams increased from 3 to 5%.
5. For Govt. buildings "levy" hiked from 5 to 7%.
6. For laying railway tracks and repair works 5%.
7. Auction of railway scrap 10% in terms of value.
8. From manual stone crusher rate hike from Rs. 5000 to Rs. 6000.
9. From machanised crushers Rs. 8000 hiked to Rs.16,000 annually
10. Brick kiln owners to shell out of Rs. 15000 a year per chimney.
11. Petrol pump owner will now be charged Rs. 25000 annually.

Bauxite mine owned by big industrial houses will be required to shell out Rs. 10 per tonne but medium–sized mining firms will pay Rs. 8 per tonne and Rs. 8 per tonne will be extorted from small time companies.

The rate charts adds that the rates for coal and iron ore mines would remain unchanged till the same is revised by the Maoists.

Zonal committee of the CPI (Maoist) will continue to remain the basic unit for collecting 'levy' and will be responsible for printing of cash receipts for the purpose besides sending the share to outfits politburo. The central committee of the terror group is responsible for fixing the share between its various committees. (*Sunday Pioneer*, December 27, 2009 Report by Rakesh K. Singh "Maoists hike protection levy")

Naxalites have developed the expertise to clone sophisticated weapons including assault Rifles of AK series. In the month of January 2010 CRPF team busted an arms manufacturing unit in forests close to Gobardaha village in Chatra district in Jharkhand and recovered a number of 'duplicate' AK-47 and AK-57 rifles of high standard.

The first big arms manufacturing unit of Maoists was busted by Andhra Pradesh in 2006 when they recovered a huge stock of rocket shells and launchers in the state. Probe later revealed that the Maoists' technical wing designed the launchers and initially made them at a foundry in Chennai. (*The Times of India,* January 18, 2010).

Differences within CPI (Maoists)

Maoists in west Bengal seem to have developed some differences among themselves on the question of the movement being led by tribals and non-tribals. One Marshall, a zonal leader and responsible for many a violence in Jangalmahal area has come out openly against Koteshwar Rao alias Kishanji branding him a 'non-tribal leader' and 'outsider' who has on locus standi to lead the tribals' fight. Marshall alleges that the sons of soil, who arrest the front lines of dangerous tasks and carry out Maoist policymaker's orders are being sidelined by the outsiders like Kishanji. Marshall intends to float a new armed outfit to fight for the tribal cause and claims to have around 150 armed men with him. He hails from Purulia village. (*The Times of India*; February 8, 2010 Bengal Maoist ranks split vide open).

Activities of CPI (Maoists)

February 15, 2002 : Sanjay Singh, Forest service officer killed by MCC local area commander stating that killing was planned by local forest mafia.

December 19, 2002 : In Singhbhum district if western Jharkhand MCC in a military action killed 18 armed policemen and wounded 38 others. All their weapons and ammunition taken away by Naxals.

October 1, 2003 : Peoples War attempted on Andhra Pradesh Chief Minister's life (Shri Chandra Babu Naidu) at Alipiri near Tirupati.

February 6, 2004 : 500 Rifles looted from District police Armoury in Koraput (Orissa) by about 180 Maoists, besieged police station, district Jail and Treasury. Killed four policemen.

January 5, 2005 : Maoist attacked Kajra Railway station in Munger (Bihar)- Jamalpur Rail division.

January 5, 2005 : Six policemen including local superintendent of police Shri K.C. Surender Babu were killed in Munger district.

January 16, 2005 : Mahendra Singh CPI-ML murdered in Jharkhand, a day after he filed his nomination papers to seek re-election for a fourth consecutive term from Bagedar constituency in Girdih district.

January 22, 2005 : A former member of parliament belonging to Lok Janshakti party, Rajesh Kumar was killed while campaigning for the February 2005 Legislative Assembly election.

2005 : 14 police personnel were killed in two Naxalite blasts in Gondia and Gadchiroli districts.

November 13, 2005 : Jehanabad Jail break by Maoist freed 375 prisoners including Ajay Kanu and 130 Naxalites. Looted 185 rifles and 200 rounds of ammunition from Giridih (Jharkhand) Armoury.

February 9, 2006 : Maoist killed 8 CISF Jawan and looted 14 tonnes of explosives, 14 SLR rifles. Raided main store of NMDC at Hirauli in Chhattisgarh's Dantewara district.

February 28, 2006 : 55 civilians killed, 14 injured and 125 kidnapped at Dantewara. A landmine was planted by Maoist at Eklagoda near Errabore.

March 13, 2006 : 50 Maoist hijacked a train going from Barwadih in Jharkhand to Mughalsarai (UP). They stopped it in jungle's of Jharkhand, held passengers hostage. Police suspected it to be retaliation for the death of an area Commander Jagannath Koiri in nearby Palamau 10 days previously.

March 24, 2006 : About 500 Maoist (armed) attacked Orissa State Armed Police Camp in R. Udaigiri. They killed 3 policemen and looted arms apart from freeing 40 prisoners. Raided Police Stations, barracks, subjail and Treasury, blasted Jail Compound.

April 26, 2006 : 200 Maoists attacked the villagers of Manikonta. 95 were abducted and thrashed 2 villagers were lynched. 13 of them were executed and remaining released.

July 17, 2006 : 25 persons killed and 18 injured when over 800 armed Naxals attacked a village in Dantewara district of Chhatisgarh.

October 2006 : Budhini Munda @ Shobha, wife of Prashant Bose alias Kishenji, second in the CPI (Maoist) hierarchy was arrested by Police near Ramjodi, near Lathikata Police along with her body-guards.

November 11, 2006 : 185 Rifles looted from Home Guards Training Center.

December 10, 2006 : About 25 maoists boarded a train from Tee nagar to Kharargpur, snatched a couple of rifles from railway guards, took away Walkie-Talkie of the Engine Driver and looted Rs. 1,00,000 which was the salary of the Railway Staff.

March 15, 2007 : Naxals killed 16 officers of CHHATISGARH Armed Force, looted 48 Rifles, killed 39 special Police Officers (SPO), injured 12 at Rani Bodli village. It was one of the biggest armed attack by maoist in Bastar.

May 14, 2007 : Dr. Binayak Sen was arrested from Bilaspur on the charges of carrying messages and letters from maoist ideologue Narayan Sanyal who was arrested on January 3, 2006 at Bhadrachalam (Khamam district of AP) to underground Maoist leaders. A Calcutta- based businessman and their associate Piyush Guha was arrested on May 6, 2007 in Raipur. He was found to be in possession of Maoist publications and three letters purportedly written in Jail by Sanyal and delivered to him by Dr. Binayak Sen. He was granted bail by the Supreme Court on May 25, 2009. Raipur sessions Court in Chhattisgarh held him guilty of sedition U/S 124(a) of IPC, read with section 20(b) of IPC and sentenced him to life imprisonment. He was granted bail by Supreme Court of India on April 15, 2011 sifting' he may be a sympathiser. That does not make him guilty of sedition". He was released on a personal bail bond of

Rs. 50,000, a surety for Rs. 50,000 and on condition that he surrender his passport and attend court whenever summoned.

July 2007 : Sriramulu Srinivasulu was arrested from Bariguda forest in Kalimela area of Malkangiri district of Orissa. He was released on bail by Orissa High Court on April 21, 2011 and asked to leave the state within 24 hours. His release was one of the demands of the CPI-Maoist in Malkangiri collection R.V. Krishna's abduction case on 24 February 2011.

August 2007 : Padma alias Padmakka wife of Bhaskar Rao alias Balakrishna, a senior member of the Maoist Andhra-Orissa Border zonal committee was arrested in Bijapur Chhattisgarh and booked u/s 302, 149 of IPC and 27 (1) Arms Act. She was acquitted in August 2009 but re-arrested. She hails from Hyderabad. Her release was demanded by CPI Maoist for releasing Malkangiri collector R. Vinod Krishna IAS, who was abducted on February 24, 2001.

September 7-8, 2007 : Maoist exploded a landmine at Vakalu in Nellore district as former chief minister of Andhra Pradesh N. Janardhan Ready along with his wife passed in a motor cade. He was a target as he had cracked down on left wing extremism in early ninetees and Maoist held him responsible for killing about 400 naxals.

October 26/27, 2007 : Maoists posing as CRPF personnel massacred 17 people including former Chief Minister Babulal Marandi's son Arup Marandi Chilkari village in Girdih district.

October 29, 2007 : Five policemen killed after Naxals surrounded a police party in Bijapur district of Chhattisgarh.

November 2, 2007 : 15 policemen killed in Bijapur district.

December 16, 2007 : Chhattisgarh Dantewara prison break where 299 prisoners escaped. Over 105 were suspected Maoists.

December 20, 2007 : 12 security personnel were killed at Kistavam in Dantewada prison break. 110 Maoist escaped from Jail.

2008

February 8 : 6 policemen were gunned down.

February 15: Maoist attacked Nayagarh and Daspalla towers killed 14 cops. A 28- page booklet circulated by Maoists on "Operation

Ropeway" termed the attack as historic and complete success. Maoists took away 11 AK-47s, 75 self loading Rifles, 250 INSAS Rifles 6 LMGs, 69 9 mm Pistols and many. 303 Rifles and muskets.

March 25 : 17 Naxals including top Dalam Commander killed in Darelli forest. Dalam Commander was Gajerla Ravi alias Ganesh North Telengana Special Zonal Committee member.

April 13 : Maoist attacked Jha Railway station as part of a wider plane of people's Revolution to target government infrastructure including Railway stations, dams, roads etc., all over India. This information was revealed when police recovered a hard disc from a laptop of Malti alias K.S. Priya, wife of Dandakarnya special Zonal Committee spokesperson Vijay Reddy alas Gudsa Usendi on January 22, 2008 from Durg. She was arrested alongwith Prafulla Jha, former Journalist and Meena Chaudhury Whose husband was supposed to be a top Naxalite. The Hard Disc revealed that the Naxalites were highly trained and expert, extremist cadres. CPI (Maoist called a 24-hour 'Jharkhand Bond'.

April 15 : Same day they raided Fesar railway station Aurangabad district in Bihar. In fact, during 2005-08 daring attacks like Jharkhand Jail break (2005) Rani Bodli Police Post attack (2007) Dantewara Jail break (2007), killing of MP Sunil Mahto and Nayagarh attack look place.

April 24 : Dandakarnya Special Zonal Committee members of CPL Maoist set 47 vehicles of Essar Steels in the premises at Kadampal locality on fire in Chhattisgarh. The terror was struck by 100 women wearing Green uniform. They claimed that the land, water and forest belonged to Bastar tribes and they alone have the right to enjoy them.

May 11 : Promod Mishra hailing from Aurangabad district and incharge of operations of entire north India and a member of politburo was arrested on May 11, 2008 from Dhanbad. During his interrogation he had revealed that Nepal Maoist leader Prachandà had visited and inaugurated 9th congress of CPI (Maoist) in the forest area of Bhimbandh in Jamui district of Bihar in 2007. Earlier 'Prachand had said "the debate over links between the Maoists of the two countries was a figment of imagination" (*The Pioneer,* in dtd May 14, 2008

"Arrested Maoist leader belie Prachand's claim" article by Amarnath Tiwari from Patna). Promod Mishra further said "the party is planning to expand its base to Punjab and Haryana with an aim to attack the government's vital installations there. His party colleague and a member of Politburo, Misira Besr arrested in 2007 near Khunti confirmed Promod Mishra's statement that his organisation had decided to shift its operation from rural to urban areas in Northern India. (*The Indian Express,* May 15, 2008 "Arrested Maoist leader says bid to expand base"–report by Manoj Prasad. Promod Mishra was made Operational Incharge of New Delhi during 9th Congress of the Maoists held in the forest of Bheemband in Bihar for 10 days in 2007. (*The Times of India*, February 18, 2008 "Naxalites have 60 crone budget for struggle"–Vishwa Mohan.

June 15 : Maoists are very sensitive about police informers. On June 15, 2008 Maoist beheaded Anand Ram Koram former member of their organisation who had surrendered to the police. police and also warned his colleague who too had surrendered alongwith him.

(*Pioneer*, June 16, 2008) in Dhanora Tehsil in North Gadchiroli.

June 16 : Naxalites slit the throat of Laxman Parlipal.

June 19 : Three SPOs abducted by Maoists following an encounter on June 18 were killed under Banda Police station limits of Dantewada district, Chhattisgarh. Alongwith SPOs five policemen were also abducted and were let off warning them to keep off Salwa Judum and the Police. 3 SPO's who were shot dead were Gopal, Bhadru and Lakshmaiah.

June 29 : Maoists attacked a launch carrying 60 Grey-Hound Commands of Andhra Pradesh in Balimela reservoir located in Malkangiri (Odisha). The Motorboat sank and the 38 Greyhounds Commandos lost their lives.

July 16 : Maoist blew up anti-Landmine vehicle on Kaliamela-Motu Road near Malkangiri village-17 SOG Jawans were killed by Maoists.

July 29 : 36 Grey Hounds Cops killed in Malkangiri by Maoists.

August 23 : 15 Policemen killed in Bijapur.

August 26 : A Divisional Committee member of CPl (Maoist) Suresh Harami surrendered before Gadchiroli. Police alongwith Dalam Commander and a Deputy Dalam Commander.

August 28 : A hard core Maoist Shankar Bhuiyan alias Sanjay Ram was arrested in Jharkhand. Bhuiyan was sub-zonal commander. Police, while searching his hide. out stumbled upon a training manual of maoists-200-page book divided into two sections- contained minute details of planning and assault strategy in different terrains. The book had graphical and political depiction that would even a layman understand how to use a particular weapon and the strategy to be adopted under different situations. Bhuiyan revealed that Maoist in Jharkhand were trained in guerrilla and Jungle warfare by former Army personnel. (*The Times of India*; September 3, 2008, "Ex-Armymen are training Maoist" by Sanjay Ojha. In Orissa Sabyasachi Panda, Secretary of the State Organising Committee of CPI (Maoist) conferred that they killed Swami Laxman and Saraswati who was indulging in anti - Christian activities. He further said most of the Maoist Cadre were Christians in Orissa (*The Pioneer*, dtd October 6, 2008) and Lakhmananand was working to revive Brahmanism. Maoists posters warned against parivar (BJP, VHP, RSS) in Orissa. Maoist held Bengal to ransom. They became active in all the 17 districts of the state, openly threatend the government to withdraw of the CRPF stating "Call CRPF, face bloody reprisals".

August 29 : CPI (Maoists) claimed to have killed VHP leader Swami Lakhmananand Saraswati on August 23, 2008 for his "fascist activities."

August 29 : In a landmine blant by CPI (Maoist), 6 CRPF men were killed near Cheribeda village in Dantewada district of Chhattisgarh.

August 30 : 11 policemen killed in Jharkhand's East Singhbhum.

Aug-September 2008: CPI (Maoist) expelled its best known leader in Orissa, Sabyasachi Panda for his alleged role in fuelling riots in Kandhmal district in Aug-September 2008. (*The Hindustan Times*, January 17, 2008)

October 10 : 12 CRPF Cops killed at Kongupelli in Bijapur.

October 26 : 80 Maoists killed 4 policemen in Gadchiroli.

November 7 : 11 Security personnel killed in Bijapur (Chhattisgarh).

November 10 : 10 Mizo Bn soldiers were killed in Chhattisgarh.

November 2 : Maoists made an a attempt on West Bengal Chief Minister's life at Kalaichand near Forested Lalgarh area.

November 14 : Maoist shot dead Sgt. Mustafa Ali when he was on a mission to evacuate 3 BSF personnel in Chhattisgarh.

December 2 to 8 : Maoists celebrated PLGA'S foundation week at Raipur. And observed 26/11 by saluting victims of 26/11 of Mumbai Terror with a gun-salute to them in the dense forest of Latehar in Jharkhand.

December 25 : They torched CPM leader's houses at Madhupur under Shalboni police station in West Medinipore district. Maoist had rival group called M 2 whose complete nomenclature was idealist-Democratic Guerilla Army. Hindu (Maobadi), according to Orissa police, formed this Hindu Maoist Army. (*The Times of India*, January 6, 2009)

2009

February 1 : Naxalites gunned down a team of 15 Maharashtra policemen in Chhatisgarh-Maharashtra border. A women named Narmada was reported to have led the attack. (*The Hindustan Times* February 3, 2009)

February 9 : Eight cops killed in Maoist attack in Nawada village bordering Jharkhand. in Bihar's Mahuliland village Naxals killed 10 policemen.

February 15 : Secretary of state committee of CPI-(Maoist) Konakuri Ilaich alias Sambaasivdu who had planned the October 2003 landmine blast to kill the then Chief Minister Chandrababu Naidu surrendered before Hyderabad Police (*The Indian Express,* February 17, 2009).

February 28 : A group of 60 Maoists blew up Bhalulata Railway near Rourkela.

March 19 : Prabhat Kumar Panigrahi, a homeopath doctor having links with rss was gunned down by Maoists in Rudiguma village in Kandhamal district of Orissa. The assailants left behind posters in the name of CPI (Maoists) which stated:" All those who misuse religion to incite communal riots and interfere in the dietary habits (e.g. opposing beet eating) of the local people will meet the fate of Saraswati. (*The Hindustan Times*, March 20, 2009).

March 24 : Around 100 armed rebels of CPI (Maoist) destroyed a police outpost and a nearby rest-house in Malkangiri district on Podia Block.

April 8 : 2 cops killed in Bastar by Maoists.

April 9 : Maoist slit throat of Somnath Madkami of Samruddha Odisha candidate from Malkangiri Assembly seat. His body was found near Arshaguda village (*The Hindu*, April 10, 2009).

April 10 : Nine CRPF men killed in Dantewada.

April 11 : 5 CRPF men killed in Khunti (Jharkhand).

April 12 : 200 Maoist target NALCO mine and a CISF post in Damanjodi killed 11 CRPF men in Orissa.

April 14 : Maoists abducted 3 Rly officials in Jharkhand.

April 15 : 2 CRPF men, 2 civilians and 5 Maoist killed at Bidania Ghat in Latehar.

April 22 : A train was hijacked at Hehegarha by 400 Maoists.

April 22 : Blew up Chiyanki Railway station in Palamau district in Jharkhand.

April 24 : Maoists gunned down a village head of Talkonda, Kasha Madhi under Malkangiri police station in Orissa.

The Indian Express daily newspaper of March 16, 2009 reported that Kasansur Area Committee of CPI (Maoist) claimed that a group of about Maoist killed G.itabai Topo on suspicion of her being a police informer. Her throat was slit open.

The Maoists have imposed their own rules that require delivering death sentences and implementing them in most brutal manner in "liberated zones". Informers most of them identified as CPI(M) cadre are dragged out of homes or even school and killed to cleanse the territory of dissenters to the Maoist regime. The Week of December 14, 2009 has probably seen the highest number of such killing, averaging between two and three every day. (*The Pioneer* dated December 22, 2009 Report by Shikha Mukherjee "CPM admits to misrule."

May 11 : Maoists blew up a police Jeep in Dhamtari killing 13 injuring 12 in Chhattisgarh.

May 13 : Shimoga (Karnataka State) police arrested two Maoists A.S. and H.S. in Chitradurga. They were 'Wanted' in Maland region.

May 16 : A CRPF, Jawan abducted from a bus while he was proceeding on leave in Chhattisgarh.

May 20 : Maoists blew up a govt building in Gaya.

May 21 : 16 Cops killed by Maoists in Gadchiroli (Maharashtra).

May 24 : Patel Sudhakar Reddy heading the Intelligence unit of the party was nutralised in Prakasam district of Andhra Pradesh. Sudhakar Reddy alias Sagar was a Central committee member and central Military Commission member. He belonged to Kurti Ravulu Cheruvu in Maddakal Mandal of Mahboobnagar district. He went underground in 1982 while studying Law at Osmania university. Carried a reward of Rs. 12 lakh on his head as he was wanted in several cases including attempted assassination of former Chief Minister Chandra Babu Naidu at Alipiri near Tirumala in 2003 and N. Janardhan Reddy in Nellore in 2007 and the assassination of former Home Minister A. Madhava Reddy in Nalgonda district in 2007, Sudhakar Reddy was also allegedly involved in the murder of senior IPS officer K.S. Vyas and Umesh Chandra in Hyderabad and last years (2008) Balimela attack in which 36 Grey. Hunds personnel died when the Maoist sank a boat on the Andhra-Orissa border. (*The New Indian Express*, Bangalore; May 25, 2009). K. Venkataiah, State Committee member was also killed on May 24 in Tadvai forest in Warangal district. Rights groups claimed that the encounter was stage-managed.

JUNE

7 : A police station at Baipariguda in Koraput district of Orissa was demolished. Police vehicles set ablaze.

7-19 : Ram Bhuwan Patel and Dhanjay Verma both Jawans of Chhattisgarh Armed Force were kidnapped by Maoists from a hilly stretch in Bijapur district on June 17 and slit their throat.

20 : Koteshwar Rao @ Kishan, the brainchild behind Lalgarh operation gave a call to the state govt of West Bengal stating. If the left people government wants discussion with the left of Lalgarh, the operation by the police and the security forces against them should end by this afternoon" He gave this call in the wake of Lalgarh operation by W.B. police and the security forces. Maoists and their associates had formed police Santrosh Birodhi Janasadharaner Committee (PSBJC) and People's Committee against Police Atrocities (PCAPA).

CPI (Maoists) spread their activities in the Kudremukh National forest in west Ghats of Karnataka state where besides their hideouts a training centre was also located. (*The New Indian Express*, Bangalore : Dated June 23, 2009).

In the month of June 2009 CPI (Maoist) Politburo issued a memo to its cadres ordering them for expanding the guerrilla war and Naxal influence to newer areas of Orisa.

Ahead of Home Minister Chidambaram's, Jharkhand Police in a statement said they have information that some of the Maoist leaders have amassed huge poverty over the years. CPI (Maoist) Politburo member Promod Mishra owms a palatial building in Dhanbad. (*Deccan Herald*, June 30, 2009).

22 : Maoist's detonated a remote-controlled device on an anti-Land mine vehicle at Chakulia on the Bengal - Jharkhand border.

25 : Ahead of Home Minister's visit to Orisa Naxal attacked Kakiriguma Railway station and ransacked it, blew up with landmines three mobile phone towers across Kakiriguma, looted post office at Narayanpatna.

26 : Security forces reclaimed control of Kadasole village located to the north of Lalgarh in West Midnapore from Maoists.

JULY

12 : Maoist killed 30 policemen including a Supdt. of Police in three separate incidents at Rajnandgaoin district in Chhattisgarh. SP's name was B.K. Choubey).

August 24 : (i) Lalgarh was called 7 as Naxalbari II

(ii) Red rebels torched 7 dumpers, 1 ten-wheeler Truck.

(iii) Amitabh Bagchi (55) alias Anil alias Sumit-da, a politburo member of CPI (Maoist) was arrested by Ranchi police alongwith 25 year old. Karthik alias Tauhid Mula, a Central Committee Member.

Both of them were produced in the court of Chief Judicials Magistrate in Ranchi who remanded them to Central Jail there. However CPI (Maoist) spokesman claimed that the two leaders had been in police custody since August 19, 2009. Later on both of them were granted bail by Jharkhand High Court. Both of them had well established criminal antecedents. Bagchi was held with incriminating documents 19 every year in the form of levies and plans for savage attack on Government properties and machinery across the country.

From Mullah Tauhid's possession details about transactions of arms were recovered.

September 7 : Commandoes of Special Operations Group (SOG) arrested a hard core Naxalite Mala Madakami, a member of Potturu Dalam, from Kaliamala Jungle. She is a resident of Kangurkonda under Kalinda police station.

September 9 : (i) Maoist target Topadihi Station Master.

(ii) Blow up Kalta police outpost, Mobile towers.

(iii) Abducted railway employees were released on September 11, 2009.

Maoists used children in armed struggle against the state taking a cue from the Taliban and Khmer Rouge (*The Pioneer*, September 18, 2009).

Naxals are noting but cold-blooded murderers (Ministry of Home Affairs, Government of India. (*The Times of India*, September 20, 2009).

September 19 : Asit Sarkar, a senior district leader was shot dead by unidentified person Bin Garbeta (West Bengal).

September 20 : Kobad Ghandy, politburo member of CPI (maoist) and in charge of spreading Naxal influence in urban areas was arrested from South Delhi.

September 30 : Francis Induwar, Special Branch Police Inspector posted in Khunti district of Jharkhand was kidnapped by CPI (maoists) cadre. Police found his decapiciated body on October 6, 2009 on Jamshedpur-Rajnchi highway. A note to the effect that they would expect more of the same treatment if their demands were not met was found with the body.

October 3 : Maoists demanded release of Kobad Ghandhy, Chatradhar Mahto and Chandra Bhushan Yadav.

October 4 : Six Naxals were killed in Police encounter at Tadgaon in Gadchiroli district. Koteshwar Rao @Kishanji No. 2 of CPI (Maoists) said that the Gadchiroli killing was a part of a avenge the murder of senior Maoist military strategist Marang by alleged CPI (M) cadres and the police. Gadchiroli was only an exercise to alert the police against such misadventures. (*The Pioneer*, October 10, 2009).

October 6 : Police Inspector Francis Induwar was executed in Taliban-style murder with the head chopped off.

October 8 : 300 strong band of Maoist guerillas ambushed a police patrol of 40 men and giuned down 17 police. Men in the jungle of Gadchiroli. Tarakka, wife of Maoist central committee member and Maharashtra Incharge Mullajhola Venugopal alias Bhupati was involved in planning the operation in her capacity as south Gadchiroli Division committee member. Apart from Tarakk of Eaitu, the dreaded local commander-in-chief of Maoist and member of Dandakarnya special zone committee was instrumental. (*The Time of India*, October 10, 2009)

October 9 : Maoist backed People's Committee Against Police Atrocities (PCAPC) Chief Chhatradhar Mahato and the party Treasurer revealed that leftist ultras were giving arms Training to about 200 teenagers in the interior wooded regions of Lalgarh-Ramgarh area. The training camps were run in the dense forest of Bhalukbasara, Barapelia, Adharia, Kumarbandh and Salboni. (*The Pioneer*, October 9, 2009).

In order to establish their (Maoists) rule, absolute and total rule they have made sure that government's belated attempt to develop Naxal interested area thwarted. They started to uproot electric poles, dug up roads, blow up bridges and Railway tracks and school buildings etc. so that police be unable to track them.

October 10 : A central committee member Narla Ravi Sharma alias Arjun alias Mahesh and his wife B. Anuradha alias Rajitha were arrested by Hazaribag police. Both belonged to Mehboobnagar (Andhra Pradesh) and have been running the Maoist outfit in Bihar and Jharkhand since 1999.

(*The Times of India*, October 16, 2009). Narla Ravi was expert in military tactis. He had enrolled for his Ph.D. in agriculture from Delhi university. He joined the organisation in 1997 whereas his wife Anuradha was an employee of a public sector bank and joined her husband in the people's war in 2004. (*The Hindustan Times*, October 16, 2009).

October 13 : The panel cabin of Bansipur Railway station was ransacked by Maoist during the 'bandh' they called in Bihar.

October 20 : Officer-in-charge of Sankrail police station Atindra Nath Dutta was abducted by a gang of thirty Maoists on October 20, 2009. Koteshwar Rao @ Kishenji said "If the government assures us that our demands will be met", we will release Dutta. Maoists killed two of Dutta's colleagues-Dibakar Bhattacharya and Swapan Roy inside the police station. (*The Hindustan Times*, October 20, 2009). Maoists took away 6 Rifles, 3 Revolvers, 19 MM Pistol and huge amount of cartridges from the police station. They also looted Rs. 9.23 Lakh from SBI Branch. Government succumbed to Maoists' pressure and freed 23 Maoists prisoners for release of Antindra Nath Dutta on October 22, He joined his duty on November 10, at Midnapore HQ.

Bengal PWD Minister Kshiti Goswami confessed that he spoke to the CPI Maoist leader 'Kishenji'. When police had surrounded Kishenji on October 21 night from all the four sides near Puranpani, the ruling party of West Bengal chose Atindranath's life over Kishenji's arrest.

October 25 : Kundan Pahan of Platoon-39 who had shot Francis Induwar was shot on October 25, 2009.

October 27 : Maoist laid seige to Bhubaneshwar-New Delhi Rajdhani Express at Banstala, 8 km Term from Jhargram. The driver was abducted. "Kishenji' denied Maoists' participation in detaining the train but Justified the action of supporters of the Police Santrosh Birodhi Janasadharan Committee (PSBJC).

November 4 : Maoists attacked Essar Group Guest House in Malkangiri district of South Orissa.

November 5 : Union Home Minister proposed a comprehensive offensive against Maoists. Maoist Top gun 'Kicheg' in response to rising pressure from Government said on November 5th. that they are ready for talks provided the terms and conditions set by them are met. He said the centre will have to withdraw para military forces from Andhra pradesh Maharashtra, Chhattisgarh, Orissa, Bihar, Jharkhand and west Bengal and treat Tribal's problems in a sympathetic way. (Pioneer, November 6, 2009). Maoists refuse to laydown arms, demanded repeal of special Acts such as Unlawful Activities Prevention Act, Armed Forces Special Powers Act and Vigilants and anti-Naxal group like Salwa Judum disbanded.

November 7 : Maoists gunned down a former Legislator of the CPI (M) Subhas Soren at Gopiballabhpur in Lalgarh region of West Bengal and the other two victims were Lakshaman Das Manoranjan Mahali and Jayram Hansda. Posters of Communist Party of India (Maoists) were found near the bodies which were lying on the road connecting Jhargram and Belpahari. They have been given the ultimate punishment for being police informers, Kishenji said. These 3 were extorting funds about Rs. 15 Lakh. Our Binapur Area committee arrested them on November 5, 2009 and after a long trial they decided to eliminate them.

December 23 : Paulush Surin a Naxalite Zonal Commander of breakaway CPI (Maoist) faction won from Torpa in the state Assembly elections. He defeated Koche Munda of BJP from Torpa Assembly seat in khunti district.

December 27 : West Bengal police apprehended a CPI (Maoist) by name of Mohammed Khalek @ Gautam Das. He was arrested with a cache' of arms while he was en route to Lalgarh of West Midnapore. He got these arms from Sentu, an arms dealer based out of Suri Birbhum (*The Hindustan Times*, dated December 28, 2009).

December 14 : Maoists chopped off the arm and slit the throat of a police Chowkidar in Jharkhand village in front of his family accusing him of being a police informer.

December 20 : About a dozen Maoists attacked power generation project at Baliamela Hydroelectricity project in Malkangiri.

100 Maoists blew up a double-storey school building in Dev block under Dhibra police station. In December 2009, Maoists Largeted more than 20 school buildings in Bihar and Jharkhand in which at least 10 were blown up through dynamite in Gaya, Aurangabad,

Jehanabad, Jamui, Munger and Rohtas districts. In these areas, government often used the schools to station para-military forces against them. (*The Pioneer*, December 22, 2009) school children made emotional appeal to Maoists of Bihiar asking them to stop attacking their schools and depriving them of education.

December 22 : Maoist party chief Ganpathy sent a letter to senior colleagues expressing serious concern at the unfailing regularity with the party was loosing its senior cadres. Worried over the reach of the intelligence agencies he cautioned the senior leaders not to come into contact with anyone and suggest that they meet their 'couriesrs' just once in a month. The devastating effect of the series of arrests was evident when the Maoists central committee postponed it politburo meeting as mentioned by Ganapathy. He said "I strongly feel that remaining CCSMs did not learn any small lesson for our losses suffered at top". (*The Hindu*, April 10, 2010).

2010

January 7 : Three aides of Maoist leader Kishenji were arrested with 17 others in Salbani near Lalgarh in a raid at Lakhanpur village. Gopal Mahato, Haripal Mahto @Bhuwaneshwar and Malik Mehato @ Joker were the confidants of 'Kishenji'.

January 9 : 'Kishanji' brands Jyoti Basu former CM of West Bengal as the main culprit and a negative mode of communist movement in the whole country.

Prime Minister Man Mohan Singh described the Maoist "as the biggest internal security threat facing the country". Trinamool Congress MP Kabir Suman sent a fax letter to the Prime Minister on January 16, 2010 stating that "he does not agree with this notion of the PM and that the poverty, lack of education and medical treatment, lack of basic social and economic development and lack of opportunities pose the real threat to the national security."

The ultimate goal of Maoists remains "seizure of power at the centre to change the constitution and establish new democracy"L Koteshwar Rao alias Kishenji says without expansion we can't retain our existing bases" and as such want expansion of their bases and creating new bases at the same time. Kishenji desires statehood for Telengana.

January 14 : Milli Panda alias Subhasree Dass, wife of Sabyasachi Panda alias Sunil, Secretary of Orissa State Organising Committee of the Maoist was arrested and lodged in Bhubaneshwar Jail. Her release was demanded by CPI Maoists for releasing abducted IAS office collector of Malkangiri Vineel Krishna.

January 23 : West Bengal police raided hideout of Kishenji located in the forest area near Tumurkota village in Kotwali Thana area. A laptop, his diary and cell phone and large cache of arms was recovered but Kishenji escaped. Police came close to capturing Kishenji four times but he always gave a slip to the police. In an open letter to Mamta Banerjee in response to the call on January 15, 2010 allowing 7 days time to Naxalites to hold talks, Kishenji said "If you want to come to 'Jangal Mahal.' for talks without bringing the police you are always welcome. If the central government or a political party gives a proposal to lay down arms and sit for talks that is not possible. Giving up arms is not on our agenda."

January 24 : Maoist issued threats to teachers in Orissa not to go to school on the Republic Day and have been forcing closure of schools on January 26. They said teachers who go to school Would be punished with death.

January 25 : Maoist attacked police camps at Chendupatha and Satnala under Barikul PS in West Bengal.

January 25 : In Orissa life was disturbed because of the 2 day economic blockade enforced by Maoists. At various places they put up banners calling Republic Day as 'Black Day'.

February 7 : STF of UP Police arrested 8 activists of CPI (Maoists) in Kanpur. Half truckload of printed material, CDs and pen drive and Rs. 8.16 Lakh in cash was recovered from them. The arrested persons were :

1. Balraj alias B R @ Arvind @ Baccha Prasad, head of Northern Regional Bureau of CPI (Maoists). He was close associate of Kobad Ghandy.
2. Bansidhar alias Chintan Da, a politburo member. He holds M. Phil degree from J.L. Nehru, University of Delhi and was in Jail for 3 years. Hails from Champaran district of Bihar.
3. Naveen Prasad Singh

4. Ambrish
5. Deepak Ram
6. Shiv Raj Singh alias Arjun
7. Rajindra Kumar Phulara alias Arvind
8. Kripa Shankar alias Mano.

(*The Pioneer*, February 2, 2010 and *The Times of India,* February 9, 2010).

February 13 : In Jharkhand CPI (Maoists) People's Liberation Guerilla Army kidnapped a BDO Prasant Kumar Nayak on February 13 from his office in Dhalbhumgarh and threatened to kill him with in 72 hours if three women cadres and some tribals are not released and returned to them. He was released on February 19 by Maoists at Asthi village in Gudabanda area on Orissa border.

February 15 : In view of Naxal operations launched by Security Forces under order of the Home Minister, ultras expressed a desire for a peace talk on condition that some of their top jailed leaders like Narayan Sanyal, Amitabh Bagchi, Sushil Roy and Kobad Ghandhy are released from custody. Home Minister Chidambaram asked them to stop violence first and then the government will talk.

Sushil Roy had managed to obtain bail in all the six cases against him from Patna High Court. But later on a band of 40 Maoists struck a Police Camp at Silda in West Midnapore on February15 killing 24 Eastern Rifles personel and looting arms and ammunition. Koteshwar Rao alias 'Kishenji' calling it a pay back for anti-Naxal drive stated "we are calling it" a "Peace Hunt". This is our reply to anti-naxalite operation the union government has launched. The Silda ambush was foretold on February14 by Asit Mahato PCPA leader stating "there will be an assault within 24 hours".

February 17 : They killed 11 people and injured half a dozen villagers in Bihars Jamui district Phulwaria Karasi village under Sikandara police station.

February 21: Kishenji, "supported the Eastern Frontier Rifles troopers grievances against the west Bengal government," "They are justifiable aggrieved. It was because of the government's faulty planing that 24 soldiers were killed". Kishenji further side." By taking action against special inspector general Binoy Chakraborty, the government can't solve the problem of basic weaknesses in the EPR".

(*The Hindustan Times,* February 22, 2010)

A Maoist squared leader Kajol Mahto alleged to Have taken part in the raid of Silda Camp of EPR on February 15, 2010 was arrested on December 3, 2010 from Pathartuntuni in Salboni PS area.

February 21 : A key facilitator of Kobad Ghandy, Arvind Joshi was arrested from Kanpur.

February 22 : Kishenji who had opposed talkes with the government made a sudden turn around offering a 72-day cease-fire saying there would be no leftwing violence if the security forces stopped their operation in Bengal, Bihar, Jharkhand and Orissa. The deadline was to begin on February 25 lasting till May 7, 2010. Union Home Minister Shri Chidambaram said to Maoists that they should fax him the truce offer but 'Kishenji' retorted by saying that he should give a telephone call on 9734695789 on February 25. This mobile number belonged to a constable whose name was Sisir Kanti Nag and who had been abducted by the Maoist demanding release of the PCAPA leader Chatradhar Mahto on September 26, 2009, Orissa government described Kishenji's proposal as a ploy to re-group his cadres.

February 22 : PCPA founder-president Lalmohan Tudu was killed by the forces alongwith two other PCPA cadre.

March 2 : Police picked up Venkateshwar Reddy alias Telgu Deepak alias Gaurang, military right hand man of maoist Kingpin Kishenji from Sarsuna in Behala, in south Kolkata. Reddy was a senior member of People's War Group and later the People's Liberation Guerilla. (*The Pioneer* March 3, 2010). Reddy, at the time of his arrest was a member of Military Commission and hailed from Prakasham district of Andhra Pradesh. Police stated on March 4, 2010 that during his "interrogation, Venkatesh admitted that he was tasked with setting up a safe corridor between the forested areas of West Bengal's south-western district known as Jangal Mahal and Nandigram. He is also reported to have said that the Trinamool Congress had provided Maoist with arms and that they, in turn, gave supporters of the party arms training during the movement in

Nandigram. (*The Hindu*, March 5, 2010). Koteshwar Rao alias Kishenji again offered to hold talks with the govt. on truce and demanded lease of Deepak first. Kishenji said "the arrest of Telgu Deepak on March 2 will strengthen our resolve to fight state sponsored terrorism. We will make our movement in the country stronger and sharper. We are still ready for talks, but the government is not interested. Their after for talks is just eyewash. The oppression by the joint forces will not succeed. We will continue our movement as long as the people are with us. "(*The Pioneer*, March 6, 2010). Telgu Deepak holds a diploma in electrical engineering. He severely indicted leaders of his own organisation. He accused them of hiring goons to carry out attacks on security forces and misusing 'levies' to fund their lavish lifestyle. However his claim could not be verified. (*The Hindustan Times*, March 8, 2010). He also disclosed that close on the heels of releasing A.N. Dutta, the abducted officer-in-charge of Sankrail police in West Midnapore late last year (2009) 'Kishenji' had travelled to Mayanmar to hold partnership parleys with Tripura National Liberation Front (TNLF) leader. In Myanmar 'Kishenji' struck a huge deal with TNLF and procured a large consignment of arms and had dialogue with ULFA and other groups but he could get arms only from TNLF. The reason for his visit, as per Reddy's statement, was that the Maoists were currently short of arms, And these arms were used in Silda attack in which 24EFR Jawans were massacred. (*The Sunday Pioneer*, March 7, 2010). Strange, Deepak was found to be a devotee of lord Venketeshwar (Balaji of Tirupati) though Naxalites do not believe in God or religious things. He gave out another important information starting that Maoists have infiltrated Kolkata and its suburbs once again entrenching themselves in some of the very areas that were their strongholds during the first phase of their movement 40 years ago and that they have raised an action squad of trained fighters picked from areas with sizeable scheduled cast, scheduled tribe population and brought them to city. (*The Hindustan Times*, March 9, 2010)

Deepak was a suspected mastermind of February 15, 2010 on EFR camp at Sildah.

Maoist have set up several frontal organisations in the city. Matangiri Mahila Samity (Women's outfit), Bandimukti committees,

Lalgarh Manch etc. They do not accept their Maoist links but demand immediate release of political prisoners including Maoists. Deepak is an expert trainer and explosive specialist who had planned and triggered most of the landmines attacks including the November 2006 strikes on Chief Minister Budh Dev Bhattacharya's convoy at Salbani near Lalgarh. Deepak is also reported to have told the police during his interrogation that the Moaist's Lalgarh line is an alter ego of what they call "Philippine Model" which involves blockades, traffic discretion, taking hostages, intermittent killings of political people to strike a general fear punctuated by regular extractions of concessions from the Governments as an image-building exercise among the poor masses. He also told the police that a group of 4 Philippine had visited Lalgarh zone for more than a week and held a number of camp last year (2009) to train the Maoist cadres in modern guerrilla warfare, particularly the hit and run tactics and how to melt away in the crowds after committing a crime. They even trained in Danda karnya. The Philippines were contacted by Kobad Ghandhy who was the Chief of Maoist International Affairs till his arrest. Maoist chalk out their plans well in advance-may be three to four months ahead and work on them but they have prompt-reaction-team of experts who chalk out alternative plans. (*The Pioneer*, March 9, 2010).

Deepak further added that an International Organisation called 'Confederation of Communist parties' has been formed to back and help Maoist across the globe. It has offered to back the Indian ultras logistically. Maoist have picked up strategic contacts in countries like Peru, the Philippines, Venezuela and Bangladesh in this attempt to trigger rebellion in the armed forces. CPI (Maoists) general secretary Ganpathy had visited Peru which has a strong Maoist presence for this very purpose, according to Venkateshwar Reddy alias Deepak. (*The Pioneer*, March 10, 2010).

March 5 : Meanwhile Union Home Secretary Mr. G.K. Pillai while speaking at the Institute of Defence Studies and Analysis in New Delhi on March 5, 2010 disclosed that Maoist engaged in an armed liberation struggle was to overthrow the Indian state by 2050 as indicated by documents seized from them. After every attack they do a post-mortem and analysis. The analysis is as good as anything that the armed forces of any country does. He further stated that

Naxalites destroy school buildings, health centres and blast mobile towers. The Maoist influence was spread over 34 districts in eight states. Mr. Pillai further said that the rebels were looking to regroup and building their own army to implement their plans. (*The Hindu*, March 6, 2010).

True to the statement of the Home Secretary, Maoist backed their true offer to holrd talks with the govt, 12 people were killed in 18 incidents of violence across five states. A day after Shri. G.K. Pillai's statement that Maoists had plans to overthrow the Indian state by the year 2050, Koteshwar Rao alias 'Kishenji' claimed (March 6, 2010) that it would be achieved much before 2050. However following up their offer of a ceasefire in February 2010, Maoist named Social activist and writer Ms. Arundhati Roy, a dissident Trinamool Congress MP and popular Bengali singer-poet Isabir Suman and B.D. Sharma, a former MP bureaucrat who worked for tribal welfare in the improverished Bastar region. (*The Hindustan Times*, March 8, 2010).

March 5 : Headmaster Ranjit Duley was abducted by the militant wing of police Santrash Birodhi Janasadharan Committee (PSDJC) from Sarenga in West Bengal's Bankura district. He was released unharmed on March 8. (*The Hindu*, March 8). Ranjit Duley's younger brother had been gunned down six months ago. The Maoists demanded release of their 6 men in lieu of Ranjit. When the government did not relent, Maoist released the Teacher for a ransom of Rs. 50,000 (*The Pioneer* March, 10, 2010).

March 9 : Union Home Secretary Mr. G.K. Pillai while speaking at a seminar said "Govt. is ready to take criticism. Govt. is responsible. Govt. is accountable but the Maoists are not accountable to anybody". "There were people and NGOs who often criticise the Government for its acts against Maoists but hardly utter any word when there ultras indulge in violence. We must be willing to call a spade a spade. If Maoists are murderers please call the Maoist murderers." He also said Maoists have murdered 159 innocent civilians between June and December 2009 in west Midnapore district of West Bengal. But I did not see any criticism of that. Had the Government killed 159 people, lots of people would have called it a genocide. Why don't they call it a genocide by Moaists?" he asked.

March 10 : 'Kishenji' warned the West Bengal government "It its war, prepare to bleed? He threatened that "rebels could blow up Writers Building anyday" "We have explosives and skill to blow Writers Building and CPMs Alimudin street Headquarter to Smithereens. If the centre can deploy forces, we will get our Comrades from Chhattisgarh, we are redeploying our forces (in anticipation of Greenhunt). If police have leads on our strength and weaknesses, we are also identifying target where we can hurt them most.' Kishenji also came down heavily on West Bengal Governor M.K. Narayanan for "highlighting Maoist killings only "Why are we being singled out? If killing is the issue then CPM should be banned first. As many as 30000 opposition activist were killed during the 30-year left rule. Why is the Governor referring to only 169 killed by Maoists?"

A 129 page document titled "strategy and tactics of the Indian war" which was cleared by the Central Committee of Maoists in 2004 was seized by the security forces in March 2010. It states "our presence today in key industries is extremely low. It is a pressing need that we enter key industries such as transport, communications, Railways, ports, power, oil and gas, and defence equipment. This is crucial for our revolution." The Maoist are carrying their fight against the Indian state into urban India. They plan to create industrial unrest, build an urban cadre base to reinforce armed operations in rural areas and build a network of sympathisers for public, legal and logistic support. The target-Gurgaon, the Mumbai-Pune and Ahmedabad-Surat industrial belt and the Kolkota-Bhilai-Ranchi-Dhanbad region, according to the information gleaned from the captured Maoist leaders Kobad Ghandy. Amitabh Bagchi and Balraj by the police. (*The Hindustan Times*, March 12, 2010).

March 8-11 : In a 4-day joint anti-Maoist operation in the border area of Jharkhand's East Singhbhum and West Singbhum district, security forces demolished a Cpi (Moaist) training camp in a hilly area near Belpahari in Bengal. (*The Hindustan Times*, March 12, 2010).

March 12 : Central Committee member Shakamuri Appa Rao @ Ravi and Telangana Regional Co-ordinator Solipeta Kondal Reddy @ Tech Ramanna were killed by police in two separate encounters in Andhra Pradesh. Appa Rao was killed in Nallamalla forest area while

Kondal Reddy was killed in Kodishala village of Warangal district. Appa Rao carried a reward of Rs. 12 Lakh on his head while Konda Reddy carried a reward of Rs. 5 lakh. Sakamuri Appa Rao was both an ideologue and a military strategist. He was arrested in Hyderabad in 1993 and Jailed for 7 year along with Patel Sudhakar Reddy (Central committee member recently killed in Warangal). He jumped bail in January 2000 and went underground to work, Nallanmala forest and work with Andhra-Orissa Border Special zonal committee. Kondal Reddy hailed from Chittarpur village in Medak, district. He had worked as a secretary of the south Telangana Regional Committee coordinating the Naxalite movement in south Telengana district. (*The Hindu,* March, 13, 2010). On the basis of information in their diaries, Andhra Pradesh police unearthed a massive dump of arms and ammunition and recovered 3000 hand grenades and other material. (*The Pioneer,* March 16, 2010).

March 19 : Maoist activist N.K. Singh arrested from Bhavnagar area. He said Maoist were encouraging movements for creating new states in Vidarbha and Telangana. They are trying to spread their influence in Gujrat. (*The Hindustan Time*, April 8, 2010).

March 21 : Maoist blew up a road bridge in Ghatshila subdivision of East Singhbhum.

March 22 : A 48-hour 'Bandh' called by Maoist in Bihar, Jharkhand, Orissa, West Bengal, Chhattisgarh, Andhra Pradesh and 3 districts of Maharashtra in protest against Operation Greenhunt and killing of their two leaders by AP police in fake encounter.

March 22 : A top Maoist leader L.S.N. Murthy (65) alias Krishna Rao, arrested by Andhra police was living in Basant Gaon, New Delhi till September 2009 before he went underground. Murthy was in touch with Arvind Joshi, a Ph.D. scholar having links and arrested with Kobad Gandhy in Delhi on September 20, 2009.

March 23 : Kanu Sanyal hanged himself to death at the age of 81 years at his village hutment in Hathigada in West Bengal's Darjeeling district which was built for him by his late elder brother. Kanu used to sleep on the mud floor and did not have even a bed to sleep on. All he had as worldly possessions were a couple of plastic chairs and a cot for guest who still kept visiting him. Expenses on his food etc. were met by his party. *The Hindustan Times*, reporters Drimi Chaudhuri and Snigdhendu Bhattacharya wrote a befitting tribute to him on March 24, 2010 edition that "Kanu Babu is the one and only example as to how politicians should lead their life."

March 24 : Maoist owned up to blowing the Railway track between Paraiya and Kastha station on the Grand Chord section but denied targeting Rajdhani Express.

March 25 : Maoist politburo member Koteshwar Rao alias Kishenji was suspected to have been seriously injured during a 7-hour long gun battle between security forces and the rebels at Lakhanpur, Hathilot forest in West Bengal's Paschim Mednipur district. (*The Hindu*, March 27, 2010) It in known as Hathilot forest encounter.

Top Maoist leader Bikram alias Ahishek Mukherjee a former Jadavpur University student was blown to bits alongwith other three rebels in an encounter with Cobra Commandos in Hathilot forest of Jangal Mahals' Lakhanpur. His senior comrade Bikash alias Sashadhar Mahato was also injured seriously was and was dragged deep inside jungle by guerilla squads. Bikash is the brother of jailed PCPA leader Chhatradhar Mahto. (*The Pioneer*, March 27, 2010).

March 27 : In a threat e-mail Maoist warned of attacking Orissa Chief Minister Naveen Patnaik and targeting vital offices and installations if the state government did not stop its operations against the ultras. The e-mail further said "we will reply to each bullet (that) hit comrade Kishenji and comrade Vikram, Maoist leaders (*The Hindustan Times*, March 29, 2010).

April 5 : Sonbhadra (UP) Police claimed to have arrested a Naxal operation, Ram Sajeewan A K.A. Jaswant A.K.A. Guruji as he was trying to cross over from Bihar early in the morning of April 5. A.38 bore revolver and half a dozen live cartridges were recovered from his possession. (*The Pioneer*, April 6, 2010).

Maoist are trying to find a toe hold in Sonbhadra, Mirzapur and Chandauli districts of UP.

April 6 : 76 CRPF personnel were killed by CPI (Maoist) consisting about 1000 Naxalites in a well planned attack, in Termetola, Chintalnar forest, Chhattisgarh's Dantewada district. This included 15 commandors of the Cobra Force. Godsa Usendi, spokesman of the outfits Dandakarnya Special Zone Committee stated that about two companies (300 men) of People's Liberation Guerilla Army (PLGA) participated in the operation. They snatch 75 CRPF weapons including 21 AK-47, 7 SLR, 6 LMGs, and 1 Stengun, 2 2-inch Mortars each. Usendi further said 'we meticulously planned the operation for 5-6 months after observing the movement and other activities of the security forces.' He claimed that the operation had 3 objectives:

1. of crippling Op. Greenhunt.
2. avenging the killing of the top leaders like Patel Sudhakar Reddy and Shakhamuri Appa Rao in fake encounters.
3. saving the people of Bastar region.

(*The Pioneer,* April 9, 2010)

Koram Ramesh alias Singanna, Commander of the 8th company of Danadakarnya Special Zonal Committee (DKSZC) arrested in Bhadrachalam forest on March 16, 2010 gave Sample indication of the preparations going on for the big strike. He was apprehended along with his wife Madakam Aithe, a section Commander and Muchika Jogaiah, commander of military platoon of the party and his wife Hassi in the Thatilanka reserve forest. They furnished significant predictor of the Maoist mission. (*The Hindu*, April 10, 2010).

The Hindu of April 7, 2010 (report by K. Srinivas Reddy) reported that sources believes that four central committee members hailing from Andhra were behind the attack. Their names:-

1. Katakam Sudarshan alias Annand, head of the Central Regional Bureau (CRB). He hails from Adilabad district.
2. Kadari Satyanarayan Reddy alias Kosa. Secretary of the Dandakaranya special zonal committee (DKSZC)
3. Thippri Tirupathi alias Devuji who guides the CRB in military issues and
4. Mallojula Venugopal alias Bhupathy, a member of the CRB and In-charge of Dandakarnya. He is brother of Mallojula Koteshwar Rao alias Kishenji. All these 3 hail from Adilabad district.

April 10 : One Vikram of banned Maoist CPI issued a press statement from Purulia district of West Bengal threatening to launch more severe attacks on security forces and government establishment if the anti-Naxalite operations are not stopped immediately. They also urged families of the para military forces and policemen to bring their near and dear ones back home from the war front. (*The Hindustan Times*, April 11, 2010)

The Times of India of April, 2010 carried a news item under the caption '*TOI* reports from Maoist country'. The Maoist empire has a turnover of more than Rs. 1500 crore a year. Every paisa comes from extortion, drug and robbery. Every truck consignment has a price. In Jharkhand, for instance, the going rate is Rs. 5 per sack of vegetables.

April 14 : In an interview with Jan Myrdal and Gautam Navlakha, Ganpathy the Maoist leader listed 3 demands for any kind of talks:-

1. All-out war has to be withdrawn.
2. The ban an the party and Mass Organisations has to be lifted and
3. Illegal detention and torture of comrades has to be stopped and they be immediately released.

(*The Hindu,* April 14, 2010 interview by Siddhartha Vardarajan)

April 23 : Ajay Kumar Singh, a Maoist operative involved in many Maoist activities in Taryani area of Bihar including the Torching of a police jeep on March 23, was arrested from Govindpuri in South East Delhi.

April 26-27 : Gopal Mishra and his wife Kanchan Bala alias Anu were arrested from their residence in Shahdara area East Delhi. They were involved in promoting the organisational activities in Delhi.

May 17 : Naxals blew up a bus on Dantewada Sukhma road in Chhattisgarh killing 15 policemen and 20 civilians.

May 28 : Maoist blew up track near Jhargram de-railing Jnane-shawari Express and killing 148 persons. Indian Railways later admitted to have incurred a loss of Rs. 10 billion in attacks by Maoist during the year 2010.

June 16 : Ranja Forest encounter in which atleast 12 Maoists were killed.

June 17 : Abdul Shakil Pasha, a close aide of Kobad Ghandy was arrested from R.K. Puram area of South East Delhi.

June 29 : Maoist killed 26 CRPF men in an ambush in Bastar (Narayanpur district of Chhattisgarh).

July 2 : Spokesperson of the central committee of CPI (Maoist) Cherukuri Rajkumar alias Azad alias Gangadhar Madhu, Vijay, Dinesh was killed by Andhra Pradesh police in Adilabad. Comrade Abhay was named as his successor on July 20, 2010. CPI (Maoist) Dandakaranya SZC Spokesperson Gudsa Usendi (real name Katta Ramchandra Reddy) also stated that they would honour Arrad's life and legacy and all the martyrs week from July 28 to August 3. 'We shall also honour Shakamuri Appa Rao and comrade Suryan as People's Liberation Guerrilla Army (PLGA) Commissioner who was killed on May 8 at Narayanpatnam (Orissa) this year". (*The Hindu*, July 21, 2010).

Hem Chandra Pandey, the accomplice, killed with Maoist leader Azad in Andhra Pradesh had his base in Shastri Nagar area in Delhi.

On January 13, 2011 Swami Agnivesh and Bineeta Pandey wife of Hemchandra Pandey moved Supreme Court for a judicial enquiry into the alleged encounter killing both Cherukuri Rajkumar and Hemchandra Pandey claiming that it was not a genuine encounter and that Azad and Pandey were killed in blatant violation of their right under Article 14 and 21 of the Constitution.

July 26 : Seven Maoists including Sidhu Soren, secretary of peoples committee against police Atrocities (PCPA) and his girlfriend Bela Karmakar were gunned down by a joint team of CRPF and special Anti-Naxal force in the jungles of Metela and Koina in Goaltore police station after 5-hour long encounter. The other deceased were Arjun, Rakhal and Sanatan. Sidhu was convener of Sidhu Kanu Gano Militia, the armed wing of PCPA.

(*Deccan Chronicle,* July 27, 2010)

(He was founding commander-in-chief of Sidhu Kanu Gano Militia).

August 4 : A top Maoist Udaiji alias Rajeshji, a member of Bihar Jharkhand Special Area Committee (BJSAC) of CPI (Maoist) was arrested by the Ranchi police and special task force from the posh residential colony of Ranchi. Udaji carried a reward of Rs. 5 lakh on his head and was arrested from Burdwan Compound area. (*The Pioneer,* April 3, 2011).

August 16 : Andhra govt. extended ban on CPI (Maoist) by another year w.e.f. August 17, 2010 under Andhra Pradesh Public Security Act 1992 which would also be applicable to all the frontal organisation of Maoists which includes:-

1. All India Revolutionary Student Federation.
2. Viplava Karmika Samakhya.
3. Singareni Karmika Samakhya.
4. Radical Students Union.
5. Ryot Coolie Sangham and
6. Radical Youth League.

August 21 : Musafir Sahni 1/c of Bihar Jharkhand North Chhattisgarh Regional Unit of CPI (Maoist) was arrested. (*Times of India*, August 22, 2010).

August 27 : A top CPI (Maoist) women commander of Jhargram area Ms. Shobha and Mandi alias Uma who levelled a charge of rape and sexual exploits in an exclusive interview to *Times of India*, on August 24 surrendered to the police in West Midnapore. She had commanded 25-30 armed Maoist squad members. She had joint People's War Group in 2003.

August 29-30 : More than 200 armed Maoist including women in green military dress attacked the search team of Bihar police that were combing forest area of Bihars Lakhisarai district and killed 10 security men, injured 10. The guerilla looted 30 rifles. (*The New Indian Express*, Bangalore, August 31, 2010). Kavaiyah police outpost officer 1/c Bhulan Yadav was among those killed by the rebels.

September 2 : Maoist executed an Assistant Sub-inspector Lucas Tete and warned the Government that the other three policemen 51 Rupesh Kumar, ASI Abhay Yadav and Havildar Ehteshan Khan abducted by Maoist would be killed unless their eight Maoist namely Jai Paswan, Vijay Chaurasia, Prem Bhuian, Promod Barnwal, Ram Vihar Tanti, Ramesh Tikri, Arjun Koda and Rattu Koda are released.

September 6 : The abovesaid three policemen were released by the Maoist after Bihar Chief Minister assured them safe passage.

September 19 : Seven cops were found missing and abducted from Bhopalpatnam area of Bijapur. Bodies of 3 policemen were discovered two days later with Maoist literature. As per hand written demands of Maoist they asked the Government to initiate peacetalks, stop operation Greenhunt and alleged atrocities on people and released named people. Policemen who went missing were-ASI Sukhram Bhagat, Head Constable B. Tikri, Constable B Toppo, Subhash Patre, Nanddal al Kaushal, Narendra Khosle and Daularam Sodi.

September 26 : Ms. Arundhati Roy said "The war on Naxals is a conspiracy to acquire their ancestral land for industrial use. The deployment of security forces in the Naxal affected states is a violation of the human rights." While addressing a 2-day seminar organised by the Jharkhand Alternative Development Forum and the Operation Greenhunt Virodhi March in Ranchi (*The Hindu*, September 27, 2010).

September 30 : Four cops namely ASI S. Bhagat, B. Toppo, Subhash Patra and Narendra Khosale, abducted by Maoists were set free by them following personnel appeals by Chhattisgarh Chief Minister Raman Singh, Maoist ideologue Varavara Rao and social activist Swami Agnivesh.

October 1 : Home Minister Shri. Chidambaram urging Nationwide condemnation of the 'Kangaroo Court' run by Maoists in certain parts of the country said such courts known as 'Jan Adalats' has risen to 48 in the current year upto August 31, 2010 up from 38 in the corresponding period last year. They had executed 21 persons this year (2010) compared to 11 last year.

October 4 : Four security personnel were killed in a powerful triggering of an explosive at a market place in Perimili village in Gadchiroli's Bhamvagarh Tehsil. CRPF Inspector Nivruth Yadav, Const. Anand Gajge and two Gadchiroli Sub Inspector Mahendera Kumar Nalkul and Shashikant More died on the spot.. Maoist rebels even robbed the slain policemen of arms and ammunition. (*The Indian Express*, October 5, 2010 and *The Pioneer*, October 11, 2010). Maoist seem to have prior information of the movements of policemen.

October 7 : Central committee of CPI (Maoist spokesman Abhay issued a statement to mark 6th anniversary of the outfit. (It fell on September 21 but the statement was released later). It read "from May 2009 to July 2010, eight topmost comrades including politburo member and beloved leader Azad and 10 state level leaders had either been caught and killed by the enemy or put behind bars". Assessing the progress of the revolutionary movement in India, Abhay said that despite the movement suffering setbacks in Andhra Prdesh and north Chhattisgarh and heavy losses in north Orissa, it had notched many successes elsewhere. The biggest loss was the death of Azad who had been rendering multifaceted services most efficiently in many fields. But he conceded that the losses since May 2009 had been more serious. Despite the reverses, Abhay said, the revolutionaries managed to inflict serious losses on the security forces at Singanamaugu and Mukauram (Dantewada) in Chhattisgarh, Laheri in Maharashtra, Sankrel and Silda in West Bengal, Gumla, Vishnupur and Lateshar in Jharkhand, Gaya and Tandwa Bazar in Bihar and Potakal and Baipharguda in Orissa. The successful strikes, he claimed had 'broken down the initiative of the enemy'. The struggles in Kalinganagar, Singur and Nandigram had desired impact on the ruling classes, he said and the Lalgarh and Narayanpatna struggle had taken place on a higher scale. In this background, the Maoist party called for a broad united front of all resistance struggles in the country. (Report by K. Srinivas Reddy in *The Hindu*, of October 9, 2010).

October 8 : The Maoist triggered an improvised explosive device (IED) under Maruti Gypsi vehicle carrying four ITBP personnel- HC Jaidip and Const. Dinesh Singh, Shiv Prasad of 38 Bn CRPF were killed in the blast on the Maharashtra-Chhattisgarh Border. Two school boys and two civilians were also killed. (*The Hindu*, October 9, 2010).

October 9 : Revolutionary folk singer Ghaddar launched his new political outfit "Telengana Praja Front" declaring that the front would not be like other political parties and will not contest elections. "He gave the slogan of self respect, self rule and equality" as the focal theme of the front. What it that the people of Telengana want? He questioned. It is the self respect and self rule. They want that their state should be ruled by themselves and not by the outsiders." (*The Pioneer*, October 10, 2010).

October 9 : CRPF and Chaibasa police arrested a CPI (Maoist) Central Technical Committee member Nulla Bhikashpati from Bangaon in Jharkhand. Bhikashpati hails from Warangal district of Andhra Pradesh and was associated with Naxals since 1991. (*The Hindu,* October 11, 2010).

October 2010 : In yet another spine chilling incident of red terror, the Maoist operating in Jangal Mahal area burnt alive a women after she tried to organised villagers to revolt against them-the villagers were even prevented from claiming the body which was rotting for four days. (*The Pioneer*, October 10, 2010).

October 22 : A senior Maoist leader Foren Singh Sardar who had been active in West Bengal and Jharkhand for more than 15 years was arrested by Bankura and Jhargram police. (*The Hindu*, October 23, 2010).

October 25 : Three ultras of CPI (Maoist) dressed in black military fatigues showed up outside the house of Dansar Kovachi in Kanker (Chhattisgarh) and shot him dead. A note recovered from his body, accessed by Jouranlist Aman Sethi of *The Hindu* stated that Sansai has been killed for violating the Maoist diktat by tilling his field beyond the allotted 35 acres. "No one can till the land" read the note "nor can it be leased out for farming". (*The Hindu* January 3, 2011).

November 6 : The Latehar unit of CPI (Maoist) opposed the panchayat polls in Jharkhand by distributing handouts saying "people will face consequences if they participate in the elections."

November 8 : While enforcing a shut down to protest US president Barrek Obama's India visit, the Maoists triggered blasts at a Railway Station Satbahini in Jharkhand's Palamau district. CPI (Maoist) also gave a call for nation wide 24-hour shutdown at midnight on November 7 to protest Obama's visit. (*The Hindu,* November 9, 2010).

November 2010 : CPI (Maoist) general secretary Muppalla Laxman Rao alias Ganpathy in an e-mail sent to the correspondent Aman Sethi of the *Hindu* stated that his party had consolidated control over areas under their influence, raided hundreds of weapons and ammunition rounds from state armouries and developed West Bengal's Lalgarh and Orissa's Narayanpatnam into emergent guerrilla zones. Terming Comrade Azad's death, Rao stated "Azad's loss had caused a very big hunderance in achieving our goals" and had a grave impact on the Indian revolution." Ganpathy, nonetheless insisted that the party was still attracting educated cadres that would be able to fill the void created by Azad by training. Ganpathy, in the same e-mail dismissed press reports that Maoists were sourcing weapons from China, Myanmar and Bangladesh. He said "our weapons are mainly country made. All the modern weapons we have are mainly seized from the Government armed forces when we attack them.' He denied that Maoist had been exorting money from the mining industry and corporations but admitted that the party extracts levies from local businesses. It mainly collects Sonations from people and funds from the Trader's in our guerrilla zones. (We) also collect rational levy from contractors who take up various works in our areas."

Srinivas Reddy, a correspondent with *the Hindu* whose reports are always timely and accurate and has access to the Naxals writes that Maoists have conceded that they were unable to strengthen the revolutionary movement in urban areas for a variety of reasons and that the current focus of Maoists leadership was on consolidating the movement among the peasantry and later extend it to urban areas. (*The Hindu*, November 10, 2010 article by Aman Sethi and Srinivas Reddy from Hyderabad under the headline "Maoists consolidating control", says CPI (Moaist) leader.

In a statement CPI (Maoist) general secretary Ganpathy laid down condition for talks with the centre, although it said the atmosphere was not conducive for such deliberations now. He demanded that the centre immediately stop Op. Greenhunt, withdraw paramilitary forces, lift the ban on Maoist outfit and its front organisations and create democratic conditions for the party to work. (*The Pioneer*, November 10, 2010).

A poster written by a newly formed tribal platoon of the Maoist, near Lalgarh warning fellow comrades using the name of 'Shaheed Kishenji' to extort money and do other wrongful works that hit the interests of the tribal population in general (*The Pioneer*, November 13, 2010). It seems that 'Kishenji' is dead. There was an encounter in March 2010 between a gang of Maoist led by Kishenji and the police in which the 55 year old party politburo member was seriously injured and was carried from one place to another often being treated by village quacks, a doctor who treated him even confessed to have treated him inside the forest. (Report by Saugar Sengupta from Kolkata "Maoist poster says "Shahid Kishenji" cops foxed" *The Pioneer* November 13, 2010). Subsequently an e-mail purportedly sent by the Central Military Commission on the People's Liberation Guerilla Army of the Maoist to Orissa Chief Minister's office threatened to blow up government installations and vowed to reply to each bullet hitting at "Kishenji and comrade Vikram."

Maoist Technical Committee zonal head in the Jharkhand state Nalla Vishakhapathi who belongs to Andhra Pradesh and was arrested during a recent operation in Saranda forest and claimed to have been engaged in manufacturing and testing of rockets and motors, proposed to show the police their arms manufacturing plants and thus show case their capacity to overpower forces engaged in anti-Naxal operations. According to Vishakhapathi Maoist have set up an underground unit to produce armament. (*The Pioneer*, November 16, 2010. Report by D.P. Sharan from Ranchi).

November 13-14 : Patmakka @ Nirmala alias Sirisha wife of Maoist leader A.K. Kiraju Hargopal alias Ramakrishna in Orissa who was on her way to meet her ailing husband along with two other women was arrested by the Police in Dudhari village in Koraput district. Ramakrishna is secretary of Andhra Odisha Border special Zone committee and Central Committee member of CPI (Maoist) (*The Pioneer*, November 16, 2010). [Her name is K. Padma]

December 3 : Sudip Chongdar alias Kanchan alias Batash, who appointed secretary of CPI (Maoist) of West Bengal committee following arrest of the former secretary Himadri Sen Roy in February 2008, was arrested from Kolkata by Special Task Force (STF) of Kolkata police along with three associates namely Anil Ghosh alias Bijoy, Barun Sur alias Vidyut, Bimal Ghosh alias Shankar Mallik alias Buchu. Chongdar hails from Garhbeta in Paschim Medinipur district and was instrumental in organising Lalgarh movement in 2008. (*The Hindu*, December 5, 2010).

December 4 : A woman Maoist leader Kalpana Maiti alias Anu member of state committee and wife of senior Maoist leader Asim

Mondal alias Akash was arrested from Howrah station on the basis of information obtained from the 4 arrested Maoist on December 3. (*The Hindu*, December 5, 2010).

In July 2005 a Central Committee member known by non-de-plume 'Dhurba' had said that the party work was going on in North and South 24-parganas, Howrah, Kolkata, Behrampur, Murshidabad and Malda districts and that the their mass base in Malda, Bardhman, Murshidabad and Nadia in ready and after five (5) years they will launch their strike. This object probably was responsible for their concentration in and around Kolkata.

December 5 : From their (above said Maoist) interrogation, it emerged that Maoist have close links with the Peoples Revolutionary Party of Kanglaipak (PREPAK) including assistance in training and supply of arms. PREPAK was formed in 1977 with the objective of expulsion of outsiders from Manipur. It also came out from their interrogation that CPI (Maoist) politburo member Kishenji is alive and living with the Dandakarnya area but outside West Bengal. Earlier he was suspected to have been seriously injured in an encounter in the Hathilot forest area of Paschim Medinipur district on March 25, 2010. (*The Hindu*, December 6, 2010).

The interrogation of the these five senior most Maoist leaders revealed a Chinese supply route that stretches from Northeast to Junglemahal. According to STF sources, they have seized nearly 200 manpacks wireless communication devices which include around 50 high-end static satellite phones. These satellite phones works in the radius of 25 kilometers. These devices were used by the Maoists for communication purposes. The use of cell phones had become suicidal for them as they were being easily tracked by the police. Maoist leaders were also reported to have told the interrogators that a central committee member had visited China. (*The Indian Express*, December 8, 2010).

Sudeep Chongdar alias Kanchan, State secretary arrested by Kolkata police on December 3, 2010 alongwith four other top leaders face, among others, charges of rape brought against him by one Maoist women who had lodged FIR in the Salboni police station of west Midnapore on October 10, 2010. One of the reasons she cited for leaving CPI (Maoist) was gangrape by several top leaders apart from Kanchan. She had surrendered in September 2010. Others who are accused in fir of rape charges include Sashadhar Mahato, aStateCommittee member and a key functionary of Lalgarh movement, brother of Chhatradhar Mahato–chief of People's Committee Against Police Atrocities-who is now in custody. Sashadhar is also wanted in Janeshwari Express derailment case that claimed 148 lives. Bikas alias Mansaram Hembram head of the state Military Commission is also one of the accused of rape. She said in her FIR that for training was taken to several camps in 2003. In one training camp was raped by several Maoist squad members. I tried to complain to our senior leaders but they did not listen. In April 2010 I was in a camp in Salboni when I was gangraped by Bikash, Sashadhar and Sudip Chongdar in presence of my husband Kamal Maity." (*The Indian Express*, December 9, 2010). (The women Maoist concerned in Shobha Mandi alias Uma).

December 5 : A Naxal pamphlet pertaining to the People's Liberation Guerrilla Army week, observed in December 2010, was found near the gate of Model Mill premises in Nagpur.

December 5 : A booklet seized during a raid on Naxal leaders Azad and Hemchandra Pandey in Nagpur titled "Shahri kaam ke bare mein" published in the year 2008 regrets that they have not paid adequate attention to the urban areas and identified nine different belt for its urban action plan :

1. Ahmedabad - pune corridor
2. New Delhi, Bangalore, Chennai, Coimbatore-Eroade belt
3. Hyderabad-Kolkata industrial cities of central India
4. Cities on the Gangetic plains and central India.

The document said "we have failed to understand the clash between the urban and rural agitations and we are guilty of utter neglect of urban work. Along with a deeper and wider support we have failed to develop a strong and impactful undercover system (Gupta Pranali) to keep the party safe in urban areas. As a result, we are feeling a serious crunch of able and experienced cadres". About "battle "perspective" it says "we must have an elaborate revolutionary struggle plan" both armed and otherwise for urban areas which will be suitable for a long term people's war that is first liberating rural areas and later taking control of urban areas". It says "with these long term perspective, we must develop a strong undercover party, a revolutionary united front and urban guerrilla squads and militia. We must be able to send cadres to rural areas who could be sourced from workers recruited from unorganised sector. Urban organisations will also help establish supply lines to our organisation in rural areas for many things such as arms and ammunition, machines and their parts and medicines". "Encouraging ghettos of the urban disadvantaged sections on the lines of Muslim ghettos, it says. The Muslim ghettos have been caused by increasing Hindu fascism. For the Muslims, it has become a necessity so that they can unitedly defend themselves. All the plans of our party must take the process of ghettoisation seriously."

The document critically looks at the nine urban areas it aims to target for its urban plan. "The Ahmedabad-Pune corridor is engineering, chemical, textile, auto, communications and electronic hub. The working class here is most diverse since it comes from all the parts of the country. "Delhi is basically dominated by North Indian workers while Bengaluru is an IT hub". "Creating a strong and undercover party by harnessing the struggle of the disadvantaged working class, creating a joint front of working class with other sections of the urban society such as the Dalits and women and undertaking military activities." are the three main tasks laid down in the document. (*The Indian Express*, of December 7, 2010 Report by Shri Vivek Deshpande from Nagpur. "Naxal turn urban."

December 12 : Following the arrest of Comrades Sudip Changdar, Kalpana Maity and Dwijen Hembram on December 4 from Kolkata, posters demanding their unconditional release appeared in prime locations of Kolkata. The posters also demanded immediate withdrawal of Operation Green hunt and removal of Unlawful Activities Prevention Act. Posters also exhorted people to be united against 'criminals' behind Commonwealth Games scandal and 2G Spectrum Scam. It also sought people's support so that the PLGA could be transformed into a full fledged Army-PLA. Posters also asked people's to observe the PLGA week and support the CPI (Maoists so that their movement can be translated into a mass movement. (*The Indian Express*, December 13, 2010).

December 16 : Ranchi police arrested wanted Naxal Maoist Gurua Pahan from Ambedkar Nagar district of UP where he had gone to meet his wife and arrange a job for himself.

December 17 : A women Maoist squad member Sambari Hansda alias Seema who entered the Eastern Frontier Rifles Silda Camp in Paschim Medinipur district disguised as a dancer on February 15, 2010 and carried out reconnaissance prior to the massacre of 24 Jawan was arrested from Lakhanpur forest in the west Medinipur district. She was arrested alongwith another women ultra Hapan Murmu who was involved in the attack on the Sankrail police station in the Same district on October 20, 2009.

December 17 : Maoist gunned down seven Forward Block men including a Panchayat Pradhan for their alleged role of 'police informers'. They were shot dead by Maoist at Jhalda in Purulia district of West Bengal on December 17, 2010.

December 17 : Three Maoist belonging to Peoples Liberation Guerilla Army (PLGA) the military wing of CPI (Maoist were killed in exchange of fire with the police in the forest area in between Cheruvuru and Yegajanaba villages under Balapam Panchayat in Chintapalli mandal of Vishakhapatnam district. One Reserve sub inspector was injured.

December 18 : Four Maoist Shivam, Sudhir, Vikas and Khuglesh were arrested from Pirmukam village in Katihar district. Maoist literature, banners, posters were recovered from them.

December 18 : Two CPI (Maoist) cadres were killed in an encounter between Naxalites SOG in Sundergarh district in Orissa.

December 19 : Samarji, Area Commander of Chotanagpur are of CPI (Maoist) handed over the body of special operation Group personnel Laxman Kissan killed in gun battle between the two sides in Orissa's Sundergarh district, to his family. Samarji said Kissan was injured in the gun battle and that they saw him in critical condition but could not give him medical help.

Meanwhile the absconding Chasi Muliya Adivasi Sangh (CMAS) President Nachika Linga demanded that all the CRPF camps in the rural areas should be immediately closed down.

December 21 : Maddela Adellu alias Anand, a Maharashtra state committee member (MCM) and his wife Kurma Rambai alias Saritha, Killo Raju alias Chkkudu Raju and Sreendri Subha Rao alias Srikanth both tribals and natives of Kannavaran village in Vishakhapatnam district in Andhra surrendered before police. Surrendered Maoist Anand said he worked for the party for 20 years and was now frustrated over the Statemate in the party activities in Maharashtra for a long period. "I have lost faith in the Maoist ideology and have decided to spend my remaining life with my family". (*The Pioneer*, December 22, 2010.)

December 21 : Bokaro police and CRPF together raided the township area of Chanderpura and arrested Devendu Singh alias Anandji alias Subodh, a member of special Area committee Bihar-Jharkhand, Ramkumar Pandit alias Langrazonal commander (Technical cell) and Jai Prakash alias Dineshan active member of CPI (Maoist) all resident of Jahanabad (Bihar). The raiding team also uneathed a maoist's explosive chemical laboratory at 35 km from district HQ of Bokaro. Liquid and solid state explosivs, 14 China made Motorola Walkie-Talkie, huge Naxal literature, Cds, battery timer and amplifiers were seized from the spot. The arrested Naxals are reportedly close to Arvindji alias Nishant alias Dev Kumar, a member of Naxal Central committee as well as CHC and CMC. On November 10, 2009 when a joint team of Patna police and Bokaro police jointly raided a house in Bokaro steel city and recovered huge arms and ammunition, it came to their notice during investigations that Arvindji is responsible for the supply of arms in Jharkhand, Bihar and Chhattisgarh. (*The Pioneer*, December 22, 2010).

December 21 : Naxals triggered a blast on Aheri- Sironcha state highway in south Gadchiroli injuring seven policemen three of them seriously and grievously.

December 24 : Prime Minister Manmohan Singh, while addressing IPS probationers said "Naxalism and terrorism are major challenges before the nation. The tribal areas of the central India are in the grip of Naxalite menance and if it is not controlled, the country would have to bid good bye to its ambitions of sustaining a growth rate of 10-11% per annum.

December 24 : Three cadres of CPI (Maoist) were killed in an encounter with SOG at Narayanpatna Block in Koratput district.

December 24 : Raipur Sessions Court in Chhattisgarh pronounced Dr. Binayak Sen, Piyush Guha and Narayan Sanyal "guilty of criminal conspiracy to commit sedition under section 124(a) read with 20(b) of IPC and sentenced them to life imprisonment. They were also convicted u/s 39(2) of the Unlawful Activities (Prevention) Act 1967 and sec. 8(1) (2) and (5) of the Chhattisgarh Special Public Security Act, 2005 which charged them with supporting, aiding and abetting in the activities of a criminal organisation CPI (Maoist) which carry sentences upto 5 years. Binayak Sen was also found guilty of belonging to a banned organisation under section 20 of the UAPA which carries a sentences of 10 years. The sentences were to run concurrently. In May 2007 (May 15, 2007) Dr. Binayak Sen was accused of acting as a courier between the alleged Maoist leader Narayan Sanyal and Kolkata businessman Piyush Guha and imprisoned for two years before getting bail on the directions of the Supreme Court. (*The Hindu*, December 25, 2010).

Dr. Binayak sen is a physician and general secretary of PUCL Chhattisgarh and national Vice President of PUCL. his bail plea was rejected by Chhattisgarh High Court on February 10, 2011 but Supreme Court granted him bail on April 15, 2011.

December 25 : Maoist triggered a landmine and resorted to indiscriminate firing killing Bishram Kumar of Cobra Force of CRPF land wounding four others inside the Dekai Hill forest of Purulia district in the wee hours of December 25, 2010.

December 25 : Maoist set ablaze a proclain stationed near Chatti village in Chintur mandal. It belonged to a Road contractor. It was suspected that Sabari dalam members were involved in the incident. (*The Hindu*, of December 27, 2010).

December 26 : Gaya police in Bihar foiled a Maoist plan to attack the divisional jail and arrested 6 hardcore ultras namely zonal commander Bhushan Sharma alias Vipinji, Suresh Yadav alias Chandanji, Yugula Yadav alias Yogeshji, Ashutoshji, Arun Paswan alias Rameshji and Jitenderra Singh alias Tiger when the police raided several places in Rampur in Gaya district. The dreaded Naxals had made a comprehensive plan to repeat the Jahanabad Jail break incident in 2005. The arrested Maoist were involved in the killing of the SHO Mithelesh Prasad in Gaya. One AK-56, two regular carbines, two countrymade pistols, 249 live cartridges besides Rs. 59000/- in cash, seven mobile phone were seized from them. (*The Pioneer*, December 27, 2010).

December 26 : Maoist reportedly belonging to Venkatapuram Area committee and police exchanged fire near Kurnapalli village in Charla mandal of Khammam district in Andhra Pradesh (*The Hindu*, December 27, 2010).

December 26 : A day ahead of Home Minister P. Chidambaram's visit to Naxal effected areas of Maharashtra, police arrested two Naxals. Bhimrao alias Bhanu alias Bhaskar Bhovte and his wife Sunanda alias Megha alias Vanaje Vasant Ramteke, both state committee members. They were chased are caught by police party on the Gondia-Bhandara road. Bhimrao who is active in Naxal Cadres since 1987 is from Chapra Shipura in Amravati and Sunanda who joined the movement in early nineties is from Pathri village in Chandrapur district. (*The Indian Express*, December 28, 2010).

713 civilians were killed by Naxalites groups in the year 2010 as compared to 591 in 1999. Security forces lost 285 personnel as compared to 317 in 2009 while the casualties on Naxalites side was only 171 in 2010 again significantly less than 219 in the year 1999. (Statement by the Home Minister on January 4, 2010).

In the year 2007, 1737 people and in 2008, 1769 people were killed by Naxal groups. Naxals have influence in 20 states (223 district) across the country.

The home minister was critical and concerned with increased Maoist violence. He criticised the liberal media for giving hype to these murderers and respectability. "Maoist believe in violence which has no place in a democracy. A strong head, a stronger heart and staying power is required to tackle them. There can be no half-way approach. Most people still think there could be a compromise or some kind of median approach, this is immature and foolish... This is expected because as long as we did not engage them, they were happy and expanding. They will continue to expand unless we challenge them" he said.

Consider what Shri Chidambaram the Home Minister said on February 1, 2011 while giving on overview of internal security at the Chief Minister's Conference in New Delhi. He said CPI (Maoist) remained a powerful and determined adversary and had added at least four companies to the People's Liberation Guerilla Army (PLGA), armed wing of Naxals. "In 2010, left wing extremists killed 718 civilians of whom 323 had been branded Police informers". "Unlike our security forces, the Naxals cadres are not constrained by the rules of law or rules of conflict. In areas they dominate they act as the judge, Jury and executioner. I regret that no representative of civil society has called for an equity into the rutal and unlawful killing of civilians and other acts of depredation committed by the CPI (Maoist)." Reiterating that there was no dilution of the governments, two pronged approach of development and police action to ceontain Naxalism, he said the offer of talks "remains valid on condition that the CPI (Maoist) abjure violence."

On the question of complaint of non-development of the areas by the state and central government, Mr. Pranab Mukherjee, the Union Finance Minister had slammed the argument that the Maoist violence is an offshoot of lack of development starting that it is "more imaginary than actual." He said Maoists are engaged in a political project to capture power by using guns. Development is needed-lack of development may swell Maoist cadre-But they do not run charitable institutions..... They are political elements and want to capture power..... he added.

Home Ministry figures show that the Red Brigade was targeting economic establishments during the past three more. They carried out 909 attacks on mines, steel pipelines and roads. Another target was Railways. Because of actions of ultras, Railways in Jharkhand Bihar were almost crippled. Naxals carried out 129 attacks during 2008-2010 against trains, stations and tracks. Blowing off the Railways stations, stations blastingthe tracks and removing fish-plates has become the ritual for Naxals. Yet another target is destroying telephone exchanges or towers, power transmission plants, mobile cell phone towers. They have not spared even school buildings, Panchayat Bhawans, bridges, culverts and roads leading to forests. Though they have been demanding removal of security forces from school buildings but they themselves have been destroying these temples of learning particularly in Bihar and Jharkhand. They were not allowing construction of forest roads. For the past three years, as many as 325 Maoist attacks were aimed at scuttling construction of forest roads and culverts. Minister of state for Home Affairs Gurudas Kamat stated in Lok Sabha on March 8, 2011 that out of 909 attacks on economic targets, a majority were on construction of roads 325 Maoist attacks were directed/ aimed at this goal. They carried out 159 attacks on telephone exchange, 61 Panchayat Bhawan, 135 school buildings and 33 power transmitters were destroyed. Railway lines passing through Jharkhand were attacked 37 times by Maoist and 35 attacks were faced by Bihar Railway lines. 52 strikes were done in Bihar against telephone exchanges while Orissa communication facilities were sabotaged 39 times, 30 attack were against telecommunication centres and towers in Jharkhand and 27 in Chhattisgarh.

More of Jawans of security forces were gunned down by Maoists. Government banned CPI (Maoist). CPI-ML, MCC and all their fronts and formations under the UAPA.

Maoist banned / prohibited entry of government staff into the "cut off" area of 6 panchayats and number of tribal hamlets on Orissa- Andhra border thus bringing developmental actvities to a stand-still. This warning was issued to the district authorities of Malkangiri on March 7/8, 2011.

According to a cable from U.S. Embassy by Ambassador David Mulford on December 8, 2005 (47006 confidential) "Despite Indian's rapidly expanding economy, Naxalite groups in poor rural areas and their educated urban sympathizers continue to spread and have extended their areas of influence into 12 states, proving they can launch spectacular attacks on government facilities," "Indian's scheduled tribes and scheduled castes who live in these remote areas, often face lives of desperation and view Naxalties as the only groups willing to defend them. There is no chance Naxalites could threaten the Indian state and GOI is unlikely to Cradicate Naxalism through police action. The most likely prospect is a continuing and blood statemate." "Although Naxalities claim to represent the interests of Indians opposed scheduled castes and scheduled tribes, the leadership is almost entirely from the upper castes, including some highly educated individuals. The same applies to the extensive Naxallite support network, including above ground organisations of educated middle class persons from academia, the media and the legal profession."

Another cable, sent on December 20, 2005 (48157 confidential) by charged affaires Robert Blake said the government unwillingness and inability to make the difficult decisions required to prevent destruction of the forests and to end the exploitation and victimisation of tribals plays into the hands of the Naxalites. Most tribals have little or no ffaith that the GOI will protect them, and over time may see little alternative but to turn to the Maoist as the best of a bad set of choices". (*The Hindu*, March 24, 2011).

In Chhattisgarh 143 civilians were killed in Maoist violence in 2010. On October 25, 2010 the Manpur Division of the CPI (Maoist) kiled one Dansai Kovachi from Karaki village. A note recovered from his dead body said he was killed because he allowed his daughter Uma (27) and Nirmala (20) to join the police force in 2007.

The note recovered from his body also stated that Dansai had been killed for violating the Maoist diktat by tilling his fields beyond the allotted 35 aeres. "No one can till the land, nor can it be leased out for farming". (*The Hindu,* January 3, 2011 article by Aman Sethi)

In Chhattisgarh, Maoists adopted a new tactics of calling frequent 'Bandhs'. In the past three months rebels called 'Bandh' five times. On October 22, 2010 the bandh affected transportation in parts of Kanker, Narayanpur, Bijapur and Dantewara district as the rebles dug up roads and put up blockades. On November 8, 2010 rebels protested the visit of Us President to India. Buses were off road, in Sarguja district that day. A month long 'bandh call' was given on December 2 to 31, 2010 to commemorate the 10th anniversary of PLGA paralysing communication in all of Bastar and Rajnandgaon. There were 11 strikes against NMDC mines in 2010 alone.

In Maharashtra, Naxalites shifted focus from rural to urban areas including semi-urban areas for recruiting SC/ST students. It was reported that between 10 and 15 hostellers from Chandrapur City from Mumbai including 3-4 girls have already been recruited in 2010, Naxals already started focusing on hostels in places like Rajpura, Brahamapuri, Mul, Soali and Nagbhid in Chandrapur district and Wani in Yavatmal. (*The Indian Express,* January 3, 2011)

An 'alert' accessed *The Indian Express* and circulated by Maharashtra Police in March 2011 detailed Naxalite strategy to intensify recruitment in urban Maharashtra and Gujrat. Interrogatija report of a top arrested Maoist leader revealed that Naxalites have created a new 'Agit Propaganda Team' besides 'Golden Corridor Maharashtra Area Committee'. While the Golden Corridor Committee has been formed to 'target industrial' centres in Maharashtra and Gurjarat', the 'Propaganda Team' has been assigned the Job of "planning and carrying out regular extortions activities for the purpose of funding their legal democratic front". The Western Maharashtra Area Committee in believed to handle Naxalite operations in Western Maharashtra, Mumbai, Pune as well as certain areas to the north such as Nashik. (*The Indian Express*, March 10, 2011).

Incidently, when Hemchandra Pandey and Azad were raided police, a booklet "Shahari kaam ke bare mein" published in 2008 was found from their possession. It said it was a blunder not to have looked at urban areas with the kind of seriousness its deserved. It defined Nine (9) belts for it urban action plan :

1. The Ahmedabad-Pune Corridor
2. New Delhi
3. Bangalore
4. Chennai
5. The Coimbatore-Erode belt
6. Hyderabad
7. Kolkata
8. Industrial cities of Central India
9. Cities in Gangetic plains.

Government's Initiatives - (West Bengal)

On June 15, 2010 West Bengal State Government announced a policy to lure Maoist to surrender with arms, if any. In fact, it was on the lines of Union Govt guidelines.

1. One time payment of Rs. 150,000.
2. Vocational training for three months.
3. Monthly stipend of Rs. 2000 for each surrendering cadre of Maoists.

4. If arms were also surrendered than Rs. 15000 for an AK-47, Rs.25000 for a machine gun and Rs. 3000 for pistor/Revolver.

But till December 26, 2010 only 5 five Maoists had surrendered. In West Bengal alone there was considerable increase in Maoist violence in the year 2010. In 2009, 158 people including 134 civilians, 15 security forces personnel and nine Maoist were killed whereas it increased to 425 people including 328 civilians, 36 security forces personnel and 61 Maoist fill December 26, 2010. West Bengal Governor M.K Narayanan had commented "The Maoists are getting the upper hand in people's mind because they are getting encouragement from a section of civil society".

2011

January 1 : Suspecting Bautu Laxmaiah (25), who had surrendered before police in 2006, to be a police informer, two rebels dragged him out of his house in village Sarvaipet in Mahadevpur area and shot him dead.

January 2 : Three persons Mangal Mahato, Dilip Mahato and Jagdish Mahato were arrested from a jungle near Lakhanpur village in Salboni in West Midnapore. They were working with Maoists.

January 2 : Five suspected Maoists were killed in an encounter by special operations Group (SOG) of State Police in area in Amka-Kalapani mining area of Jaipur district in Orissa. The area comes under Kalianganagar Sub-Divisional Committee of the CPI-Maoists. (*The Indian Express*, January 3, 2011).

January 3 : 300 kg of explosives, 3000 live bombs were recovered by police from a hideout at Baliapal near Gopiballabhpur in west Midnapore district.

Police also picked up four Maoists from Belapahari near Lalgarh and three others from Beliapal including Amiya Kisku and Prafulla Ravi Dass of PCAPC. Police recovered a gun and 10 rounds of ammunition from them.

January4. Police shot down a Maoist of notorious Tofa squad at Bakshibandhn west Midnapore. Another Maoist was injured and taken into custody.

January 6. Peoples Liberation Front of India (PLFI) rebels killed five members of a family living in Taisera and four members from another family of Bunta Mahua Toli in Gumla district of Jharkhand. All the nine victims were earlier associated with PLFI.

January 6. Five Maoists - all minor girls of 12 to 15 years of age- including a local Deputy Commander surrendered in Keonjhar district. All of them were members of Kaling Nagar division committee and were active since 2008.

January 9. Nine Maoist which included four women and Ravi, the leader of Kashipur dalam of Basthare division were killed by Orissa Police in an encounter in Rayagada under Kashipur Police station. All were in the age group of 20-25. Police claimed to have recovered an INSAS rifle, two. 303 Rifles and some country made guns from the Naxal hide out when police raided the camp located at the foothills near Dabramali village on Kashipur-Kalya Singhpur area of the district.

In an another incident, two self styled Maoist Area Commanders and another rebel were killed in an encounter with SF at Hurbung near Jhumra Hills in Bokaro district of Jharkhand.

January 13. Nepal Maoist leader Babu Ram Bhattarai, on his return to Kathmandu after a week-long visit to India dismissed reports that the Maoist consider India as "Principal. enemy" and said "We are ready to consider India's genuine security concerns".

January 14. Maharashtra Police and CRPF exchanged fire with Maoists in the remote forest of Gotekasa in Gadchiroli (Maharashtra). No loss of life was reported.

January 18. A Press release signed by Bikram, state committee member of CPI (Maoist) dated January 12 and to Media Houses on January 17 made an appeal to Ms Mamta Banerjee to resign from Cabinet and quit UPA Government to obtain the full support of the Maoist during the forthcoming polls and that the outfit would not boycott the polls in West Bengal.

January 18. Jailor Mohammed Sansuddin and wardens Louis Tigga and Kamal Ram of Chaibasa Jail in Jharkhand were arrested for allegedly facilitating the escape of three CPI Maoist commanders-Raghunath Hembrom, Sandip and Dhirendra Mahato-three years ago.

January 22. In a press release January 22, 2011 Maoist spokesperson Gudsa Usendi said that the union government was preparing to use the Army to wage war on its own people. Maoist said that the development of the Army would result in the imposition of the Armed Forces (Special Powers) Act (AFSPA) in Chhattisgarh and to a "Civil War" in Central India. (*The Hindu*, February1, 2011).

January 22. 25. Maoists abducted five personnel of Chhattisgarh Armed Forces (CAF) from Narayanpur. A civilian was also kidnapped by the rebels. On being granted leave, they were on unscheduled visit and going in a passenger bus which was stopped and searched by Maoists. The abducted personal were Head-Constable Ramadhar Patel, Raghunandan Dhruv, T. Ekka, Constables Mani Shankar and Ranjan Dubey and Civilian Gulchand. Rebels later released him after verifying his credentials.

January 28: An ITBP Jawan Bhoop Singh was killed in a Naxal attack near Khunera in the Ambagad police limits in Rajnandgaoan (Chhattisgarh).

January 28: Nine Maoists were killed in an encounter with Jharkhand Police in Luhur Jungle of Latehar district in an hour-long battle under Babadi police station. The CPI (Maoist) were later identified as zonal commanders Basant Yadav and Dev Dut. Five 315 Rifles, two pistols, a self-loading rifle with cartridges, three mobile sets and an Indian small arms systems (INSAS) rifle were seized from them. Yadav was a sub zonal commander of Koel Sankh Zone of CPI (Maoist) and was wanted in over a dozen cases including an attack on Latehar SP Kuldeep Dwivedi on July 16, 2010 in which five Jawans were also killed. (*The Pioneer*, Jan, 29, 2011).

January 30 : Two hard-core Maoists identified as Linga Madkami (35) of Teehguda colony and Dula Madhi (25) of Kanaguda village under Kalimela police station in Malkangiri district, belonging to Kaliamela dalam unit were arrested by police. A gun and a directional mine was recovered from their possession.

February 2 : Top Maoist leaders of Jharkhand Regional Committee (JRC) a military wing of CPI (Maoist) held a top-level secret meeting of its commanders at Marang-buru under Arki police station on February 2 to plan the organisation's military strategy for Jharkhand for 2011.

February 2 : Through media reports CPI (Maoist) came out with a list of demands to set free the five personnel of CAF abducted on January 25, 2011. The demands were :

(i) Stop efforts for setting up the proposed Army Training school near Abuj Maad region in Narayanpur district. (This area is spread over nearly 4000 square kilometers where Maoists are said to have over a dozen arms Factory and Training Camps).

(ii) Release of 15 villagers detained by police.

(iii) Scrapping all MoUs with major Industrial Houses.

(iv) Disbanding the operation Green Hunt, Area domination exercises by the forces.

(v) Withdrawal of central paramilitary forces from school building.

(vi) Compensation to villagers whose houses were damaged during operation by the security personnel.

In total eleven demands were placed by comrade Nitu of East Bastar Divisional Committee who also claimed that the five abducted policemen were in their custody and would not be released till all the demands are met by the government.

(*The Indian Express,* February 3, 2011)

February 5-6 : Reports originated by Sayantanee Chowdhury from Ranchi that appeared in *The Pioneer* of February 7 and 28, 2011 stated that Ninety Maoist Commandos and leaders including Annal da, Chief of JRC, Kundan Pahan, notorious Zonal Commander of South Chotanagpur zonal committee, Prasad sub zonal commander of Podahat sub zonal committee, Navin Manjhi Zonal Commander etc. reportedly met at Marangburu forest over Gitil Bero and Rabo Hills under Arbi Police station. The organizer of this meet was Kundan Pahan. A fierce encounter on early morning of February 5 ensued in which six jawans including ASP (Operations) Vijay Kumar were injured.

February 6 : Bikram of CPI (Maoist, in a statement released in the form of a CD to a section of electronic media in Kolkata stated that if Ms. Mamta Banerjee truly wants to work for the benefit of the people, she should resign from the Union Cabinet.

February 7 : Bharat Bandh was called by the Maoist against price rise and scams in different sectors. Communication was paralysed and shutters of business establishment were down.

February 7 : Naxalites blew up a police outpost under construction and felled trees to block the National Highway in Bijapur district during their one-day Bharat Bandh against price rise and corruption.

February 8: Area Commander of CPI Maoist Samir Khalko alias Nuansa Xalxo (35) was shot dead at Mundatola chowk under Chandiposh police station in Sundargarh district in Orissa encounter.

February 8: Comrade Niti, Commander East Bastar Divisional Committee said that they would release the five policemen (abducted on January 25). "All the five police men are safe. They were produced before a January Adalat (the people's court) of the Communist Party of India (Maoist) which accepted their apologies taking their poor family background into consideration and on humanitarian grounds" "we will handover the hostage to Swami Agnivesh and Gautam Nav-Lakha in the presence of Media". The government agreed to suspend the search operations for 24 hours as the people involved in the negotiations.

February 10 : Jankhu alias Biju, chief of Dandakarnya area and member of Pipragarh dalam was arrested by a team of ITBP and local police from Jamree village in Rajnandgaon. 4 kg of explosives and a gun was recovered from him.

February 10 : About 50 Maoist including women attacked a newly constructed police outpost at Subaranagiri under Kotgarh police station and set it on fire.

February 11 : In the presence of Swami Agnivesh and four other Rights activists viz V. Suresh, a Chennai High Court lawyer, Kavita Srivastava PUCL Secretary. Gautam Navlakha, Rights activists and Harish Dhawan PUDR, member, CPI Maoist released 5 policemen, who were abducted on Ja. 25, in the forest of Dhoudai in Narayanpur district in Bastar. A banner hung between trees at the venue of release read "In the name of humanity, on admitting to their mistakes and renouncing their jobs, a people's court has decided to free the five policemen. Prabhat, a member of the East Bastar Regional Committee of CPI-Maoist said "Had we abducted a Minister's son, the administration would have immediately agreed to all our demands. But these (the policemen) are poor people, no one cares about them, so we decided to let them go.

February 11 : Three Maoists including Area Commander of Digha in Jharkhand, Mohd. Muslim, one Nepali were killed at Akhayatila Nala, forest near Bisra in Sundergarh district in Orissa when they opened fire on a police party.

February 12 : A former women Maoist Kandri Lohar was shot dead and her four years old son Kanha's throat was slit. Their bodies were found in a field in Sundergarh district in Orissa. Kandri who hailed from Sagjodi village in Jharkhan's West Singhbhum district joined MCC wars christianed Madhuri, she was assigned the duty of guarding the Maoist Training Camp in Sar and a forest. But after 2-3 months she was disillusioned and fled from the rebel camp and returned to her village in February 2005. She had joined Home Guards in 2009. (*The Indian Express*, February 13, 2011).

February 12 : Orissa Police claimed to have arrested three Maoists from Assam one of when was former member of ULFA – After an encounter at Saranda in Sundergarh district. The arrested Maoist Aditya Bora was from ULFA and was head of Upper Assam Leading Committee of CPI-Maoist floated last year. The other two arrested were Ashiqui Sabar and Tingaaays Oram. (*The Indian Express*, February 13, 2011).

February 16 : Asit Mahato, one of the prime accused in Janeshwari Express carnage and Spokesperson of People's Committee Against Police Atrocities (PCAPA) was picked up by the special task Force of Kolkata Police from Bankura. Janeshwari carnage happened on May 28, 2010 in which 148 lives were lost.

February 16 : Malkangiri (Orissa) Collector R. Vineel Krishna I.A.S. and a Junior Engineer Pabitra Majhi of Kudumuluguma Block of Malkangiri district were abducted by CPI Maoist's armed Cadre in the evening hours of February 16, 2011 at Janata Pai village in Malkangiri. Maoists sent a note to the Orissa government listing five demands for release of these two abducted persons :

(i) An immediate halt to operation Greenhunt and withdrawal of para-military forces from Orissa.

(ii) Release of all political prisoners in Orissa.

(iii) An end to police atrocities against the state's tribal population.

(iv) Suspension of contracts signed with multinationals companies particularly in Niyamgiri.

(v) Compensation for the families of two Maoists—Taringe Ganglu and Sirka Ranola who died in Koraput Jail because of Jailor's complicity.

Guerillas also demanded :

(i) Distribution of land titles in three places in Orissa including Narayanpatnam where Adivasis are struggling to retain ownership over about 2500 acres of land and compensation for villages submerged in the Baliamela reservoir.

(ii) Polavaram Dam project to be scrapped.

(iii) Tribal status for the Konda Reddy community.

(iv) Ban on bauxite mining in the Deomali Hill of Koraput district.

On February 17, Bhaskar, Secretary CPI (Maoist) Andhra-Orissa Border Special Zone Committee (AOBSZC) through a letter demanded release of :

1. Sriramulu Srinivasulu, member AOBSZC. (He is former Chief of Revolutionary Writers Association, arrested in July 2007).
2. Ganti Prasadm. Who is leading the co-ordination Committee of the martyrs families. He was earlier with CPI-ML People's War).
3. K. Padma alias Sirisha (Kundula Sirisha) alias Nirmala wife of Akkaraju Hargopal alias Ramkrishna, a Central Committee member. (She was arrested on November 13, 2010 from Semiliguda in Koraput district while she was on her way to Narayanpatnam to meet Ramakrishna and their son Prithavi. Hargopal is @ Ramakrishna is the general secretary of Andhra–Orissa Border Special Zonal Committee.
4. Central Committee member Ashutosh. (His real name is Moti Lal Soren. He was arrested in March 2009 from Rourkela).
5. Sobha wife of Kishenji (Her real name is Budhini Munda alias

Shoba alias Sheela Budhini. A tribal from Jharkhand, she is founding member of Nari Mukti Sangh.

6. Ishwari Anduluri, she is Padma's cousin comes from Vishakhapatnam and was arrested in Naranpatna on November 13, 2010.
7. Several Leader of Chasi Mulia Adivasi Sangh of Narayanpatna like Gananth Patra.
8. Tapan Mishra.

Orissa Government agreed to suspend anti-Maoist operations in Malkangiri and expressed its willingness to hold talks with Maoist representatives to ensure safe release of Krishna IAS and Manjhi JE. Chief Minister Naveen Patnaik appealed to Maoists to release the Collector and the Junior Engineer.

Meanwhile Maoist named the persons who will negotiate on their behalf with the Orissa government.

1. Prof. Hargopal, Kakatia University in Andhra Pradesh.
2. Prof. R. Someshwara Rao, a retired economics Profesor of Sambhalpur University, presently Hyderabad based.
3. Social Activist Dandapani Mohanty.

From the Orissa Government side, negotiations were done by :

1. Home secretary U.N. Behera
2. Secretary (Panchayat) S.N. Tripathy

Negotiations began on February 20.

On February 21, the Naveen Patnaik Government accepted following 8 of the 14 demands made for the release of the Malkangiri Collector and the Junior Engineer.

1. The government recommend tribal status for Konda Reddy Nukku Dora Communities.
2. The government would stop Polavaram multipurpose project (Orissa is already opposed to it).
3. The government would return tribal land, appoint special officers in Koraput, Malkangiri.
4. Would build new canals in Potteru irrigation on project' govt. to give Rs. 50 lakh.

5. Government agreed to compensate for deaths in Koraput, Rayagada jails as per High Court orders.
6. Would agreed to write to Jharkhand, Chhattisgarh for release of two ill women comrades.
7. It would minimize impact on tribals of bauxite mining in Maliaparbat, Deomali.

(*The Indian Express*, February 22, 2011)

Though deadline for acceptance of the demands was given by Maoists for release of 2 abducted persons, Bhaskar, Secretary of CPI Maoist (AOBSZC) extended the deadline twice.

After three days of negotiations, Naxals freed Junior Engineer Pabitra Majhi on February 23. After his release he said "we were kept in a forest somewhere in the cut-off areas. We changed locations a few times but were treated well. They fed us rice and dal. Nobody tortured us. The collector is in good health……"

Malkangiri collect R. Vineel Krishna was set free on February 24 near Daliamba village in Chitrakonda in Malkangiri. He gave a statement that "the Maoists took care of my well-being and dignity."

Strangely, through Manjhi' Maoist sent a new set of demands. But the tough attitudes of mediators of Maoists side themselvews saved the situation and did not agree to such fresh demands. Their refusal to be abided by the new demands saved the situation and the episode ended. On March 4, 2011 Orissa High Court granted conditional bail to four Maoist whose release had been demanded by Maoists for Malkangiri collector's release from captivity. Padma Andaluru, Ramkrishna, Roja Mandangi alias Sarita Gokul Kuldipia were granted bail to meet Maoists demand. Ganti Prasadam refused to go out on bail demanding release of 700 odd tribals and 135 activists of Maoist-backed Chasi Muliya Adivasi Sangh lodged in different jails in Orissa.

February 26 : Six hardcore Maoists were killed and one arrested after 6-hour long encounter in Marjhidih village under Jaipur police outpost of Katoria in Banka Bihar. Police Chief claimed that a hardcore Naxal Golu alias Joseph was gunned down in police encounter.

February 28 : About 60 Maoists of Company 6 of CPI Maoist' in an ambush, killed an ASI Narayan Mandal at Tandwa under Chatra district. A Home Guard Jawan Gonda Turi and one Jawan Nand

Kishore sustained injuries but later succumbed while on way to hospital in Ranchi. The attack was carried out by Maoist Commanders Azad, Manohar and Ankit to claim lost ground in Tandwa and Simaria area.

March 3 : Police Constable Sarkar Hembram was abducted from the Jhargram region. His body was recovered from Jamshola village in Beliabera area of Jhargram sub division on March 19, 2011.

March 10 : Shashadhar Mahato alias Kisan, a member of Bengal–Jharkhand–Orissa border Regional Committee and brother of Chhatradhar Mahto the Jailed leader of PCACA of Lalgunj was killed in an encounter at Chandsora village in Paschim Medinipur's Jhargram (West Bengal). He was close to Maoist politburo member Kishenji and carried a reward of Rs. 2 lakh on his head. He was main accused of Gyaneshwari Train blast.

March 11 : A five-day operation (March 11 to 16, 2011) in Konta Block against Maoist was launched into the forest of Dantewada in Chhattisgarh by about 350 armed troopers of CRPF's Combat Battalion for Resolute Action (COBRA) and Koya Commandos of police. Three Koya Commandos were killed in Maoist ambush, three villagers killed and media reported that three women were criminally assaulted. A surrendered Maoist claimed that the guerillas were running an arms factory at Morpalli–a two hour March from the police camp at Chintalnar (*The Hindu* March 23, 2011). On March 11, Police force went into action to destroy the arms factory. While police made the night halt at Timapuram on March 13, Maoists numbering 70 or so attacked it next morning i.e. March 14 which was led by Area Commander Ramana. The ambush lasted three hours. Maoist claimed that only section commander Muchaki Ganga was killed. Koya Commandos spent the night at the village itself and left for Chintalnar on March 15. Villagers claim that before they left the same company of Koyas surrounded Tarmetla and burnt about 200 structures including homes, granaries and woodsheds. Dantewada Collector R. Prasanna set up a 5-member committee on March 25 to look into the incident.

March 13 : CPI Maoist called for a 48-hour shutdown in West Bengal, Jharkhand, Orissa and Bihar beginning from March 13 to protest the killing of its Commander Sashadhar Mahto.

March 13 : Naxalites chopped off the hands and gouged out eyes of Santosh Mishra, a mentally challenged 26 years old missing man from Madhubani district of Bihar for about six months, before shooting him dead in the Kasansur are of Gadchiroli.

March 14 : In an encounter in Darmaha village in Bihar's East Champaran district, six Naxalites were killed and eight others were arrested. At least 30 Maoist were feared killed in Dantewada of Chhattisgarh. Three policemen were also killed in Dantewada. In Jahanabad, a fierce encounter between security forces and members of Jharkhand Regional Military Commission led by Commander of South Chotanagpur Zonal Committee Kundan Pahan took place at Jorabeda village under Arki police station of Khuti district. 14 weapons were recover from Naxalites

(*The Pioneer,* March 15, 2011).

March 19 : In an exchange of fire with Maoist squad led by Suchitra Mahato wife of Maoist leader Sashadhar Mahato who was killed on March 10, at Amapuli in Binpur, police recovered three rifles one carbine small fire arms and important documents.

March 19: A member of notorious Gautam Rana squad Maoist Debdulal was arrested from Ghritbani village. During interrogation he revealed that kidnapped police constable Sarkar Hembram (March 3) has been killed and buried by the rebels.

March 24 : About 50 ultras blasted a state run school in Tetrain village in Deo police station in Aurangabad district of Bihar.

March 25 : Collector R. Prasanna constituted a 5-member committee and announced that the District Administration would deliver emergency rations of grains, cloths, cooking and edible oil to the effected villages. It was alleged that SPO's at the Salwa Judum camp of Dornpal assaulted truck owner Kapur Chand Rajput accusing him of aiding Maoists.

March 26 : A large group comprising Special Police Officers (SPOs) of Chhattisgarh police and members of Salwa Judum attacked social activist Swami Agnivesh as he attempted to deliver relief to a village alleged by torched by security forces in Chhattisgarh's Dantewada district. Agnivesh said the first attack occurred when a crowd of SPOs and Judum members surrounded his vehicle pelted him with raw eggs, knocked off his turban and pushed him around. But the crowd accused Agnivesh of turning a blind eye to the plight of victims of Maoist violence. Resultantly, Senior S.P. Police Dantewada, Mr. S.R.P. Kalluri was transferred to allow an independent enquiry into the allegations. Dantewada Collector R. Prasanna was also transferred. (*The Hindu,* March 27, 2011)

The agitated crowd while blocked the way of Swami Agnivesh asked him why human rights activists never showed up whenever Maoists killed innocent people. "What about our human rights, are we animals ? Why don't you see the condition of widows whose husbands were killed in Maoist violence? Why you people always cry hoarse over small incidents which directly or indirectly effect the Maoists"

(*The Pioneer*, March 27, 2011)

March 28 : A Special team of Ranchi police picked up a Naxal cadre Chotu Singh Munda alias Chotu Sarkar who belonged to Local Guerilla Squad (LSG) in Tomar in Ranchi. He was working as a labourer at cotton mill in Shahada, Nandurbar in North West Maharashtra. He was active member of Kisan Krantikari Committee (KKC) and was Area Commander of his outfit which was part of MCCI. He had blown off a police jeep in which Dy SP Promod Kumar Sinha and two constables were killed on July 1, 2008.

March 28 : Two top Maoists – Pallojula Parmeswara Rao alias Nandu alias Papanna and Korukonda Dalam surenundered to Orissa Police.

CPI (ML) (PW) AND MCCI – MERGED, COMMUNIST PARTY OF INDIA (MAOIST) EMERGED

Press Statement:

CPI (ML)(PW) and MCCI – Merged

Communist Party of India (Maoist) Emerged

On September 21, 2004, amidst the thick forests in some part of India, the formation of the Communist Party of India (Maoist) was declared at a public meeting before an assembly of peoples' guerrilla fighters, party activists and activists of mass organisations. The two parties, the Maoist Communist Centre of India and the Communist Party of India (Marxist-Leninist) (People's War) were merged to form the new unified Party, the CPI (Maoist). However, this merger declaration has been withheld from the media for security reasons and is now being released to the entire people of our country and the world. The formation of this new Party has fulfilled the desires and aspirations of the oppressed masses of the country for a genuine proletarian party that can lead them to revolutionary change for the establishment of a new democratic society, advancing towards socialism and communism.

This unified party has been formed after thoroughgoing discussions held between the high level delegations of the two parties initially and then finalised by the Joint Central Committee meeting of both the parties. Through these thorough-going and constructive discussions, held on an equal footing, five documents have been drafted and finalised. These documents are: Hold High the Bright Red Banner of Marxism-Leninism-Maoism, the Party Programme, Strategy and Tactics of the Indian Revolution, the Political Resolution on the International and Domestic Situation and the Party Constitution.

In addition to these documents it has also been decided that our beloved leaders and teachers of the respective parties, the late Com. Charu Mazumdar and Com. Kanai Chatterjee, will be recognised and highlighted as the founding leaders of the unified party. It was also decided that both these parties, stemming from the turbulent period of the decade of the 60's, particularly from the great Naxalbari uprising, livingly inherited all that was revolutionary in the long history of the Indian communist movement. The peculiarity of the situation is that both these parties continued to flow as two separate streams of the revolutionary communist movement, wedded to the same cause of carrying forward the Indian revolution over the past 35 years. All these steps taken together clearly disclosed a unified understanding on almost all ideological and political questions of line. The line established provided a principled basis for the unity achieved by both the parties.

Basing on this unity the Joint Central Committee meeting finally resolved to unite the two parties into a single unified party, which will henceforth be called as the Communist Party of India (Maoist). Com. Ganapati was unanimously elected as the general secretary of the new party.

The formation of the unified Communist Party of India (Maoist) will certainly prove to be a new milestone in the history of the communist movement of India. A unified Maoist party based on MLM continued to be a long and highly cherished need of the revolutionary minded and oppressed people of the country including all our ranks, and also all Maoist forces of South Asia and internationally. Today this long-cherished desire and dream has been transformed into a reality.

The new Communist Party of India (Maoist) will continue to act as a consolidated political vanguard of the Indian proletariat. Marxism-Leninism-Maoism will be the ideological basis guiding its thinking in all the spheres of its activities. It will continue its struggle against right and left deviations, particularly against revisionism, by taking this as the main danger for the communist movement as a whole. It will still seek to unite all genuine Maoist groups that remain outside this unified Party.

The immediate aim and programme of the Maoist party is to carry on and complete the already ongoing and advancing New Democratic Revolution in India as a part of the world proletarian revolution by overthrowing the semi-colonial, semi-feudal system under the neo-colonial form of indirect rule, exploitation and control. This revolution will remain directed against imperialism, feudalism and comprador bureaucratic capitalism. This revolution will be carried out and completed through armed agrarian revolutionary war, i.e. protracted people's war with the armed seizure of power remaining as its central and principal task, encircling the cities from the countryside and thereby finally capturing them. Hence the countryside as well as the PPW (Protracted People's War) will remain as the "center of gravity" of the party's work, while urban work will be complimentary to it.

Since armed struggle will remain as the highest and main form of struggle and the army as the main form of organisation of this revolution, hence it will continue to play a decisive role, whereas the UF will be built in the course of armed struggle and for the seizure of power through armed struggle. Mass organisations and mass struggles are necessary and indispensable but their purpose is to serve the war.

We also hereby declare that the two guerilla armies of the CPI(ML)[PW] and MCCI—the PGA and the PLGA—have been merged into the unified PLGA (Peoples' Liberation Guerrilla Army). Hereafter, the most urgent task i.e. principal task of the party is to develop the unified PLGA into a full-fledged People's Liberation Army (PLA) and transforming the existing Guerrilla Zones into Base Areas, thereby advancing wave upon wave towards completing the New Democratic Revolution. The formation day of the PLGA is to be December 2, the day when a people's army was formed for the first time ever in our country in 2000, on the first anniversary of the martyrdom of the three CCMs, com. Shyam, Mahesh and Murali.

Apart from this the unified party will continue to pay added attention to building a new wave of revolutionary mass movements on various political and other issues of the people. It will involve all the vast sections of the masses in these struggle directed against imperialism, feudalism and the comprador bureaucratic bourgeoisie. The vicious imperialist offensive on our country has resulted in mass destitution of an already impoverished people, particularly in the countryside, which has even witnessed thousands of suicides. The CPI (Maoist) will mobilize vast sections of the masses against the growing onslaught of the imperialists on the country, against state repression together with mobilising support for all the movements directed against imperialism and feudalism.

The new party will also continue to support the struggle of the nationalities for self-determination including their right to secession and condemn the brutal state repression on these movements. It will pay special attention in mobilising and organising the women masses as a mighty force of the revolution, and will fight against all other forms of social oppression, particularly untouchability and casteism. It will continue to expose, isolate and defeat the more dangerous Hindu fascist forces, while exposing all other fundamentalist forces. It will continue to do so while keeping the edge of the people's struggles directed against the new Congress rulers in Delhi along with the CPI/ CPM and their imperialist chieftains.

It will continue to expose and resist the expansionist designs of the Indian ruling classes along with their imperialist chieftains, particularly the US imperialists. It will more actively stand by the side of the Nepali people led by the CPN(Maoist), and vehemently oppose the Indian expansionists and US imperialists from intervening in Nepal with their military might. It will also continue to support the people's war led by the Maoist parties in Peru, the Philippines, Turkey and elsewhere. It will continue to support all people's struggles directed against imperialism and reaction. It will also support the working class movement and other people's movements the world over. It will continue to stand by the side of the Iraqi and Afghan people in their mighty struggle against the US imperialist-led aggression and occupation.

The Unified Party will continue to hold high the banner of proletarian internationalism and will continue to contribute more forcefully in uniting the genuine Maoist forces at the international level. Besides, it will also establish unity with the oppressed people and nations of the whole world and continue to fight shoulder to shoulder with them in advancing the world proletarian revolution against imperialism and their lackeys, thereby paving the way towards realising socialism and then Communism on a world scale.

Thousands of our martyrs have laid down their valuable lives for these lofty aims. The Central Committee (Provisional) of the unified Party-CPI (Maoist)—pledges that it will continue to advance along the path illuminated by them and thereby mobilize all its existing and latent energies in transforming the dreams of the martyrs into a reality.

With revolutionary greetings,
General Secretary General Secretary
Central Committee Central Committee
Maoist Communist Centre of India CPI (M-L) [People's War]
Date: 14-10-2004

(Published in People's march, Ernakulam, Volume 5, No. 11-12 November-December 2004).

SALWA JUDUM

Naxalites grabbed the opportunity when the tribals of Bastar Chhatisgarh, constantly harassed and exploited by corrupt police, corrupt officials of forest, Revenue and greedy traders and petty businessmen, looked towards them for being emancipated from their cruel actions. Naxalite came to their rescue albeit temporarily. They had their own agent to entrench themselves in tribal areas. And the exploitation of tribals gave the desired wish. Once these Naxalites firmly and nicely ensconsed themselves, they started doing the same thing which the tribals were vexed with. Naxals even forbade the tribals to pluck the tendu leaves and took the trade into their hands, thus depriving the poor villagers/tribals of their livelihood. Naxalites monopolised the tendu leaves trade and tribals were forbidden the enter that domain. So much so, Naxalites started interfering in every field of tribal life including the tribal customs which was utterly disliked by them. On June 6, 2005 agitated tribals started a movement under the leadership of a Congress worker Mahendra Karma which was named as Salwa Judum (All together) and was aimed against the interference by Naxalites into the domain of tribal social customs, culture and practices including tendu-leaf trade etc. State government also extended a supporting hand and asked the tribals to move away from their villages temporariy and take shelter in government provided camps but asked them to develop skills to counter Naxalites and defend themselves. Government also provided them with licences to acquire guns and other available weapons.

This move of the state government was utterly disliked by Naxalites and they started a tirade, criticising the Salwa Judum. They attacked Salwa Judum camps and wanted to nullify the resistance by tribals gathered in there camps. Naxalites even killed a Congress leader Laxman Kashyab, President of Block Congress Committee at village Talnar under Mirtur PS in Bastar region for supporting Salwa Judum. CPI (Maoist) branded Salwa Judum as the greatest set back in June 2006 which the Naxal movement had faced since 1972 and resolved to isolate it at all levels simply to crush it.

Right from its inception in June 2005, Salwa Judum had been opposing Maoist outfit, says Shri Vishwa Ranjan, Director General of Chhattisgarh Police. (*The Pioneer*, September 3). In June 2005 the tribals of 20 to 25 villages in Bijapur district especially those belonging to the Maria tribe, became so restive when the Maoist declared that none should gather 'tendu' leaves. This dictate adversely affected the seasonal employment in the area. When the villagers opposed the Maoist decree, the Maoist retaliated with people running to police stations and police camps for safety. Later some youths living in the camps decided to take out processions to other villages and held rallies against Maoist suppressions. The first such rally was at Mathwada weekly market in Bijapur area on June 18, 2005. There was a quick and violent retaliation by the Maoist who killed three (3) tribals who had attended the rally. As these rallies gained momentum Mahendra Karma, Congress MLA from Maria tribe hailing from Dantewada, took over the leadership of the movement which was later named as Salwa Judum (Peace marchers). "Mahendra Karma earlier had led the Jan Jagran Abhiyan in 1990-91 against the Maoist. Even in 1994-95 unrest against Maoist oppression was noticed in Dantewada – Bijapur regions but was crushed by the Maoists with brutal force." Jan Jagran Abhiyan activists were killed by Maoist when they returned to their villages during May 17-22, 2006.

Asian centre for Human Rights became the first organisation that demanded winding up of Salwa Judum in March 2006. It was followed by Committee against violence on women, human rights forum. National Human Rights Commission also recommended scrapping it in its report to the Supreme Court on September 19, 2008, accusing it of the grave human rights violations. However, Supreme Court appointed NHRC investigation into Salwa Judum justified government–sponsored arming of civilians by calling it a "spontaneous revolt of the tribals against years of atrocities and harassment suffered by them at the hands of Naxalites". The 118-page report submitted to Supreme Court also dismissed most of the allegation of human rights abuses made by the petitions in the Apex Court (*The Times of India,* October 6, 2008). Shri Vishwa Ranjan said (*Pioneer*, September 3, 2008) Quote "Just before the Supreme Court commenced its hearings a news item appeared in all the papeprs that the Administrative Reforms Commission has castigated Salwa Judum in its report." The fact is that the Administrative Reforms Commission had only stated in its report htat Salvwa Judum has been unsuccessful in containing Maoist passion and violence and that the poor tribals are being crushed between the legal power of the state and illegal power of the Maoist. What the Maoist network did not project was that the same report talks of the necessity of employing a large number of tribal youth as Special police officers. But how could they have projected this? It would have knocked out a major portion of their argument in the

Supreme court. Further, the Maoist know that very few people still actually go through the report submitted by the Commission. Soon another report was planted in media by the Maoist network stating that the expert committee of the Planning Commission has castigated Salwa Judum. The whole report was planted in a manner that it look as if the Planning Commission itself had castigated the movement. No one noticed that this committee was constituted in 2006 and worked overtime to produce its report in April 2008 just before the Supreme Court Commenced its hearing of the Salwa Judum petition.

Around 40 to 60000 people were accommodated in 23 Relief Camps in Naxal-effected Bijapur and Dantewara district. SPOs were about 3800 to 4000 at a monthly stipened of Rs. 1500. But Gautam Navlakha, Civil Rights Activists says when Salwa Judum was launched, 644 villages de-populated, nearly three lakh people rendered homeless and thousands hearded into camps. In this area (Bastar) Corporations were given land, forest and water resources to exploit. A conscientious citizen living in proximity to a war zone, witness to a people resisting the loss of livelihood and loot of their resources, cannot remain mute. Binayak Sen incurred the wrath of the state for precisely that reason. The last straw was exposing the massacre of peasants on March 31, 2007 i.e. Six weeks before his arrest—(*The Economic Times*, May 29, 2009 from Bangalore) at Bilaspur town. Dr. Binayak Sen of Chhattisgarh was arested on May 14, 2007 under the Chhattisgarh Special Public Security Act on a charge of acting as a courier between a jailed Maoist, Narayan Sanyal and a businessmen Piyush Guha. Dr. Binayak Sen a gold medalist from Christian Medical College Vellore had established a Clinic alongwith his wife Ilina at Bagrimala village.

Prof. Nandini Sunder, Historian Ramchandra Guha and former bureaucrat EAS Sharma had filed a motion in the Supreme Court to have an independent committee monitor the plight of about 40000 tribals caught in the crossfire between Maoist, the state police and Salwa Judum. Chhattisgarh government asserted in the SC on October 28, 2010 that the Salwa Judum movement does not exist in the state and therefore the question of disbanding it does not arise. But the petitioners stated in an affidavit that the Salwa Judum had been revived in October 2010 under a new name of "Dandakarnya Shanti Sangharsh Samiti".

Salwa Judum in Gondi dialect means "Purification hunt. The government means it as "Peace march". 'Salwa Judum' refers to a controversial tribal vigilante group, armed, trained and assisted by the Chhattisgarh government in its battle against the banned Communist Party of India (Maoist). A public interest litigation, currently being heard by the Supreme Court, hold Judum members responsible for 537 murders, 92 rapes and 103 acts of arson.

(*The Hindu*, March 27, 2011)

APPENDICES

APPENDIX A

People's Daily (July 5, 1967 Editorial) Spring Thunder Breaks Over India

A peal of spring thunder has crashed over the land of India. Revolutionary peasants in the Darjeeling area have risen in rebellion. Under the leadership of a revolutionary group of the Indian Communist Party, a red area of rural revolutionary armed struggle had been established in India. This is a development of tremendous significance for the Indian people's revolutionary struggle.

In the past few months, the peasant masses in the Darjeeling area led by the revolutionary group of the Indian Communist Party have thrown off the shackles of modern revisionism and smashed the ita that bound them. They have seized grain, land and weapons from the landlords and plantation owners, punished the local tyrants and wicked gentry, and ambushed the reactionary troops and police that went to suppress them, thus demonstrating the powerful might of the peasants' revolutionary armed struggle. All imperialists, revisionists, corrupt officials, local tyrants and wicked gentry, and reactionary army and police are nothing in the eyes of the revolutionary peasants who are determined to strike them own to the dust. The revolutionary group of the Indian Communist Party have done the absolutely correct thing and they have done well. The Chinese people joyfully applaud this revolutionary storm of the Indian peasants in the Darjeeling area as do all Marxist-Leninists and revolutionary people of the whole world.

It is an inevitability that the Indian peasants will rebel and the Indian people will make a revolution because the reactionary Congress rule has left them with no alternative. India under Congress rule is only nominally independent; in fact it is nothing more than a semi-colonial, semi-feudal country. The Congress administration represents the interests of the Indian feudal princes, big landlords and bureaucrat-compradore capitalists. Internally, it oppresses the. Indian people without any mercy and sucks their blood, while internationally it serves its new boss, US imperialism, and its number one accomplice, the Soviet revisionist ruling clique, in addition to its old suzerian British imperialism, thus selling out the national interests of India in a big way. So imperialism, Soviet revisionism, feudalism and bureaucrat-compradore capitalism weigh like big mountains on the backs of the Indian people, first of all on the toiling masses of workers and peasants.

The Congress administration has intensified its suppression and exploitation of the Indian people and pursued a policy of national betrayal during the past few years. Famine has stalked the land. The fields are strewn with the bodies of those who have died of hunger and starvation. The Indian people, above all the Indian peasants, have found life impossible for them. The revolutionary peasants in the Darjeeling area have now risen in rebellion, in violent revolution. This is the prelude to a violent revolution by the hundreds of millions of people throughout India. The Indian people will certainly cast away these big mountains off their backs and win complete emancipation. This is the general trend of Indian history which no force on earth can check or hinder.

What road is to be followed by the Indian revolution? This is a fundamental question affecting the success of the Indian revolution and the destiny of the 500 million Indian people. The Indian revolution must take the road of relying on the peasants, establishing base area in the countryside, persisting in protracted armed struggle and using the countryside to encircle and finally capture the cities. This is Mao Tse-tung's road, the road that has led the Chinese revolution to victory, and the only road to victory for the revolution of all oppressed nations and people.

Our great leader Chairman Mao Tse-tung pointed out as long as forty years ago: "In China's central, southern and northern provinces, several hundred million peasants will rise like a mighty storm, like a hurricane, a force so swift and violent that no power, however great, will be able to hold it back. They will smash all the trammels that bind them and rush forward along the road to liberation. They will sweep all the imperialists, warlords, corrupt officials, local tyrants and evil gentry into their graves".

Chairman Mao has explicitly pointed out long ago that the peasant question occupies an extremely important place in the people's revolution. The peasants constitute the main force in the national democratic revolution against imperialism and its lackeys; they are the most reliable and numerous allies of the proletariat. India is a vast semi-colonial and semi-feudal country with a population of 500 million. The absolute majority of which is the peasantry. Once aroused, these several hundred million Indian peasants will become the invincible force of the Indian revolution. By integrating itself with the peasants, the Indian proletariat will be able to bring about earth-shaking changes in the vast countryside of India and defeat any powerful enemy in a soul-stirring people's war.

Our great leader Chairman Mao teaches us: "The seizure of power by armed force, the settlement of the issue by war, is the central task and the highest form of revolution. This Marxist-Leninist principle of revolution holds good universally, for China and for all other country".

The specific feature of the Indian revolution, like that of the Chinese revolution, is armed revolution fighting against armed counter-revolution. Armed struggle is the only correct road for the Indian revolution; there is no other road whatsoever. Such trash as "Gandhism", "parliamentary road" and the like are opium used by the Indian ruling classes to paralyse the Indian people. Only by relying on violent revolution and taking the road of armed struggle can India be saved and the Indian people achieve complete liberation. Specifically, this is to arouse the peasant masses boldly, build up and expand the revolutionary armed forces, deal blows at the armed, suppression of the imperialists and reactionaries, who are temporarily stronger than the revolutionary forces, by using the flexible strategy and tactics of people's war personally worked out by Chairman Mao, and to persist in protracted armed struggle and seizing victory of the revolution step by step.

In the light of the characteristics of the Chinese revolution, our great leader Chairman Mao has pointed out the importance of establishing revolutionary rural base areas. Chairman Mao teaches us that in order to persist in protracted armed struggle and defeat imperialism and its lackeys, "it is imperative for the revolutionary ranks to turn the backward villages into advanced, consolidated base areas, into great military, political, economic and cultural bastions of the revolution from which to fight their vicious enemies who are using the cities for attacks on the rural districts, and in this way gradually to achieve the complete victory of the revolution through protracted fighting".

India is a country with vast territory; its countryside where the reactionary rule is weak, provides the broad areas in which the revolutionaries can manoeuvre freely. So long as the Indian proletarian revolutionaries adhere to the revolutionary line of Marxism-Leninism, Mao Tse-tung's thought and rely on the great ally, the peasants, it is entirely possible for them to establish one advanced revolutionary rural base area after another in the backward rural areas and build a people's army of a new type. Whatever difficulties and twists and turns the Indian revolutionaries may experience in the course of building such revolutionary base areas, they will eventually develop such areas from isolated points into a vast expanse, from small areas into extensive ones, an expansion in a series of waves. Thus, a situation in which the encirclement of the cities from the countryside will gradually be brought about in the Indian revolution to pave the way for the final seizure of towns and cities and winning nationwide victory.

The Indian reactionaries are panic-stricken by the development of the rural armed struggle in Darjeeling. They have sensed imminent disaster and they wail in alarm that the peasants' revolts in Darjeeling will "become a national disaster".

Imperialism and the Indian reactionaries are trying in a thousand and one ways to suppress this armed struggle of the Darjeeling peasants and nip it in the bud. The Dange renegade clique and the revisionist chieftains of the Indian Communist Party are vigorously slandering and attacking the revolutionaries in the Indian Communist Party and the revolutionary peasants in Darjeeling for their great exploits. The so-called "non-Congress government" in West Bengal openly sides with the reactionary Indian government in its bloody suppression of the revolutionary peasants in Darjeeling. This gives added proof that these renegades and revisionists are running dogs of US imperialism and Soviet revisionism and lackeys of the big Indian landlords and bourgeoisie. What they call the "non-Congress government" is only a tool of these landlords and bourgeoisie.

But no matter how well the imperialists, Indian reactionaries and the modern revisionists may cooperate in their sabotage and suppression, the torch of armed struggle lighted by the revolutionaries of the Indian Communist Party and the revolutionary peasants in Darjeeling will not be put out. "A single spark can start a prairie fire". The spark in Darjeeling will start a prairie fire and will certainly keep the vast expanses of India ablaze. That a great storm of revolutionary armed struggle will eventually sweep across the length and breadth of India is certain. Although the course of the Indian revolutionary struggle will be long and tortuous, the Indian revolution, guided by great Marxism-Leninism, Mao Tse-tung's thought, will surely triumph.

Appendix B
Joint Statement of the Maoist Parties and Organisations of South Asia

June 2001

We, the undersigned Maoist parties and organisations of South Asia, proclaim the formation of the Co-ordination Committee of Maoist Parties and Organisations of South Asia (CCOMPOSA) and issue this joint statement:

"Under the signboard of "globalisation", "structural adjustment"and "open market economy", world imperialism has announced its global agenda to further intensify the domination, exploitation and oppression of the people. This agenda reflects a new spiral of crisis of world imperialism, bringing about the inevitability of even more misery, horror, devastation and war, on a world scale.

The proletariat and the oppressed people of the world continue to resist this agenda by raising revolutionary struggles, targeting imperialism and the subservient reactionary ruling classes of different countries and generating a new wave of people's struggles alL over the world, particularly in the oppressed countries.

As Mao formulated, the oppressed countries constitute the storm centrEs of world revolution, and revolution is the main trend in the world today. The region of South Asia continues to provide a concentrated expression of this truth.

South Asia, with more than one-fifth of the world's population, is a simmering volcano, as recognised by the imperialists themselves. All the major contradictions in the region are intensifying and call for revolutionary solutions.

Inspired by the Great Proletarian Cultural Revolution in China, the historic Naxalbari armed uprising under the leadership of Charu Mazumdar served to ignite sparks of protracted people's war in different parts of South Asia. The drums of Naxalbari continue to reverberate throughout South Asia and beyond. The protracted people's wars, which are advancing in Nepal and India (Andhra, Dandakaranya, Bihar, etc.) and the preparations for initiating protracted people's war in the region basically derive their origins from the "Spring Thunder" of Naxalbari.

National liberation movements are also continuing in Kashmir, Assam, Nagaland, Manipur and other north-eastern areas [of India], and in Bangladesh, Pakistan and Sri Lanka. Various people's struggle against imperialism and the reactionary ruling classes are also surging forward.

The irresistible advance of the new-democratic revolution and the protracted People's War in Nepal under the leadership of the Communist Party of Nepal (Maoist) [CPN (M)], along with the protracted People's. Wars in India led by Communist Party of India (Marxist-Leninist) (People's War) [CPI (ML) (PW)] and the MaoisT Communist Centre (MCC), are changing the political geography and revolutionary dynamics of South Asia. The emerging new wave of protracted people's war is clearly visible in the South Asian region. The Indian ruling classes, under the leadership of the Bharat People's Party (BJP), are sharpening their offensive against the on-going protracted people's wars and the various nationality movements in India. Various operational command units have been formed to suppress these struggles, and the central government is directly coordinating all the various operations. The BJP, a Hindu chauvinist force, is rapidly transforming the state into a fascist apparatus and is adopting newer and newer black laws to crush all types of democratic movements in India, surpassing all its predecessors. It has also started functioning as the gendarme of US imperialism in order to fulfil its expansionist ambitions, suppressing people's movements in the subcontinent, particularly threatening armed intervention in Nepal.

The reactionary ruling classes in Bangladesh, Sri Lanka, Pakistan and Bhutan are intensifying their fascist repression of the masses and of the democratic, progressive and Maoist revolutionary forces.

In spite of vicious fascist repression, the masses continue to resist and are struggling forward in the region. The Indian expansionist state, backed by world imperialism, particularly US imperialism, constitute the common enemy of the people of South Asia. This provides a concrete political basis for building the unity of the South Asian revolutionary forces. The increasing collusion between US imperialism and Indian expansionism can be clearly seen in the politics of the region in recent years.

This can be seen clearly in the recent developments in Nepal. However, much the imperialists and their lackeys try to cover up the real politics behind the brutal massacre of the royal family of Nepal, the people know the truth. The crisis that led to the massacre is directly related to the development of the new-democratic revolution and protracted People's War in Nepal. King Birendra and the royal family were annihilated in order to ensure that state power would be in the hands of a more reliable, fascist and die-hard section of the ruling class that would be interested in the task of deploying the armed forces in an all-out, total counter-revolutionary war against the CPN (M), the People's War and the oppressed masses of Nepal. This crisis was deliberately designed to create the conditions for external intervention by Indian expansionism in the hope of extinguishing the flames of Maoist protracted people' war in Nepal. This massacre was clearly planned and executed as a conspiracy between US imperialism, the Indian expansionist state and the most die-hard fascist sections of the Nepalese ruling classes.

The CPN (M) and the massacre has effectively liquidated the traditional monarchy, placing the establishment of the People's Democratic Republic of Nepal on the people's immediate agenda.

The Co-ordination Committee of Maoist Parties and Organisations of South Asia (CCOMPOSA) has been formed in order to unify and co-ordinate the activities of the Maoist parties and organisations in South Asia to confront this developing situation by spreading protracted people's war in the region, in the context of hastening and advancing the world proletarian socialist revolution. This is a historic step of far-reaching significance.

The initiative is the result of ideas and suggestions put forward by the CPN (M) and CPI (ML) (PW). The Committee of RIM played a positive role in this process.

The Co-ordination Committee resolves to combine their efforts and raise their revolutionary struggles, with the aim of fanning the flames of protracted People's Wars in Peru, the Philippines and Turkey. We resolve to combat and defeat revisionism–both parliamentary and armed as the main danger to developing protracted people's war. We declare our principled unity and conscious determination to hoist the red flag of Marxism-Leninism-Maoism and Communism in all its splendour on the silver summits of the Himalayas and throughout the region. We undertake this responsibility as our internationalist duty contribution towards destroying the system of imperialism and achieving our final goal of socialism and communism by accomplishing the new-democratic revolution through the path of protracted people's war.

We appeal to all the Maoist forces of South Asia to join CCOMPOSA to defend and advance the on-going protracted People's Wars in Nepal and India and to achieve the victory of new-democratic revolution in the countries of South Asia.

We appeal to all anti-imperialist democratic forces to support us in strengthening the rising mass struggles against imperialism and Indian expansionism.

Signed

Purba Bangla Sarbohara Party, PBSP CC, Bangladesh

Maobadi Punorgathan Kendro, MPK of PBSP, Bangladesh

Bangladesh Samyabadi Dal (Marxist leninist), BSD (ML), Bangladesh

Communist Party of India

(Marxist-Leninist) People's War

CPI (ML) (PW), India

Maoist Communist Centre, MCC India

Revolutionary Communist Centre (Maoist), RCCI (M), India

Revolutionary Communist Centre (Marxist-Leninist Maoist), RCCI (MLM), India

Communist Party of Nepal (Maoist), CPN (M), Nepal Ceylon Communist Party (Maoist), CCP (M), Sri Lanka.

APPENDIX C

The First-ever Joint Interview of the General Secretaries of the Erstwhile CPI(ML) [PW] and MCCI

In the context of the merger and the formation of the CPI(Maoist) our magazine, People's March, interviewed Comrade Ganapathy and Comrade Kishan, the General Secretaries of the erstwhile CPI(ML)[PW] and the MCCI at an undisclosed location. This is an exclusive interview given to the People's March, the first of its kind given to the press. Both leaders first gave their Red Salutes to People's March, an independent magazine that reflects the Voice of the Indian Revolution. The interview had questions interspaced between the two leading comrades:

Peoples March: The Revolutionar Camp and the oppressed masses are naturally happy to hear about the unity. Why did it take such a long time—35 years—since the existence of your parties? Why did it take over two decades of talks for the unity process to culminate?

Ganapathy: It is true that the whole revolutionary camp, and all the revolutionary and democratic forces, and the entire oppressed masses of India will certainly feel so happy. The formation of the unified Communist Party of India (Maoist) is a new milestone in the history of the revolutionary communist movement of India. A unified Maoist party based on Marxism-Leninism-Maoism is a long delayed and highly cherished need of the revolutionary minded and oppressed people of the country, including all our ranks, and also all the Maoist forces of South Asia and other parts of the world. Now, this long-aspired desire and dream have been transformed into a reality.

As part of the world proletarian revolution, the Indian revolution has been advancing forward to establish a new democratic society by smashing the existing semi-colonial, semi-feudal system through the path of prctracted people's war. Our party has been leading not only the struggles of the basic masses of workers, peasants and the petite-bourgeoisie, and supporting those interests of the national bourgeoisie that come in conflict with imperialism and the comprador big bourgeoisie, but also fighting against all forms of social oppression, for the rights and emancipation of the oppressed nationalities, women, *dalits* and oppressed castes, minorities, etc. In this way we have won the confidence of the oppressed masses, who know that our party will stand steadfastly by them in all their woes and for their complete emancipation from all forms of oppression and exploitation. Quite naturally they will be happy with this merger. With the merger, the Party's fighting capacity grows considerably, and, as a result, its effective striking power multiplies, thereby benefiting the masses. Over this lengthy period, where the international communist movement also has faced many splits and setbacks, the Maoist movement in India has seen some advancement and much sacrifice of the best of its cadre for this great cause. So, the entire revolutionary camp and all the people are naturally happy to see our unity.

Now coming to the query: why did it take such a long time for these two streams to merge. Yes, it is true that our two parties existed separately for thirty-five years, and two decades of time for the unity talks, is a long time. But to concretely understand this, we must primarily look at the historical background, and the conditions in which these two Parties emerged and developed.

In the period after the Naxalbari uprising, there were differences, of opinions with regard to the immediate necessity of formation of the Party between the two leaderships. These differences could not be solved. So the CPI(ML), and MCC came into existence separately on 22 April 1969 and 20 October 1969, respectively. Later, the CPI(ML) was in disarray after the martyrdom of Comrade Charu Mazumdar (CM) and the setback of the movement. The Party split into many groups and there was vacuum of leadership on whom the major sections of the party could repose confidence. Apart from this, in 1976, after the demise of Com. Mao, with the seizure of power by the capitalist roaders, the counter revolutionary renegade Hua-Deng clique in China, and the Communist Party of China (CPC) turning revisionist, there ceased to be any international proletarian leadership and a revolutionary base. This had its negative impact on the Maoist movements worldwide, where a strong Right-wing and revisionist trend swept the international communist movement. It had its repercussion in India too. Because of the absence of an International leadership and a revolutionary base, the problems of unity of revolutionaries in India were compounded.

By 1980, the CPI(ML)[PW] and CPI(ML)[PU] evolved from the CPI(ML) stream, and the MCC built peasant movements and got strengthened. The CPI(ML)[PW] and the CPI(ML)[PU], from their very inception, had good relations with the MCC. The PW and MCC began unity talks from their very first meeting in 1981. However, the reason for the delay in the process was the lack of continuity of leader-ship. The arrest of Comrade Kondapally Seetaramaiah (KS), the leader of the PW, and later the internal crisis of the PW and split in the Central Committee (CC) delayed the unity process for several years. In the early 1980s the MCC lost its two top leaders, Comrades Amulya Sen (AS) and Kanai Chatterjee (KC), which had some negative impact, resulting in further delay in the unity process. Though there was basic unity on several major issues between the two Parties, there were some serious political differences on some major issues, and also a lack of maturity of the leaderships prevented the unity from fructifying. However, in this long period the revolutionary movement has developed and expanded, and the People's Guerrilla Army/People's Liberation Guerrilla Army (PGA/PLGA) got formed and guerrilla zones have been set up with the perspective of establishing Base Areas. Now, there is much more experience of both the leaderships and greater maturity in dealing with the issues and differences, and also in realising one's own mistakes. So, the situation was ripe for the big leap in the unity process. Thus, by analysing the objective and subjective factors for the delay in achieving the unity, we will take lessons from this experience and resolve, in the future, to strengthen the unity now achieved. Keeping the lessons in mind, we will also endeavour to unite the revolutionary forces who are outside to the CPI(Maoist).

PM: The M-L movement in India has a long history of splits; what guarantee is there that this will not be followed by a split? Can you give any assurance to the masses?

Ganapathy: Yes, in the past history there were many splits within the M-L movement. But splits are only one side of the coin; the brighter side was that there were continuous efforts to unify the revolutionaries. The CPI(ML)[PU], despite having its origins in Bengal, spread and strengthened by unifying several revolutionary groups. Although the CPI(ML)[PW] originated in Andhra Pradesh and Tamil Nadu, it unified with revolutionaries in almost all the states where it was working. The MCC too, had originated in Bengal, unified many revolutionaries groups in it in many states and became the MCCI.

The past could be broadly divided into three periods: After the setback in 1972, the main trend was splits; in the 1980s the main trend was the strengthening of the genuine revolutionary parties and the revolutionary movements, and degeneration of Right and Left opportunist parties and the weakening of their movements, and increasing steps towards unity; and in the decade of the 1990s the main trend was the development of the people's war and the unification of genuine revolutionary parties and forces. These efforts finally culminated in the formation of the unified CPI (Maoist) this year.

This unified party has been formed after thoroughgoing discussions, firstly held between the high level delegations of the two parties and then finalised by the Joint Central Committee meeting of both the parties. Through these deep and constructive discussions, held on an equal footing, five different documents have been drafted and finalised. These documents are: Hold High the Bright Red Banner of Marxism-Leninism-Maoism, the Party Programme, Strategy and Tactics of the Indian Revolution, the Political Resolution on the International and Domestic Situation and the Party Constitution.

In addition to these documents it has also been decided that our beloved leaders and teachers of the respective parties, the late Com. CM and Com. KC, will be recognised and highlighted as the founding leaders of the unified party. It was also decided that both these parties, stemming from the turbulent period of the decade of the 1960s, particularly from the great Naxalbari uprising, inherited all that was revolutionary in the long history of the Indian communist movement. The peculiarity of the situation is that both these parties continued to flow as two separate streams of the revolutionary communist movement, wedded to the same cause of carrying forward the Indian revolution over the past 35 years. All these steps taken together clearly disclosed a unified understanding on almost all ideological and political questions of line. The line established provided a principled basis for the unity achieved by both the parties. Basing on this unity the Joint Central Committee meeting finally resolved to unite the two parties into a single unified party.

If we examine the history, it is true that a period has been marked with serious and agonising splits, which was a depressing feature especially after the set back in 1972. But since 1980, after the emergence of the CPI(ML)[PW] and CPI(ML)[PU], there has not been any vertical split within these parties. This is in stark contrast with the splits and degeneration in the parties of Right deviation and Left sectarianism. The MCC, too, did not suffer any major split. And now the basis of unity has been principled, and since it has been achieved after thoroughgoing discussions, it has a strong foundation.

Within the party there will be differences, and as a reflection of the class struggle in society, there would be the possibility for the emergence of non proletarian trends. There will be a fight between right and wrong within the party. All internal differences will be solved on the basis of MLM and correct methods. The Marxist method of self-criticism and criticism, conducting inner-party struggles and rectification campaigns, to weed out non proletarian trends, guarantee a strong party unity, avoiding any split. History proves that in the past too, we basically solved all major internal problems in this manner.

PM: Was your unity based on the needs to face the increased repression by the state on both your parties or on genuine unity of thought?

Kishan: In my view the merger of the MCCI (Maoist Communist Centre of India) and the CPI(ML)[PW] {Communist Party of India

(Marxist-Leninist) [People's War]} and the birth of the Communist Party of India (Maoist), looked at from all angles, is an event of historic importance. The birth of the CPI(Maoist) will not only create a new revolutionary wave in India's revolutionary struggles in the development of India's agrarian revolutionary guerrilla war and people's war and the communist movement in India but will also have a positive and important impact on the international communist movement.

The above mentioned can only fructify when the newly formed Party stands on a firm political, ideological and theoretical basis. Both these parties have a 35 to 40-year-long practical experience of conducting political, theoretical and revolutionary struggles. Yet they existed as two separate streams the M-L stream and the MCC stream. To think that two such parties could take such a historic decision to unite, with just an approach to jointly facing state repression and not based on policy, could be due to subjectivism.

If you view the past 40 years' history you will see that: (i) in 1969 the then 'Dakshin Desh' Group (i.e., MCC) did not join the CPI(ML) formed under the leadership of Com. CM, and (ii) though 35 years have been traversed since 1969, and inspite of many rounds of unity talks, till the end, full unity could not be established. The question finally before us is, why? No doubt, there existed some basic differences between the two.

These two streams have existed separately for the past 35 years because of some political and practical differences, and have yet advanced independently, fighting back the massive attacks and encirclement-suppression campaigns of the state. So, how realistic would it be to think, such an important merger could take place merely with an approach to jointly face state terror?

Now I will answer your question from another angle. You must be aware of the fact that the unity talks initiated by the MCC's founder leader, Com. KC, from 1981, with the then CPI(ML)[PW], under the leadership of Com. KS, failed in 1995. After that we were able to once again take up unity talks in February 2003. In that sitting, after serious and lengthy discussions and debates on numerous basic political and practical questions, it was possible to make a major breakthrough. Based on this positive conclusion, the meeting took important decisions to carry on continuous unity talks, prepare some basic documents and conclude the unity process basing on these documents. The documents were–Hold High the Glorious Red Banner of Marxism-leninism-Maoism, the Party Programme, the Strategy and Tactics of Indian Revolution, the Political Resolution (International and Domestic situation) and the Party Constitution.

If the main aim of this merger is to counter state repression, there would have been no need to have decided to prepare the basic documents, but would have decided how to develop closer relations between the two parties to counter state terror and as to what other measures could be taken up to do so.

But that did not happen. In the course of the four rounds of bilateral discussions over the past 20 months, the drafts of all these documents were prepared. Together with this, there were detailed discussions on all basic issues through which a general understanding was reached, only after which the historic decision for merger was taken.

Therefore, it can be clearly stated that it was only on the basis of agreement on basic political and organisational issues that the historic merger process could be completed and on the basis of a strong political, theoretical and organisational line was the Communist Party of India (Maoist) formed.

Now I will speak about the last part of your question. You asked whether this unity, based on ideology, could be said to be a true unity. My answer is: it could be said yes, as also no. Because true unity based on ideology should not be seen in an absolute sense. It should be seen in a relative sense. In other words it can be said that this unity which is basically and principally based on theory is a true unity. But, together with this, there is a secondary aspect, i.e., to make it based more on theory and a true unity, struggle is also needed. In this case, the principal aspect is unity, and the non-principal aspect is struggle. Together with this, dialectical materialism shows us that true unity based on theory can only be possible through the dialectical process of unity-struggle-unity. If we look at all questions from the Maoist approach of 'One divides into two', it is only in the long process of negating the negative aspects and strengthening the positive aspects that we can further the process in a correct way to achieve true unity based on principles.

Finally, in reply to your question, I would like to make one point; it is absolutely impossible to fight state repression without a strong political-theoretical foundation and a correct Marxist military line. So, without a politically and theoretically strong Party we can't achieve any thing.

PM: Given that you had such a bad chapter which went so far as to be involved in mutual killing how were you able to resolve these serious differences and even proceed towards unity with such speed?

Kishan: The first major point in the relations between our two parties was to develop a correct understanding of this bad chapter, i.e., Black Chapter in our relations. Till such a time, as we both recognised this tension period as a Black Chapter, it was not possible to solve the problems that had developed. Secondly, it was important to develop the understanding that we ourselves were responsible for this Black Chapter. Thirdly, it was necessary to understand that we had to engage in self-criticism with full frankness and sincerity of heart and mind, and also to place this self-criticism before the general rank-and-file and also the revolutionary masses.

Even the most difficult problems can be solved if we are able to understand our own mistakes. Only after grasping this feeling, there will be no hesitation whatsoever for a genuine and objective self-criticism. Precisely, this is what happened regarding the solution to the problems associated with the Black Chapter. Today, both of us continue to engage in self-criticism with frankness on the correct aspects of this problem. We both have placed our written self-criticisms openly before the revolutionary rank-and-file and masses; and in future too, we will adopt a similar method.

Only through this process of genuine self-criticism, we have been able to convert a bad thing into a good thing.

When this problem was correctly solved, the unity process was bound to advance–and this is what, in fact, happened.

You asked as to how it was possible to advance with such speed towards unity? Well, I think, such a question is absolutely natural, given the. Black Chapter that existed. But, it must also not be forgotten that in the past, in the long fraternal relations between the MCCI and the CPI(ML)[PW] the aspect of cordial, strong and fraternal relations was principal, while the aspect of the black chapter was secondary. If you reflect on the past 24 years' friendly relations between the two parties and many bilateral meetings on the joint activities and on political issues, you will find that there is a long history of political debate behind today's unity. Therefore, if you see it in totality, this final unity may be seen to have been achieved quickly, but that is not fully so, in reality. In fact only by adopting a correct Marxist-Leninist method and after quite heated political debates over a period, could we successfully complete this process and achieve unity.

PM: There are still some revolutionary groups in the country, what is your united party's approach to them?

Ganapathy: It is true that there are still some revolutionary groups in the country and also many genuine revolutionary forces in the Right opportunist parties of the revolutionary camp. In addition, there are numerous individual comrades, who do not belong to any Party at present. But they were part of one or the other ML Groups at some point of time. They are also part of the revolutionary camp in the country. We seek to unite all genuine revolutionary groups, forces and elements that remain still outside our unified Party. So, one of the important tasks of our Party building is to unite all these forces. We will make serious efforts to realise this task in a principled manner, by conducting thorough and consistent struggles against revisionism and all non -proletarian tendencies, within the revolutionary camp, like reformism, economism, parliamentarism, postmodernism, etc., which seek to divert the masses from the path of revolution. For this we conduct polemics on political and ideological questions and tactics.

PM: What will the impact of this unity be on the people of the country?

Kishan: I think this unity and the birth of the CPI (Maoist) will have an unprecedented positive impact on whole of the masses including workers, peasants and all the toiling masses of India. In reality, the pro-people mask of the various Gandhian vote-mongering and fake Communist Parties have, to a large extent, been exposed.

For long, the people of India have been waiting for such a party that is capable of leading them in their liberation struggle. From the point of view of the masses, the emergence of the CPI (Maoist) which is equipped with the experience of conducting revolutionary class struggle and agrarian revolutionary guerrilla war, is a very important event. That is why it can definitely be said that this unity will have a positive impact on the people of the country.

But this is only one aspect concerning the birth of this new Party. Regarding other aspects it can certainly be said that with the announcement of the new Party, all the enemy and revisionist forces will go insane with anger. The above two factors will definitely occur.

PM: Now coming to other questions. What have your two parties achieved in the last 35-years long history of your existence? What is the contribution of your parties to the development of the political and ideological line of Indian revolution?

Ganapathy: If we look at the last 35 years of our past history, amongst all the confusions and setbacks that raged in the communist movement of India and in many countries, we have, to a large extent, been basically successful in applying MLM to the concrete conditions of the Indian revolution and have got many significant achievements.

The Unified Party with a collective leadership saw the emergence of an ideologically and politically mature party–a party of a new type-that has developed and steeled itself through decades of intense class struggles in the course of advancing the Guerrilla War. In the process, we have also developed the Party line in the concrete conditions of the Indian revolution. And it is only by successfully doing this have we been able to grow into the type of force that we are today. With the present unity, we have achieved unity of most of the revolutionary forces in India. This, in itself, is an outstanding achievement. Now our party has acquired an All India character which has spread to over a dozen states. In some states like, AP, Bihar, Jharkhand, and Chhattisgarh we are a significant force. The United Party has not only united the revolutionaries within India, it has forged formidable fraternal relations in South Asia by taking part in forming the Coordination Committee of Maoist Parties and Organisations of South Asia (CCOMPOSA) and also with revolutionary parties abroad, especially with those parties which are waging PPW.

For the first time in the country, our two parties have formed a People's Liberation Guerrilla Army and have developed Guerrilla Zones, and intensified Guerrilla War with a view to advance towards the formation of Base Areas. In some of these Guerrilla Zones we have been able to establish the Revolutionary People's Political Power in an embryonic form. This, alone, is a substantial achievement in the face of the enemy's fascist encirclement and several suppression campaigns. Over the years, the PLGA has been systematically strengthened from a small to a bigger force. This is reflected in the growth from small skirmishes with the enemy to bigger battles; from small formations to bigger formations; from a few in numbers to larger numbers; to the development of a more systematic structure of commands and commissions; and, its greater ability to arm itself with the seizure of arms from the enemy. The PLGA, though still small, with its heroic actions and with more than two decades of continuous and consistent armed tactical counter offensives against the state police and various Special Forces and various paramilitary forces, became the apple of the peoples' eye and a nightmare to the ruling classes.

We took lessons by thoroughgoing debates and discussions on the Party. These inner party struggles gave a better understanding on how to conduct two-line struggle on the basis of democratic centralism with the aim of achieving a greater level of unity, and with the aim of defeating the wrong line or rectifying wrong deviations. In the process of two-line struggles, the Party leadership and the whole Party got steeled and a collective leadership evolved. This is one of the remarkable achievements.

We have worked out specific policies for the various oppressed sections of the people, like the *dalits* and other oppressed castes, women, minorities, etc. from the class viewpoint of the proletariat, and have led many struggles on these issues.

In the areas where we are a force to reckon with, we have taken up issues of political, economic, social, and cultural oppression extensively and people have achieved substantial victories, including construction and developmental activities, where people's political power is being established by restricting the political power of the enemy classes. In these areas the people are relatively more politically conscious, well organised, and better off with improved working and living conditions compared to the other regions. Now, they have more self-confidence, they have gained literacy and knowledge, they are able to stand upright with self-respect against all authority and they are free from the tyranny and terror of the landed elite, government officials, etc.

Regarding the development of the political and ideological line, the united party has definitely enriched the party line. While adhering firmly to the respective parties' basic line, which was formulated in the basic documents of earlier period of both the parties, we enriched several concepts basing on the rich experiences acquired in advancing the people's war over these years, taking into account the political developments of the past three and a half decades. We firmly fought against both 'Right' and 'Left' deviations that were seen in the forging of the three magic weapons of revolution - the Party, Army and the UF - and in the formulation of tactics. It achieved a higher level of understanding regarding the concepts such as that of people's army, guerrilla zones, Base Areas and the Revolutionary United Front; on persisting along the path of protracted people's war, creatively applying the Maoist strategy to the concrete conditions in India and rejecting entirely the parliamentary form of struggle in the concrete conditions of India; building a secret Party with an underground structure with Professional Revolutionaries (PRs) forming its core; consistently adhering to the revolutionary mass line and building powerful mass movements linking them to the Protracted People's War (PPW), etc.

The united party addressed the ideological-political questions confronting the International Communist Movement today such as: the guiding ideology of the proletariat, the General Crisis of Capitalism and its impact on the world revolution, the question of the principal contradiction, the danger of world war, the understanding on the nature of the present Era, the significance of national liberation struggles and the need to unify the two streams of the World Socialist Revolution, and, finally, the danger of revisionism in the International Communist Movement (ICM). The united party thus enriched the party's understanding on the above questions concerning the contemporary world situation and the ICM and adopted clear-cut proletarian stand-points.

In a nutshell, we can say that the two erstwhile parties have continued the ideological and political legacy of Naxalbari, and, while imbibing all the positive aspects, have further developed the line. The development of the line to the concrete conditions is embedded in the now formulated documents - MLM, Party Programme, Party Constitution, Strategy and Tactics, and a Political Resolution on the current situation.

PM: What is the development of the political, organisational and military line since the 1996 Conference of the MCC?

Kishan: Even today, at the international plane, the contradiction between imperialism and the oppressed nationalities and people is the principal and decisive contradiction. Due to the continuously deepening and increasing crisis of imperialism, the inter-imperialist contradictions are also intensifying gradually. Asia, Africa and Latin America have become the storm centres of Revolution. Revolution is the main trend in the world today and revisionism is the main danger in the present era. Because of the above conditions, the world situation is day-by-day becoming more favourable for revolution.

We drew these conclusions in our 1996 Conference and we follow this even today. In our November 2002 Central Committee meeting, after much discussion and analysis we reversed our earlier understanding that 'Russia was a weak superpower' and concluded that this earlier assessment was wrong. In this meeting we also included that the US imperialism was a superpower and declared it the number one enemy of the world people.

In our analysis of the domestic situation, we had seen that under the domination of the US imperialists, various imperialist forces are in the fray to increase their influence in the country. All the governments, from the BJP alliance to the Congress and other alliances are implementing political, economic and all policies according to their wishes. Together with this, the contradictions within the Indian ruling classes are also gradually growing sharper. In fact, hardly ever before has the revolutionary situation been so excellent and favourable as today. On the basis of this analysis we decided to make the formation of our Red Army and Base Areas a basic, chief, central and immediate task and to advance in that direction with speed; and to select strategic areas to systematically organize the work there. In the midst of this, in January 2000 a serious debate and dispute developed in our CC through which it was decided to accept Mao Thought as Maoism; and we took the decision that Maoism is a completely new stage, as a third, higher and qualitative development in the history of advancement of Marxism. Besides this, through an equally intense internal struggle we took a very important decision in this meeting to unilaterally stop all clashes with the erstwhile PW. In addition to this we also took a decision to stand by our earlier understanding of Stalin, basing on Comrade Mao's assessment of him in the course of the Great Debate.

In January 2000, the decision was taken to name Mao Thought as Maoism. But after this an opportunist group emerged in our Party that opposed this decision and which sought to put hurdles in the task of building the army and base areas. By launching a relentless struggle against them we were able to demolish them. At this time we also took initiative at the international plane to forge unity with genuine Maoists, and as part of this acquired membership to RIM. Similarly, at the national level we gave primary importance to unite genuine Maoists. And in this we also achieved success. Together with this, the erstwhile MCCI made major advances in all spheres. Major leaps were taken in strengthening all party committees, including the central committee, in both quality and quantity; and also in the sphere of determining a correct direction towards giving a well organised form to a Maoist military line and military organisation. We formed the most important department like the Central Military Commission and on 22 April 2003 announced the formal formation of the People's Liberation Guerrilla Army (PLGA). In the past few years this brave army has fought many a great and heroic battle. The fight and guerrilla attacks of Tekari, Pretshilla, Topchanchi, Churchu, Chandrapura, Simrahni and Saranda are some good examples of such glorious battles. In short, it can be said that the erstwhile MCCI, after its second central conference in 1996, and particularly after 2000, carried out a sharp two line struggle in the Party and defeated the incorrect line both theoretically and practically. And in the process, compared to earlier, we have been able in taking a qualitative leap in all matters.

PM: Both your parties are confined primarily to the most backward forest belts of the country. Why in these 35 years of existence have you not been able to have much impact on the plains and urban areas, where the bulk of the population live?

Ganapathy: In absolute terms what you say is not true that we are confined to the forests alone. Of course, it is true that our movement is stronger in the forests than in the plains and urban areas. This focus is linked to our path. Depending on the specific characteristics of the Indian revolution, we decided that the path of revolution is that of protracted people's war. That is, by first setting up Base Areas in the backward areas and spreading these to the other areas and thereby ultimately encircling the cities from the countryside. So, it is according to this strategic understanding alone that work must be done in any area, whether forest, plain or urban. The forests and mountainous areas quite naturally get priority as these are the strategic areas where Base Areas can be set up. But, it is not correct to say that we have ignored the plain areas. We have built extensive anti-feudal and anti-imperialist struggles in the plain areas in AP and Bihar. Even today our Party is working in the plain areas in some states. In fact, in AP and B-J states much of our cadres, leadership and even the prestige of the movement were gained by developing the revolutionary movement in the plain areas. We built strong movements in several forest areas starting from and relying on the plain areas for our subjective forces, material help and concrete experience.

In the process, we suffered severe leadership and cadre losses due to the most cruel and fascist suppression campaigns by the enemy, and due to our shortcomings. Accordingly we are trying to formulate and change our tactics - forms of organisation and struggle and method of work - in the plain areas. Acting according to our strategic plan in building the revolutionary movement in plain areas by following the path of PPW, we have gained rich experience through our practice crimsoned with the blood of thousands of martyrs; and have also learned from the experience of the armed struggles of the oppressed nationalities of the Indian sub-continent.

Keeping in the forefront our path of revolution, i.e. Protracted People's War, we have been working in the plains, cities and villages and have consolidated our forces in the strategic areas. Before us, we have the experience of the first round of struggles of Naxalbari,

Srikakulam, Birbhum, etc.; and then we also have our own direct experience of armed struggle since the end of the 1970s. This experience has itself proved the validity of the path of protracted people's war. So, while focusing on the strategic areas, we have worked also in the plains and urban areas coordinating this latter work with that of the strategic areas. If we did not have this orientation, we too, would have gone into right deviations like so many of the other M-L parties and groups.

Revolution cannot develop according to one's own wishes; it will follow certain determined laws depending on the nature of Indian society, and the stage of the revolution. The general laws of PPW have to be applied to the specific characteristics of the Indian revolution. In the revolutionary process, it is for us to discover these laws and act accordingly in the most effective manner.

Today, we are strong in the forest areas as these are the perspective areas for setting up Bases; where we are intensifying and expanding the class struggle for the seizure of political power, even though the starting point of our work has been the plain areas.

We are also concentrating on the forest areas for the strategic needs of building a strong people's army and establishing people's political power by politically mobilising the vast masses and smashing the state power of the enemy classes. We are coordinating the three types of movement (broadly) - forest, plain and urban - with, each other, according to the principles of PPW.

The specificity of the Indian revolutionary process is that the M-L movement faced a severe setback and splits after the historic revolutionary movements of Naxalbari, Srikakulam, etc. Another aspect of this specificity is the existence and continuation of two independent Maoist streams—M-L stream and the MCC stream in the country. Yet, despite these ups and downs, we have recovered from the setback and rebuilt the revolutionary movement, and have been step-by-step unifying the revolutionary forces in the country. The unity of our two major Maoist streams is the most positive aspect of this process.

Despite these positive developments, the revolutionary forces are still weak in urban areas, and the revisionist leadership has still many influential pockets. There is a danger of revisionism which has a countrywide domination over the trade unions, a wide influence in the urban areas and even amongst the peasantry in some parts of the country, despite their feeble base. It also exists in the government and has a wide influence in three states. The revisionists, under the garb of the Red flag, propagate bourgeois ideology and politics, and adopt reformist tactics. It acts as one of the main props of the rule of the reactionary ruling classes in the country. It is one of the main sources of injecting parliamentarism, economism, reformism into the body politics of the oppressed masses and has become a major hurdle in building and developing the working class and urban movements. Due to the long influence of revisionist politics and practice in some areas there will be need for much patience, consistency and creative revolutionary initiatives to make a breakthrough.

The cities and towns are the bastions of the imperialists and the Indian ruling classes. Yet, in a few towns and cities we had built powerful working-class movements, and these movements had created panic amongst the imperialists and the ruling classes and created a positive impact on the people, particularly the working class, students and intellectuals. But, they have faced many losses. Today, though we are a weak force in urban areas, we have a presence in many cities and towns in several states and are trying to develop the working class and the urban movement, which is also being influenced by the growing armed struggles in the rural areas.

Finally, I would like to conclude that with great determination we will strive to advance and expand the Guerrilla war to establish Base Areas in the strategic areas; we will refine and develop our tactics to rebuild, consolidate and expand the revolutionary movement in the vast plains of India, to advance the People's War to drown the enemy in the great ocean of the class struggles of the vast masses; and we will rebuild, consolidate and expand the working class and urban movement in cities and towns, keeping in mind the strategic direction and the changing socio-economic-political conditions of our country.

India is a highly diverse and complex social system and a country of enormous size; here, the enemy is much stronger; and the interests of the imperialists in India are greater because of its geo-political and economic situation. Hence, the odds are heavy; so, it will no doubt take more time, particularly in the plain and urban areas. But we are taking lessons from our experiences with regard to the work in the plain and urban areas. We will concentrate our work in the strategic areas to develop the People's Army, and intensify the armed agrarian revolutionary war and establish Base Areas; coordinate this work with the work in the plain and the urban areas in a planned way with a strategic outlook by keeping in mind the dialectical relationship between these three types of areas; and we will make a breakthrough in building powerful movements in plain and urban areas. So, I firmly say that, our advance is inevitable.

PM: In what way will your unity have impact on the development of the guerrilla war in the country? How will you face the massive onslaught of the Indian state? What concrete tasks have you set yourself to achieve Base Areas?

Kishan: We believe that the direct impact of our unity will be most on the ongoing guerrilla war in the country. Also due to this, the agrarian revolutionary guerrilla war will attain a new inspiration and new dynamism, a new energy, and a new upheaval and will thereby expand and intensify throughout the entire country. Especially, when our erstwhile armies of the PGA and PLGA will unite into the newly formed PLGA, this can be said with much greater certainty.

As far as the question of countering the massive onslaughts of the Indian state machinery is concerned, we think that not only will we be able to give them a fitting reply, but also completely smash them through the creative application of our strategy and tactics to the path of protracted people's war in India. In fact, one of the reasons that determine the specific application of the strategy and tactics to the path of protracted people's war is that the enemy is strong and masses are weak. But this strength of the enemy and weakness of the masses is relative. This truth has been proved by our struggles over the last few years. Compared to earlier, we have now acquired some greater strength, while to some extent the enemy's strength has definitely reduced in relative terms. Besides, in a huge country like India, it is not possible for the enemy to deploy its forces everywhere, particularly in the distant and widespread rural areas. Therefore, facing all types of difficulties and crossing all hurdles we can definitely smash to pieces the Indian state machinery and beat back their fierce attacks if we, on the one hand, make the rural areas the main centre of our work, while on the other, if we intensify our work amongst urban workers and all the toiling masses and bring a proper balance between both these types of work. Simultaneously, we will have to recruit lakhs and crores of the masses into the military battles to conduct the revolutionary mass movements and at the same time bring a correct coordination between the two.

Therefore, one very important task before us is to bring a proper balance between the armed struggle and the widespread activities and movements of the masses and thereby develop and extend both.

No doubt, to establish Base Areas we have determined some definite tasks. For example, developing through Guerrilla Zones and Guerrilla Bases we will have to move in the direction towards establishing Base Areas. Together with this we have to strengthen in every way, the formations of all three forces of the PLGA - the Basic, Secondary and Main forces; and through a proper command system a correct coordination has to be developed between them. In addition, within a fixed time frame the military formations have to be developed from the company to the battalion level. In this way, through both qualitative and quantitative development, the PLGA has to be turned into a PLA.

If we are able to complete these tasks in a correct way, and we are able to draw vast sections of the masses into the guerrilla war and also into the various other forms of struggle, then we can definitely achieve victory in the protracted people's war, no matter how long, tortuous and difficult the process may be, facing the numerous twists and turns and ups and downs in the march forward.

PM: Now to turn to other questions linked to the political impact of your movement. Your parties did not seem to have much impact to fight against the massive imperialist penetration into the country? Why? Also there seems little impact on the fight against the monster of Hindu fascism. . . Why?

Kishan: See, from one point of view, it is true that the impact of revolutionary struggles against imperialist intervention in the country cannot much be seen. To some extent this is even a fact. Firstly our subjective force is quite less than what is needed, and even of that which exists, the strength in the urban areas and industrial areas is far less compared to the rural areas. Therefore, we have not been able to intensify the struggle against imperialism as is needed, while, on the other hand, the other so-called anti-imperialists, like the parliamentary and revisionist parties and the NGOs, are nothing but a farce and a deception.

In reality, the basis for real opposition to imperialism is only in the hands of genuine Maoists and revolutionaries. Therefore, even if at present the anti-imperialist struggle is somewhat weak, by rectifying our weaknesses in this sphere, we can definitely create and advance a strong movement against imperialist intervention, based on a correct approach to the issue. Though, on this issue, we are somewhat late, we can definitely advance this movement by adopting correct methods.

On the question of the struggle against Hindu fascism too, there are a host of fake anti-communal forces. In such a situation it is no easy task, where, on the one hand we have to draw a clear-cut line of demarcation with such forces, and on the other, create and develop a genuine movement against Hindu fascism. In the true sense, problems like communalism and Hindu fascism can actually only be solved by developing and extending the class struggle. That is why you will find that in those areas where Maoist revolutionaries have influence, communal riots there, will be seen to be relatively less.

Therefore, by focussing on worker-peasant unity and by being able to build our revolutionary mass base amongst them through patient work, will we be able to build and conduct a genuine movement against communalism, religious fanaticism and Hindu fascism in a correct way and in correct direction.

So, perhaps it is not fully true to say that the impact of the revolutionary movement against the problems of communalism or Hindu fascism is very little. But, it is no doubt true, given the way the RSS gangs are instigating communalism and provoking riots in India today, our response in giving an effective answer to them has been far less than what the situation requires. We are confident that the initiative we have now taken to rectify this shortcoming and the process we have recently started will soon bear fruits.

PM: How do you view the impact of the US/Globalisation policies on our country?

Kishan: I am of the opinion that the imperialists, particularly the US imperialist-promoted globalisation, has had a very bad impact on the life of our people and the national life of the country. These policies have pushed to devastation the living standards of every level of the people. If this is not stopped, in the next few years, it will have a horrifying impact. We believe that it is only the advancing agrarian revolutionary guerrilla war together with the development and expansion of widespread militant mass movements, that can successfully complete the people's revolution, which alone can free our country from the dangerous effects of globalisation.

PM: India is such a diverse country of nationalities, *dalits* and various castes, minority groupings, linguistic sections etc. How do you expect to unite such diverse elements, all of whom face not only class oppression but also varied forms of social oppression?

Ganapathy: Women, *dalits*, Adivasis, oppressed nationalities and religious minorities are the most important of the social sections to be taken cognisance of by the party of the proletariat leading the revolution in the concrete conditions prevailing in India. All these sections have special problems of their own and specific types of extra-economic oppression apart from class oppression. We have to pay due attention to solve their special problems, like patriarchy, untouchability and other forms of caste oppression, attacks on minorities and oppressed nationalities, etc. and approach these problems from a class view-point. We also have to link these tasks with the ongoing revolutionary movement. Towards this end, we have to not only bring these sections into class organisations along with other oppressed masses, but also evolve the necessary forms of organisations and forms of struggle for the widest mobilisation of these sections on their special problems both on a short-term and long-term basis. Broader joint fronts too should be formed wherever and whenever necessary to address the specific grievances.

However, while taking up specific tactics on the special problems related to these sections, we should keep in mind that the tactics should always serve our strategic line. We should place the specific programme for the solution of their specific problems in relation to, and in the overall context of the on-going people's war in the country. We must educate these sections how their problems are essentially class questions; how the material basis for the final solution of their problems lies in liberating themselves from class oppression; and hence, the imperative need for waging war against the common enemies - feudalism, imperialism, and comprador bureaucrat capitalism, that are oppressing the vast toiling masses in the country - unitedly with other oppressed masses under the leadership of the proletariat.

We must demonstrate in practice how the people's war and the ongoing class struggle is bringing these sections increasingly into the centre stage; how the latent potential and creative energies, the revolutionary initiative and capacities of these oppressed sections are being released in the course of the people's war and the deepening class struggle. It is only by paying special attention and making conscious efforts, based on concrete planning, by the leadership of the Party to develop the oppressed among these sections, that we can bring a qualitative change in their over-all status in the Party and position in the revolutionary movement.

By pursuing the above-mentioned general line and approach, we will be able to draw the clear line of demarcation with the bourgeois parliamentary and revisionist parties, with the reformist Non-Governmental Organisations (NGOs) and other petty bourgeois organisations, as well as with the so-called Communist Revolutionary organisations in our country with regard to the solution of the problems of these special social sections. This can be done by demarcating the wrong approaches to these issues from the proletarian approach. At the same time we must fight against the mechanistic approach that ignores these social issues and thereby indirectly acts to perpetuate all these social evils. Conscious efforts have to be made amongst the males and upper castes from the oppressed to educate them against their patriarchal and casteist views. We must also take up consistent political exposure of the various bourgeois-revisionist-reformist trends within the movements of these sections.

The Party must also fight against non-proletarian values inside itself that may manifest in subtle forms of patriarchy, casteism and caste biases, elitism and turning a blind eye to the rights of the oppressed sections. On the other hand, it must also educate comrades who may be influenced by the varied post-modernist trends, bourgeois feminism, Dalitism, narrow nationalism, etc.

It is only by remaining loyal to the politics of the proletariat and the ideology of Marxism-Leninism-Maoism and maintaining its own political and organisational independence, that the working class can give leadership and liberate the peoples from the sectarian approach to all these social evils and arouse them and bring them into the path of the revolutionary democratic struggle in its true sense (as part and parcel of the new democratic revolution). Yet, it must be understood that merely the new democratic revolution will not do away totally all these social evils. Though, the objective basis of an exploitative social system may not exist, it will continue to manifest in the superstructure in people's thinking and social/cultural norms and value. So, even after the victory of the revolution in the new democratic and socialist societies, the struggle will have to be continued in all realms of thinking and social practice.

PM: Today the dog-fights amongst the ruling classes are intensifying; how do you plan to use this to your advantage?

Kishan: The fact is that revolutionaries always utilise the growing contradictions within the ruling factions in order to advance the revolution. But it must be remembered that in India, as yet, there is no clearcut polarisation due to these contradictions and none of these contradictions have reached the level of a war. Another point is that while they fight like dogs for the spoils of office, they get united when it comes to suppressing the revolutionary struggles. But of course, there are also contradictions amongst them, as to what policy is best used against the revolutionaries - soft or strong.

That is why this question demands serious thought as to how this contradiction can be used in the interests of revolution. In order to effectively utilise the contradiction within these ruling classes to further the revolutionary struggle all the following points must be analysed and considered the concrete condition of the revolutionary armed struggle and its nationwide impact; the condition of our subjective forces, particularly of the Party, People's Army and United Front, and its impact on the people of the country; and the question of our ability to keep the initiative in our hands and our ability to effectively intervene on the varied political issues of the day.

In this matter I want to say one more thing, in the present condition I don't think it is correct to ally with one section of the ruling class parties in the name of utilising contradictions among them.

PM: Now coming to international questions. What is the significance of Maoism in the contemporary world? Can it help analyse the big changes taking place and give a perspective for the future in the present context?

Kishan: We have accepted Maoism as the Marxism-Leninism of today. Marxism-Leninism-Maoism is in itself an integrated whole. It is such a dynamic science that, with its help one can better analyse all the branches of science. With it, we can correctly analyse anything, any event and draw conclusions.

We know that Marxism does not merely interpret the world, but determines the laws that govern its change. Accordingly, what ever changes have taken place in the world today or all the changes that have taken place since the very beginning of the imperialist era, tin date, can only have been correctly analysed in the light of the theory of Marxism-Leninism-Maoism. This will apply to the future as well. Together with this, we must remember that Marxism-Leninism-Maoism is the guide to all our activities. Therefore, it acts as the theoretical guide to understand even big changes that may have taken place in any new conditions. We have to do our work not in a dogmatic way but apply it creatively.

In addition, to understand the future within the framework of the present can only be done in the light of Marxism-Leninism-Maoism. Development of the world situation takes place only through the process of passing through various ups and down, the zig-zag path and through the process of advancing through both victories and defeats. Even all advances in the world and the social system go through this process and will continue to do so.

Therefore, I am of the firm opinion that to understand today's world and find solutions to its varied problems, the use of Maoism is of a historical and international significance.

PM: How do you plan to develop relations with other revolutionary forces throughout the world? What impact will this unity have on the international communist movement?

Kishan: We, communists are internationalists. This internationalism is best reflected through our slogan—Workers and oppressed people of the world unite! For the advance of the world communist movement there is utmost necessity to establish strong fraternal relations between the revolutionary struggles of the colonial, semi-colonial and semi-feudal countries and the working class movements in the capitalist-imperialist countries. With this approach, one of our important duties is to establish strong relations with all genuine Maoist parties in the world. Earlier, both the erstwhile MCCI and the erstwhile CPI(ML)[PW] have continued bilateral relations with Nepal, Peru, Philippines, Turkey and other countries at the international level. The erstwhile MCCI had even joined the RIM (Revolutionary Internationalist Movement), while the erstwhile PW had decided to further deepen its relations with RIM.

Now when a new Party - the CPI (Maoist) - is born, by following revolutionary traditions, the party has decided to continue its deep relations with RIM and all other genuine Maoists.

As India is a vast populated country, the unity of India's two important revolutionary organisations - the erstwhile MCCI and PW - will definitely have a very positive impact at the international plane. Today there is no socialist country in the world. Today, when the reactionaries are shouting from the roof tops that Marxism and Communism have been defeated, the merger of the erstwhile MCCI and PW and the formation of a genuine Marxist-leninist-Maoist Party, is such an event, that too in a vast country with a population of one billion, that can give new life to the international communist movement. To the extent that we will be able to intensify revolutionary guerrilla agrarian war - protracted people's war - under the leadership of the new Party, to that extent new energy will be infused into the International Communist Movement.

PM : You have been always saying for the last 35 years the situation in the world is excellent for revolution. If so why are the Maoist forces in the world so weak?

Ganapathy : Yes, the objective situation is in general terms excellent. The objective situation is very excellent in the third world or backward countries or oppressed countries or semi-colonies and colonies and the revolutionary objective situation is developing in the imperialist countries. But, why is there this contradiction that you mentioned? How can we understand this?

We should understand that there is a dialectical link between the objective and the subjective factors; it is not a mechanical interconnection or a one-to-one relationship. If there was such a mechanical relation everything would be pre-determined and revolution would take place in the backward countries first only. Lenin said that, to a revolutionary situation to mature, both the objective and subjective factors must develop and then alone revolution breaks out at the weakest link. Though, today the storm centres of world revolution are the backward countries and the conditions are acute thêre, the occurrence of revolution is dependent on numerous factors. Similarly, the development and growth of genuine proletarian parties (Maoist parties) is determined not merely by the extent of poverty but by the political content of the general democratic movement in that country and the growth of genuine proletarian forces within it.

With the advent of imperialism, the crisis of capitalism took the form of a General crisis and ripened the objective condition for social revolution. The principal characteristic feature of the general crisis of capitalism in the era of imperialism is that capitalism as a whole is bogged down in a state of under-utilisation of capacity and permanent mass unemployment and inflation. The continuous massive destruction of reproductive forces through world wars and proxy wars, through under-utilisation of productive capacities of millions upon millions of people and the destruction of surplus commodities, even as millions of people languish in destitution; are all features of imperialism.

The general crisis of capitalism brought forth all the fundamental contradictions in society to a bursting point-that between capital and labour, between imperialism and the oppressed nations and people, and between the various imperialist powers and monopoly capitalist groups. The conflict of the productive forces with the existing relations of production, thus, took on an explosive form ever since the advent of imperialism, leading to fascism, world wars and social revolutions. These will continue until the final victory of the World Socialist Revolution over the world capitalist system.

The present day world is under a great disorder, turbulence and instability rarely witnessed after the Second World War. The collapse of Soviet Social imperialism and the complete integration of erstwhile bureaucratic capitalist states of East Europe, Soviet Union in the 1990s and China into world capitalist system have not mitigated the crisis of world capitalism. This ever intensifying crisis of the world capitalist system is the basis for the chaos, turmoil and instability which has become characteristic of the contemporary 'world situation. After the September 11 incident, in the name of fighting against terrorism, the US imperialism is unleashing a series of wars of aggression and carrying out attacks on the people all over the world. This has generated powerful backlash from the people, in various forms. Thus, a new situation has emerged where instability and turmoil have deepened further.

Today, imperialism is facing an unprecedented worldwide crisis, unheard of ever since the end of the Second World War. All the fundamental contradictions are further sharpening. A new tide of revolutionary struggles, national liberation struggles and various people's movements against imperialist aggression, oppression and exploitation is unfolding everywhere. There is great need to utilise this favourable situation to make great leaps in the ongoing people's war in our country and advance towards the establishment of a new democratic state and then march forward to socialism.

Vast areas of Asia, Africa, and Latin America are continuing as the storm centres of world revolution. Guerrilla war against the US occupation is intensifying in Iraq and Afghanistan. People's war, under the leadership of the Maoist parties in India, Nepal, Philippines, Peru and Turkey, is advancing. The workers and vast sections of the masses in imperialist countries are fighting militantly against the policies of globalisation and war. Genuine revolutionary parties based on MLM are emerging in several capitalist countries. All this acts to weaken imperialism.

Yet, relative to the 1960s and 70s, the proletarian movement is weaker. The principal reason for this is the growth of the revisionist trends worldwide and the betrayal of the national liberation movements of the 60s and the 70s. The reversals in the Soviet Union (1956) and then in China (1976) and the conversion of the Communist Party of Soviet Union (CPSU) and the CPC into revisionist parties fuelled Rightist and revisionist parties throughout the world. The restoration of capitalism in these former socialist societies and the disintegration of the socialist camp had a very negative impact on the advance of the world revolution. Utilising the situation of this setback, the imperialists went on ideological and political offensive against communism trying to show it as being out-dated, and floated various new forms of dissent theories. On the other hand, most of the genuine communist revolutionary forces were in disarray and ideological and political confusion rife with no international centre. It is these factors that have resulted in the relative weakening of the Maoist forces today. In addition, the massive, genocidal repression unleashed on all revolutionary forces (as witnessed in Indo-China, Latin America, and now Asia) further created impediments in growth.

But today, with the conditions worldwide becoming even more horrifying and the regrouping of genuine Maoist forces and the birth of new ones, the revolutionary situation is bound to advance. The relatively faster growth of the PPW in Nepal is a concrete example of the excellence of the revolutionary situation. If Maoist parties emerge in various countries and take concrete tactics, under a correct strategy, they are bound to advance. To do so, there is a need to correctly grasp MLM; know the nature of the imperialist era and grasp the historical task of the world working class and its Vanguard Parties; prepare the subjective forces; politically mobilise and lead the masses in the class struggles and advance the revolutionary wars to success.

PM : Finally, what message does your united Party have for the people of the country?

Ganapathy: Finally, our United Party calls on the people of India and the world over to:

Unite! Unite! And Unite! Unite all the revolutionary and democratic classes and forces of our country - workers, peasantry, petty bourgeoisie and national bourgeoisie, including all the oppressed social sections-under the leadership of the Communist Party of India (Maoist)!

Organise! Organise! And Organise! Organise in the Revolutionary. Mass Organisations, Red Army, and the Organs of New Political Power under the leadership of the Communist Party of India (Maoist)!

Struggle! Struggle! And Struggle! Struggle to break the chains of Imperialism, Feudalism and Comprador Bureaucrat Capitalism for liberation! Struggle for great victories to triumph countrywide political power! No force, however mighty, can suppress the people's struggles permanently! Ultimately Victory of the revolution is inevitable! It is the law of transformation of class society! Final defeat is only of the enemy! Final victory is only of the oppressed masses!

We give a similar call to the working class, oppressed nations and the people of all countries - Unite, Organise and intensify the struggle against imperialism and all reaction, for the advancement and success of the world socialist revolution under the leadership of the genuine proletarian Parties!

Source: *Peoples March*, Ernakulam, Volume 5, No. 11-12, November-December 2004.

APPENDIX D

Statement by Ganpathy, General Secretary, CPI (Maoist) Dated 19 February 2007

The 9th Unity Congress [of CPI (Maoist)] affirmed the general line of the new democratic revolution with agrarian revolution as its axis and protracted people's war as the path of the Indian revolution that had first come into the agenda with the Naxalbari upsurge...It set several new tasks for the party with the main focus on establishment of base areas as the immediate, basic and central task before the entire party. It also resolved to advance the people's war throughout the country...and wage a broad-based militant mass movement against the neo-liberal policies of globalisation, liberalisation, privatisation pursued by the reactionary ruling classes under the dictates of imperialism...

The Congress also passed a number of political resolutions on numerous current events like the world people's struggles to support nationality struggles; against Indian expansionism, on [the] post-Khairlanji Dalit upsurge and against caste oppression, against Hindu fascism, against SEZs and displacement, etc...

...Rise up as a tide to smash Imperialism and all its running dogs! Advance the revolutionary war throughout the world!! The Unity Congress-9th of the CPI (Maoist) finally called on the people of India to come forward in large numbers to support the ongoing people's war in the country and the embryonic power emerging, to build a truly democratic society built on justice, equality, free from the chains of imperialism and semi-feudal bondage.

—Ganapathy, General Secretary, CPI (Maoist),
19 February 2007

APPENDIX E

EXCERPTS FROM THE 'URBAN PERSPECTIVE PLAN' 2004 OF CPI (MAOIST)*

(The text has not been edited for style, consistency and grammar for reasons of authenticity. Where necessary, parenthetical explanations are provided to clarify time, a term, title or acronym.)

OUR WORK IN URBAN AREAS

INTRODUCTION

Urbanisation Pattern

The old hierarchy of four mega cities located in different regions of the country is giving way to urban corridors and clusters of new investment located mostly in the southern and western parts of the country.

With the exception of the Delhi region and adjacent areas in Haryana, Punjab, Rajasthan and Uttar Pradesh, much of the north, the east and the centre of the country have been bypassed. This vast area covering the eastern half of UP and stretching across Bihar, West Bengal, the North-Eastern states, Orissa, Madhya Pradesh and the eastern part of Maharashtra is remaining as an area of urban backwardness, with old industrial bases and high unemployment. These areas are thus the main sources of cheap migrant labour for the large metropolitan cities.

*Lifted from the book "Red Sun : Travels in Naxalite Country" by Sudeep Chakravarti.

The above inequalities are being encouraged by the policies of the government. In the earlier period under industrial licensing there were some small attempts at bringing about balanced industrial development and this led to some projects being set up in relatively backward areas like the central India minerals belt. Now under the liberalisation policies investment is not regulated and goes to the areas promising the greatest profits. Thus the main investment is centred in and around a few areas of growing urban concentration.

De-industrialisation of Major Cities

Over the years most major cities have seen a decline in manufacturing activity as compared to business activity in banking, finance, and other service sectors. This process started first with the largest cities, with the close down of many of Kolkata's jute mills and other industries from the late sixties (1960s]. This process however became very generalised from the early eighties [1980s] with the decline of the textile mills in Mumbai, Ahmedabad, Chennai, and other centres lakhs of blue-collar jobs were destroyed without the setting up of any new industries within the city. Since the last twenty years now, hardly any new industry has been located within the major old cities. New industrialisation is normally taking place on the outskirts of the main city, or in the nearby towns and cities. This is combined by an increase of white-collar jobs in the field of services, with investment normally going into these areas.

This process has led to a change in the class composition of most cities, particularly the metropolitan cities.

Since this factor is very important for our organisational perspective, plans, and tasks at the city level, all the respective committees should conduct city level class analysis regarding the situation and trend in their areas.

Changes in the Workforce

With closures of industries and the accompanying loss of jobs, many workers are forced to take up casual work or earn on their own through hawking, plying rickshaws, running roadside tea stalls and food joints, etc. At the same time new youth entering the work force do not get regular jobs immediately (unemployment rate is the highest in the 15 to 24 age group) and are forced to take casual employment or also run some small trade. This trend is increasing in recent years in the urban areas. At the same time more and more women are being employed in jobs but at much lower wage rates. This trend which had started since the early eighties in most cities has further accelerated since the liberalisation policies [in the 1990s].

The percentage of urban males in regular work has dropped and the percentage of self-employed and casual labourers has gone up. At the same time the percentage of women in regular work has gone up, though this does not affect the total size of the working class so much because women compose only 17% of the total urban workforce.

This then means a change in the composition of the working people. Firstly there has been an increase in the proportion of the semi-proletariat (i.e. self-employed); secondly there has been an increase in the proportion of women workers being paid very low wages; and thirdly there has been an increase in the casual labour force.

Besides the above given changes, another change has been the shift of jobs from the larger factories of the organised sector to the small workshops and industries. In recent years the percentage of workers in the organised sector as compared to the total workforce has fallen from 8.5% in 1991 to 7.1% in 1997 to 6.9% in 1999-2000. As the workers are divided into smaller units their potential for unionisation also reduces.

All the above changes in the workforce have been presented here at the all-India level. These changes have significant consequences for our planning at the city and area levels. We should conduct local class analysis and plan accordingly.

Division or Segmentation of Cities

Cities and towns in India, basing on the colonial pattern, have always had a rich British section and a poorer Indian section. This separation however reduced to some extent in the process of growth of the metropolitan cities. Thus it became quite common to have slums adjoining posh high-rise buildings, and hawkers and vendors occupying space right next to the offices of multinationals in the heart of the central business district. Periodically drives would be taken up to demolish slums or evict hawkers, but they would most often manage to struggle and maintain their space within the centre of the city.

This process of dividing or segmenting the city is done through various measures. These measures extend from the old measures of slum demolition and hawker eviction to new forms like closure of 'polluting' factories, banning of protests in central areas, law changes encouraging privatisation and localisation of urban finance and urban facilities, regulations encouraging concentration of development in the richer zones, etc.

The role of the state is most prominent. Bureaucrats and urban planners operating under direct instructions from the World Bank, Asian Development Bank, and other imperialist institutions have formulated laws, regulations, policies and master plans, which have given up even the earlier pretence of the slogans of equity and alleviating of urban poverty. Now the basic thrust of the plans are on 'efficiency' and 'clean and green' cities, which means basically providing sanitised five star enclaves with the best infrastructure and communication facilities for the offices, houses, and entertainment facilities of the corporate managers and elites, while pushing the urban poor along with their 'unclean' slums and 'polluting' industries to the borders of the city. The basic thrust of the National Capital Plan for Delhi and the 1993 Mega-City programme for the other 5 top cities mentioned above basically has this objective. The High Courts and Supreme Court, aided by anti-people so-called environmentalists, have also played a very active role in this process giving numerous court rulings to speed up this process in the name of 'public interest' litigation.

POLICY AND GUIDELINES

Strategic Approach in Urban Work

Role of Urban Work within the Political Strategy

...Being the centres of concentration of the industrial proletariat, urban areas play an important part within the political strategy of the New Democratic Revolution. Urban work thus means, firstly, forming the closest possible links with the working class, and, through the class struggle, establishing the party as a proletarian vanguard; further, it means the mobilisation and unification of all other sections under proletarian leadership in the struggle to achieve the tasks of the revolution.

Role of Urban Work within the Military Strategy

...It is clear that the armed struggle and the movement in the rural areas will play the primary role, and the work in the cities will play a secondary role, complementary to the rural work. However, while giving first priority to the rural work, we must also give due importance to the urban struggle. Without a strong urban revolutionary movement, the ongoing people's war faces difficulties; further, without the participation of the urban masses it is impossible to achieve countrywide victory. As Com. Mao says, 'the final objective of the revolution is the capture of the cities, the enemy's main bases, and this objective cannot be achieved without adequate work in the cities.' (Mao, *Selected Works*, Vol. II, p. 317)

Long-term Approach

The cities and big industrial centres are the strongholds of reaction where the enemy is the most powerful. In these places the police, army, other state organs, and other forces of counter-revolution are concentrated and are in a dominant position from which they can suppress the people's forces.

In such a situation, where the enemy is much stronger, we cannot have a short-term approach of direct confrontation in order to achieve 'quick results'. Rather, we should have a long-term approach.

As Com. Mao, while outlining the tasks of the Party in the urban and other white areas dominated by the reactionaries, explained, 'the Communist Party must not be impetuous and adventurist in its propaganda and organisational work...it must have well-selected cadres working underground, must accumulate strength and bide its time there. In leading the people in struggle against the enemy, the Party must adopt the tactics of waging struggles on just grounds, to our advantage, and with restraint, and making use of such open forms of activity as are permitted by law, decree and social custom; empty clamour and reckless action can never lead to success.' (Mao, *Selected Works*, Vol. II, p. 318)

Main Objectives of Our Urban Work

Work in the cities and towns involves a number of tasks. All these tasks can however be combined under three broad heads or objectives. They are as follows:

1. **Mobilise and organise the basic masses and build the Party on that basis:** This is the main activity of the Party. It is the Party's task to organise the working class, as well as other classes and sections like the semi-proletariat, students, middle class employees, intellectuals, etc. It also has the task of dealing with the problems of special social groups like women, dalits, and religious minorities and mobilising them for the revolutionary movement. It is on this basis that the masses are politicised and the advanced sections consolidated into the Party.
2. **Build the United Front:** This involves the task of unifying the working class, building worker-peasant solidarity and alliance, uniting with other classes in the cities, building the fronts against globalisation, against Hindu fascism, against repression, etc. This is a very important aspect of the work of the Party in the city.
3. **Military Tasks:** While the main military tasks are performed by the PGA [People's Guerilla Army) and PLA [People's Liberation Army) in the countryside, the urban movement too performs tasks complementary to the rural armed struggle. These involve the sending of cadre to the countryside, infiltration of enemy ranks, organising in key industries, sabotage actions in coordination with the rural armed struggle, logistical support, etc.

Of the above three, the first task of organising the basic masses is fundamental and primary. Without widely mobilising the masses it is not possible to perform any of the other tasks such as building of UF [United Front) and performing the military tasks.

Mass Mobilisation and Party Building

We need to build the broadest mass base by building various types of mass organisations, such as, open revolutionary mass organisations, legal democratic organisations, secret mass organisations, cover organisations, etc. Depending upon the situation one or other type of organisation becomes primary for that period. But keeping in mind long term approach, we need to build several types of mass organisations simultaneously. As the Indian political situation is uneven, we need to explore right combination of various types of mass organisations. While there is no possibility to form open revolutionary mass organisations in AP [Andhra Pradesh], there are several states in which still such possibility still exists.

Correctly coordinating between illegal and legal structures, we should have an approach of step by step raising the forms of struggle and preparing the masses to stand up against the might of the state.

Types of Mass Organisations

[There are] three types of mass organisations: (1) Secret revolutionary mass organisations, (2) Open and semi-open revolutionary mass organisations, and (3) Open legal mass organisations, which are not directly linked to the Party. Urban work within the third type of organisations can further be subdivided into three broad categories: (a) Fractional work, (b) Party-formed cover organisations, and (c) Legal democratic organisations.

Secret Revolutionary Mass Organisations

In our party such mass organisations were not formed as a plan. They emerged in and around the struggle areas when the open revolutionary mass organisations were forced to go underground under severe repression. Later they were consciously formed even in areas with relatively less repression. Today with the imposition of an All-India ban...mass organisations in many more areas will be built underground. Many of these organisations are principally functioning in urban areas. Though such secret organisations may be formed in any section of the masses, we have so far, in the urban areas, mainly set them up among the youth, students, and workers. It is the task of the secret units and committees to plan the forms and methods of propagating the Party line, the dissemination of Party propaganda, and the formulation and propagation of the revolutionary standpoint on various issues of the day-particularly the issues affecting the section which they are organising. These can be done through secret posters, voices, pamphlets, cassettes, booklets, and other forms of propaganda;

it can be done through personal contact by the organisation members; it can be done through planned dramatic actions like attacks on imperialist, comprador, and other ruling class targets, etc. Through sustained and effective propaganda, and planned actions, the secret revolutionary mass organisation must aim to reach a position where it influences, guides and even determines the actions and decisions of the non-Party organisations and the masses in its field of operation.

...The secret organisation performs its revolutionary role by giving calls and conducting propaganda to guide and push the open organisations in the correct direction. However this too should be avoided in areas where the field of fractional or cover work is too small or where the open revolutionary propaganda may lead to exposure that we are doing such work in that area. If it is necessary for the secret organisation members to actively work within the open organisation, they will work as ordinary open members of the organisation, while taking special care to safeguard their political identity. It is better to avoid combining of the tasks of the secret organisation activist and open organisation leader; wherever possible different comrades should be assigned these separate tasks.

Open Revolutionary Mass Organisations

These are the open and semi-open mass organisations, which openly propagate the politics of New Democratic Revolution and prepare the people for armed struggle. These organisations make use of the available legal opportunities to carry on revolutionary propaganda and agitation openly and try to mobilise anti-imperialist, anti-feudal forces as widely as possible.

Our Party has formed and run such open revolutionary mass organisations since the seventies, particularly in the period following the lifting of the Emergency in 1977. These open organisations were then the main organs of mass mobilisation both in the rural and urban areas. They were the banners under which thousands and lakhs were mobilised, particularly in the struggle areas of AP and Bihar. These mobilisations reached their peak in the 'open' periods upto 1986 and during 1991 in AP. They played the role of attracting the broad masses towards the revolution. However with the onset of repression most of these organisations were denied any legal opportunities and were forced to go underground. Direct bans were imposed in AP and Bihar, whereas serious restrictions and surveillance were placed on the organisations in other states. Thus the scope of such organisations has drastically reduced with the rise in repression on our Party throughout the country. Today only very small open bodies exist in some cities.

As is clear from experience, this form of organisation can only be used when the ruling classes, due to various reasons cannot or do not bring repression. This being the case there is limited scope for this type of organisation in the urban areas.

" ...We should expose only a small section of our forces and make sure that the majority of our cadre remain hidden from enemy surveillance.

We should on no account indulge in small demonstrations where all our activists are easily identified and even video filmed for easy targeting in future.

Fractional Work

Work of this nature can be carried out in various types of organisations. The best organisations are those which are more oriented to struggle, like trade unions, slum and other locality based organisations, youth organisations, unemployed organisations, students' associations and unions, women's organisations, commuter associations, etc. Besides there are also other organisations which are welfare oriented, community based or are self-help organisations - like workers' cooperatives, cultural organisations, sports clubs and gymnasiums; libraries, bhajan mandals, non-governmental welfare organisations, women's welfare organisations, caste based and nationality based welfare organisations, minorities' bodies, etc. There are also many organisations, which emerge on a particular issue, for a particular period, or for a particular festival, etc.

Once we have decided to do fractional work within an organisation we should strive to achieve a leading position in it. This means we should be in a position to influence and guide the decisions of the organisation. If it is necessary to takeover office bearers' posts in order to achieve this influence, then we should make attempts to do so.

Whether we take up office bearers' posts or not, the important point in fractional work is the skilful exposure of the reactionaries and reformists leading or participating within these organisations. This exposure is essential to draw the masses away from their influence. This must however be done without exposing ourselves to the enemy. The forms of exposure will thus differ depending upon the concrete situation. In vast areas where risk of direct exposure of our fractional work activists is low, we can use propaganda by the secret revolutionary mass organisation or even direct calls by the Party. In smaller areas like a single factory or slum we may have to mainly or only use word-of-mouth propaganda. Sometimes we can create artificial banners like 'angry workers', 'concerned slum dwellers', etc. for doing our propaganda. Very often we may have to use a combination of various methods. Whatever be the method it should be applied carefully, skilfully, and consistently.

The crucial point is to achieve the correct balance of making the fullest use of the legal opportunities without crossing the boundaries set by social customs, habits, existing forms of struggle, etc. Our speech and actions should suit the normal functioning of the activists and masses in the particular area.. This will of course vary from situation to situation. While it may not be abnormal to resort to gherao among many sections of industrial workers, we may have to restrict to black badges and dharnas for bank employees; while militant anti-dowry and anti-caste struggles may be normal in some areas and states, social norms in other states or areas may be such that they would draw immediate suspicion if we tried to engage in such struggles through cover organisations. We would probably have to restrict ourselves to propaganda in such situations. Thus we should plan our activities, and our issues and forms of struggle according to the concrete situation of the class struggle, so that our Party identity is not quickly suspected and exposed. We should of course not reduce ourselves to mere tails of the masses. We should be skilful enough to remain one step ahead of the masses, without getting exposed.

Party-formed Cover Mass Organisations

It sometimes becomes necessary for us to directly form mass organisations under cover without disclosing their link with the Party. Mostly, such a need arises due to the absence of any other suitable mass organisation within which we can do fractional work. An example is the case of unorganised workers, where the established trade unions have a limited presence and we often have no option but to set up our own trade union organisation to take up the unorganised workers' demands. This however is not the only area where we may form cover organisations. In fact, cover organisations can be of as many varied types as the organisations for fractional work we have mentioned in the earlier section. They can range from trade union type struggle organisations to welfare type organisations to issue-based organisations, etc.

We should be careful (especially in repression areas) not to attract the attention of the state by far exceeding the socially acceptable limits of militancy for that area. For example if the normal weapons used in the area are knives and swords we should not resort to firearms, or we should not normally resort to annihilations in a new area where there has not been any history of such actions.

We have had some experience of building cover organisations now since the last few years. We have committed various mistakes...leading to the quick exposure of our forces in many areas.

Legal Democratic Organisations

These are the organisations formed on an explicit political basis with some or all aspects of an anti-imperialist, anti-feudal programme, and with a programme of action and forms of struggle that broadly fall within a legal framework. Some such organisations may be those catering to a particular section like trade unions, student bodies, women's fronts, caste abolition organisations, nationality organisations, writers' associations, lawyers' organisations, teachers' associations, cultural bodies, etc. Others may be formed with issue-oriented programmes focussing on particular core questions like contract labour system, unemployment and job losses, caste atrocities, communalism, imperialist culture, violence on women, saffronisation of education, corruption, regional backwardness and statehood, etc.

...Actually the legal democratic organisations serve as important means to the Party's attempts at the political mobilisation of the urban masses. This is because repression normally prevents the open revolutionary mass organisations from functioning. The legal democratic movement is thus the arena where the masses can participate in thousands and lakhs and gain political experience. It thus has a very important role in the revolution, complementary to the armed struggle in the countryside. Revolutionaries in other countries, particularly the Philippines, have participated within and utilised the legal democratic movement very effectively.

...As long as the organisation adheres to the principles of legal democratic functioning, and as long as it has a broad enough base of support, it will be difficult for the state to close it down.

Organising at the Place of Residence

In slums and other poor localities there are already numerous traditional organisations in existence. Constantly living in precarious conditions, the urban poor naturally come together to help each other and unite within organisations to fight for their rights, to secure better living conditions, to solve problems among themselves and to better organise their social and cultural activities. The common types of traditional organisations are slum-dwellers' organisations, basti or chawl committees, mahila mandals, youth clubs, sports clubs, cultural bodies, committees for various festivals like Ganesh festival, Durga puja, Ambedkar Jayanti, etc. There are also some organisations that are peculiar to certain regions, cities, and areas. Since such organisations offer the best cover we should try to make the best use of these traditional organisations and mainly work from within them. Even if there is a need to form new legal organisations, we should normally give them the forms already existing among the masses.

Struggle issues are a regular feature of locality work, particularly slum work. Fights for basic amenities like water, electricity, toilets and sewerage, against corruption and exploitation of ration shop owners, adulterators and black marketeers, against slumlords, goonda gangs and other lumpens, and against demolitions are some of the regular issues. We should organise the struggles on these issues through the local committees and the slum-dweller organisations. As women and unemployed youth play a leading role in most of these struggles, the mahila mandals and youth clubs should also be involved and struggles can even be led under their banners.

A problem peculiar to slum work is the problem of imperialist funded NGOs. They are today in existence in almost all the slums of the main cities of the country. We should educate the slum masses and particularly the activists about the sinister role of such organisations and the agencies financing them. We should particularly expose them when they stand in the path of the people's struggles. However if such organisations come forward for struggles we can have issue-based unity with them. In situations of repression we can also work within them.

We should consolidate the activists emerging from the struggle first into basti activist groups and then into Party candidate cells and full cells. The basti activist groups, the Party cells and the basti Party committees are the cores for planning and leading all the activities and struggles in the bastis, for political propaganda and education, and for recruiting new members into the Party.

The situation of the urban poor in the slums and poor localities is worsening continuously. The slum population of India today stands at 4.1 crores [41 million], spread in 607 towns. The largest mega city, Mumbai, has 49% of its population in the slums. Our Party has so far paid limited attention to the organising of this section. Other revolutionary parties, particularly the Peru Communist Party (PCP) have been particularly successful in this respect. In fact the shanty towns of Lima have been the strongholds of the revolutionaries for a long period. We too should work at creating such strongholds in India's major cities.

Activist Groups

The secret activist group is a crucial unit in the Party-building and recruitment process. It is the preliminary organisational form for consolidation of the most active and sincere elements emerging from the class struggle. It is the unit through which the activities of its members are given political direction, through which they receive ideological and political education, through which their life decisions are politicised, and through which they are chosen to become members of the Party.

The activist group may be formed at the work-place - factory, mine, industrial estate, shift, department, section, office, branch, or any other level which is a unit for organising; it may be formed at the place of residence - the slum, chawl, street, society, or any other level which is a unit for organising; it may be formed in schools, colleges, or other institutions; and where the organising is based on a particular section, the activist group can be formed at the level suitable for that section.

While leading the group in the above responsibilities, it is the task of the PM [Party Member] in charge to conduct the ideological and political education of the group. While classes and joint study should be conducted, great importance should also be given to other more flexible methods like informal discussion, films, individual reading, etc. As the group develops, where feasible, there should be collective discussion on personal and family problems and this should be used to help the members to take political decisions in their personal life.

Through the above process some or all or even none of the activist group members may develop to become candidate members and members of the Party. This will lead to the formation of a cell in the same area where the activist group had been operating. Once such a cell has been formed, the activist group should be dissolved or reconstituted without exposing the cell-formation to the non-PMs... Thus the activist group is a transitory form of organisation.

Political Education

Mass organisational education should use open forms of mass education for all topics permissible without attracting the attention of the state. We should try to adopt and adapt all locally prevalent forms used by the ruling classes and other classes. These can be like libraries, street corner reading posts and other such means which can be used to disseminate progressive literature among other general books; lecture series during festivals, debate competitions, elocution competitions, etc. where our comrades express progressive views; public speaking courses, personality development courses, etc. with political topics included in the syllabus; mass organisation training camps, and the like. The level of political education possible through such methods will of course be very low, but it is very essential to be conducted on a regular basis to keep up a political atmosphere among even the more backward sections within the mass organisation.

For the more advanced sections we have of course to use different forums and methods – e.g. the activist group.

Party Structure

The essential principle forming the basis of our Party structure, particularly in the urban area, is political centralisation combined with organisational decentralisation. This means that all PMs and all bodies, particularly at the lower level, should have solid ideological-political foundations, so that they are able to independently find their bearings and take the correct organisational decisions according to the political line of the Party. This is particularly important in the urban areas because of the technical difficulties of maintaining close and constant links between the secret higher bodies and those at the lower levels engaged in direct open work.

This is also important because urban work often demands immediate and quick responses to the events of the day. With rapid advances in electronic communication and media, delays of days and sometimes even hours in politically reacting to major events can hinder the impact that our Party can have on the urban movement. This thus depends on the strength of the bodies that form the foundation of our urban Party structure - the cells and the lower level committees - as well as on the Party fractions that link the Party with the mass organisations.

Party Cell

The urban Party cell can be formed on the basis of unit of production - for workers this could be factory, shop, department, section, shift, production line, industrial estate, etc. For students and middle class employees it could be the college, school, institution, office, etc. The cell can also be formed on geographical basis (i.e. the place of residence) - this would be the slum, chawl, street, society, etc. Wherever the number of PMs in a particular unit (e.g. factory) is less than three they can be combined with adjoining units to form a cell. However this should not be done indiscriminately in the urban areas as this would lead to unnecessary exposure. Where the work is integrated a common cell may be formed. In other cases it is better to wait for further recruitment before formation of a cell.

The cell is the body leading all other organisational units within its sphere of responsibility. It performs its basic tasks under the leadership of the next higher committee. The basic tasks of the urban cell include organising the masses, politicising them, educating the advanced elements and recruiting them into the party, and preparing its members and other activists to go to the countryside to work for the success of the agrarian revolution.

The cell should develop its own secret network of shelters and meeting places. As far as possible meetings should not be held in the areas where the members do their political work among the masses. Generally cell members should not be transferred from cell to cell as this would lead to unnecessary exposure.

Where there are at least three PRs functioning in an area and are known to each other, a Professional Revolutionary Cell (PRC) may be formed... The main function of the PRC is to provide the political training and development to the PR, which would not be possible within the time constraints and other limitations of a part timer cell. Longer political education programmes, collective study and debate, and other similar activities can be conducted through the PRC. Thus it can playa positive role in rapidly developing the future Party leadership.

Layers

Layers refers to the various levels in the urban Party organisation like city committee, area committees, factory/basti/college committees, cells, candidate cells, as well as the links to the mass organisations like activist groups and fractions. Due to greater enemy threat in the urban areas it is always necessary to maintain a number of layers from the lowest to the highest levels, and it is important to work through these layers without bypassing them.

The core question for functioning through layers is to see that each layer is trained and developed to independently perform the functions at the particular level. This requires the close guidance and follow-up of the next higher level. The guidance should be directed to developing the independent capabilities of the comrades at that level as well as the team functioning of the committee.

United Front

The urban areas are the centres for struggle by various classes, under the leadership of several organisations representing them. It is essential that we unite with such struggling organisations and build up broad struggles against the ruling classes Thus a significant part of the party's work in the urban areas concerns joint front activity. This includes the formation of various tactical united fronts, as well as building the worker peasant alliance, which is the basis of the strategic united front. This extends from the task of building basic working class unity, to solidarity with the peasantry, to unity with the other revolutionary classes like the semi- proletariat and petty bourgeoisie, right up to maintaining relations and even joint activity with national bourgeois and even ruling class organisations. Let us look at the main forms of such united front activity:

Working Class Unity

Joint trade union fronts are important for increasing the fighting strength of the working class. These joint fronts may be issue-based or based on a minimum political understanding and programme. They may be organised at various levels-industry, area, city, region, all-India, and international... The legal democratic working class joint front organisations can play a very useful role in achieving this long term objective.

Industry-based Unity

Due to the multiplicity of unions in India, in most industries there is very low possibility of achieving the 'one industry, one union' principle. In such a situation we should work for or support the next best option of forming co-ordination committees of the unions within a particular industry. We should try to draw all the unions with significant membership into such bodies. Such unity can start on issue basis and can later advance to a more permanent minimum understanding.

Similarly it is necessary to unite the various factory level unions within a particular company. Such unity can start at the co-ordination committee level or be formed as a federation.

In the present globalisation scenario where the production in one country is easily transferred across international borders, international 'workers' unity is also very important and necessary. Such unity is today very weak. We should however support initiatives for building the international unity of workers within a single multinational or within a particular industry. Even where it is not possible to give the unity an organisational form we should push for solidarity struggles and strikes and do propaganda in this regard.

Issue-based Unity

Our approach in such joint fronts is to build the broadest possible struggling unity of all organisations that have a minimum common stand on the issue. At the same time there should be no compromise on basic principles. Very often joint front bodies tend to become ineffective top heavy bodies, or forums for endless debate. Our approach should be to see that the joint front builds the broadest possible unity of the masses and is not merely the joint front of a few leaders. The attempt should be to take the masses forward in militant struggle and politicise them in the process.

Area-based Unity

This unity can be for an industrial area, town/city, region, state, all-India etc. Unity in a particular industrial area or locality may be restricted to only putting up a common front against problems faced by the workers of the area like goondas, transport, sanitation, water, etc. However area unity at higher levels is normally based on some minimum political understanding. It is the unity of like-minded unions and other bodies, who agree to struggle together to achieve a common set of demands or issues or stand by common political goals. This is thus the most common type of legal democratic workers' organisation.

Workers' Platforms

Another form of uniting the working class on a political basis is to directly form legal democratic workers' organisations as forums or platforms with a minimum workers' programme. Such platforms do not principally, attempt to unite the unions, but target the worker activists of various unions and attempt to rally them politically. Such bodies use meetings, demonstrations, talks, seminars, cultural programmes and various means of propaganda to draw the advanced sections from among the workers on a political basis. They should also mobilise for agitations and struggles on political and other issues.

The aim should be to draw the widest possible non-Party forces who can be united around the programme.

Worker-Peasant Alliance

The revolutionary workers' organisation has a particularly important role to play. It has to take on the main responsibility of propaganda and agitation regarding the agrarian war. Constant and continuous propaganda regarding the progress of the rural movement, the victories achieved, and the repression it faces, and the need for solidarity of the workers with this movement should be an essential part of the work of this organisation. Since the organisation has to normally function secretly it will not be possible to organise open solidarity demonstrations by the workers. However the revolutionary organisation activists can use the method of secret shock actions for propaganda purposes to highlight issues concerning the agrarian struggle.

...We should however not organise open demonstrations in support of our movement if we expect the mobilisation to be low, as it will only result in the exposure of our forces. We should in fact plan such actions in order to mobilise non-Party forces in large numbers. Another type of programme which can be taken up through the legal democratic organisations is large joint mobilisations of workers and peasants on common issues like WTO, state repression, etc.

Unity of the Urban Exploited Classes

Besides the working class, the other exploited classes and sections of the urban areas include the semi-proletariat, the urban poor concentrated in the slums, the students, teachers, employees, and other sections of the middle classes, etc. The Party sends its cadre to organise and lead the mass organisations of all these classes. This however is not the only way by which the working class and its Party unites and provides leadership to all these classes. Solidarity struggles and united front activity are the important means by which the working class inspires and leads all other classes in struggle.

The other medium through which the urban united front is built is through joint fronts on various issues concerning the general mass of the urban population, like price rise, corruption, closure of a key industry or many industries, or various urban problems like water shortage, commuter problems, sanitation issues, etc. Such issues unite all classes but mainly involve the exploited sections.

Unity with the Semi-Proletariat

The semi-proletariat, living in extremely poor conditions, is the urban class with the greatest potential for unity with the proletariat. In recent years the new economic policies have led to a steep rise in their numbers. Many workers are being thrown into the ranks of the semi-proletariat and many rural migrants who come in search of jobs end up in petty trades or in doing sundry odd jobs. Because of their dispersed nature they are not as well organised as the proletariat. It is therefore the task of Party to organise this class and build about its close unity with the industrial workers.

White-collar Employees

In the globalisation period the ruling classes have launched a concentrated propaganda attack against this section as an overpaid, under worked section whose salaries and numbers should be reduced. Thus some sections are being forced to agree to very meagre rises in salary and cuts in earlier allowances. They have also been the target of various privatisation and VRS [Voluntary Retirement Scheme] schemes. Though they have been struggling continuously they often do not receive the sympathy and support of other sections. Our workers' unions, legal democratic and secret workers' organisations, and sometimes even the Party should make it a point to express solidarity in various ways with the struggles of the bank employees, teachers, journalists, etc.

Other Sections of the Petty Bourgeoisie

Some section or the other of the petty bourgeoisie is often in struggle. The students come out in agitations, the lawyers resort to strikes, the shopkeepers also have their protests and bandhs. When these struggles take a militant turn they face the attacks of the state. The working class should be alive to the struggles of these sections. We should, through the trade unions, legal democratic organisations and even the Party, express solidarity. Where possible we should not restrict ourselves merely to statements of support. During major struggles and repression we should make all attempts to mobilise the workers in large numbers to come out on the streets in support. Where there is sufficient support we should attempt to widen the scope of the issue and involve as many sections as possible in support.

Among the urban petty bourgeiosie students and youth constitute important category. They react to the events and historically from the anti-British movement they played a significant role. In the wake of Naxalbari their role is exemplary. Our party has good experience in organising them. While working in urban areas, we must pay necessary attention to organise them.

There is need to emphasise the necessity of uniting with intellectuals. We need to allot sufficient cadre to work among them and some special effort be put in to unite and organise them.

Relations with the National Bourgeoisie

Due to the vacillating and exploitative nature of the national bourgeoisie, its wide participation in the strategic united front generally takes place only at later stages in the revolution. However there is scope in the urban areas, for supporting or uniting with various sections of the national bourgeoisie in tactical united fronts.

These can be on various issues like reduction of taxes, cut in electricity rates, anti-small industry policies and court decisions, protest against entry of multinationals and foreign goods, exploitation of ancillary producers by big industry, etc. Our support can take the form of propaganda or even extend to militant mobilising of workers on the issue.

Another mode of unity could be through joint from bodies with national bourgeois organisations. Mostly such unity will be issue-based like preventing relocation or closure of industries, opposing anti- small industry laws and tax increases, etc. However as the anti-globalisation and anti-WTO movement picks up we will have to try our best to draw the more progressive sections and organisations of the national bourgeoisie into the movement.

The ceaseless attacks of the imperialists and their Indian agents are daily pushing the national bourgeoisie into more conflict with the ruling classes. Thus today the practical possibilities of unity from below are growing. These possibilities are greater in cities with a stronger national bourgeois presence like the Delhi belt, the Coimbatore-Erode belt in Tamil Nadu, Surat in Gujarat, etc.

Front Against Repression

[An] excellent form of building broad fighting unity against repression is to take up particular cases of brutal state repression and immediately mobilise all sections of the masses in militant struggle. Police firings, lock up deaths, rape by security forces, are some of the examples that can be used to rouse the masses into open battle. There have been many instances like the Rameeza Bee case and others, where such incidents proved to be the turning points for building not only militant struggle but also much broader democratic movements. In some cases where the above methods lead to broad movements we can work with others for the formation of organisations of a more long term nature with a broad anti-fascist repression programme.

United Front Against Hindu Fascist Forces

An important call of the Ninth Congress is to build a broad UF of all secular forces and persecuted religious minorities such as Muslims, Christians, and Sikhs against the Hindu fascist forces. Since a large proportion of the minorities are urbanised and since the attacks of the Hindu fascists are as yet mostly concentrated in the cities, this UF has basically been the responsibility of the urban organisation. This task has appeared in our documents now from many years, but very little has as yet been done. One of the explanations for this failure is the weakness of our urban organisations, but the other more important reason is our neglect of work among the minorities.

The above UF cannot be built merely by uniting some secular individuals on the basis of a political programme. In order to be effective it has to involve the masses, particularly the masses from the minorities. This, therefore, means that we must have substantial grassroots work among the minorities, particularly the Muslim masses who are the most numerous and the worst victims of the Hindu fascists' atrocities. However due to extreme ghettoisation in almost all Indian cities, this is only possible if we take a conscious decision to shift out at least some forces from Hindu dominated areas and base them in the slums and localities inhabited by the Muslim poor. This would be the first step to building any united front.

Front Against Globalisation, Liberalisation and Privatisation

The line of action for building anti-globalisation fronts should...rely primarily on the working class, while rallying around all other sections in the struggles against the imperialist policies.

Other classes and sections of importance we should try to draw into the anti-globalisation front are the peasants' organisations and the farmers' bodies, slum bodies, students' organisations, intellectuals, writers and cultural activists, pro-people environmental groups, teachers and other middle class employees' associations' etc. The scope of the anti-globalisation movement is so large that it includes practically all classes who are part of the strategic UF. While the separate organisations formed by these sections against various aspects of globalisation objectively form part of the movement, we should nevertheless try to draw all such organisations into common united struggle on a common anti-imperialist programme.

Reactionaries like Swadeshi Jagran Manch, revisionists like CPI, CPI (M) and foreign funded NGOs are some of the forces involved in anti-globalisation movement. These forces are linked to the ruling classes or part of them. We must keep away from the reactionaries in any joint front. With regard to the revisionists who are part of ruling classes, we ourselves should not invite them into any joint front, but if they are part of a front called by others, we need to keep away because of their presence. The revisionists and foreign funded NGOs may participate to some extent but there is always danger of them attempting to sabotage the movement at higher levels of struggles. We must be alert to this danger.

MILITARY TASKS

As explained earlier, the urban movement plays a secondary and complementary role in the military strategy of the revolution. While the main military tasks are performed by the PGA and PLA in the countryside, the urban organisation too performs tasks complementary to the rural armed struggle. Due to the spread of urbanisation, the growth of a number of mega cities, and the sharper division of the cities into rich and poor sections, the possibility and importance of urban military operations increases. These however yet remain second to the rural military tasks. The varied military tasks performed in the urban areas relate to, (1) the defence of the urban movement, (2) help by the urban organisation to the rural armed struggle, and (3) direct military operations conducted under central direction. These thus form the main categories of military tasks and forms of organisation in the urban areas.

Defence of the Urban Movement

The nature of urban work being primarily legal and defensive, the military tasks directly related to the urban movement are basically defensive in nature and will remain that way till the final period of the [r]evolution. However even a defensive urban movement requires the military type organisation of the armed defence of the urban masses against the peoples' enemies. These enemies are of various types - goonda gangs acting in the service of the ruling classes, Hindu fascist organisations and their militias, vigilante gangs specifically organised by the state to attack activists and sympathisers of our movement, state forces themselves, etc. Without standing up to such forces it would not be possible for an organisation to survive and develop. While we cannot and should not, at this stage, organise for armed offensive confrontation with the state we should definitely build such defence organisations as are suited to the concrete situation.

Open Self Defence Teams

Wherever necessary the legal organisations should organise self defence against the local enemies. Examples of such self-defence teams are union self defence against lumpen strike breakers, basti self defence teams against goonda gangs, mahila organisation self defence teams against eve teasers and molesters, mohalla all-community self defence during communal riot situations, mass self defence against slum demolition, etc. Open self defence teams should be organised in such a way as to mobilise sizeable sections of the masses in this task, particularly motivating the youth to participate in large numbers. When such defence is organised systematically involving the broad masses, it greatly strengthens the legal organisation, gives confidence to the rank and file and the local leadership, and releases the creative energies of the masses. If such activity grows in an area it gives rise to new creative forms of militant mass fighting. Conversely it demoralises and paralyses the enemy, and prevents him from using his old forms of repression.

Often such open self defence is organised on a temporary basis for a particular situation or period. However wherever possible we should plan and attempt to give this mass self defence a permanent form and structure, allocating specific responsibilities, and linking with the mass organisational committees. Such bodies can run vyayamshalas, martial arts centres, sports clubs, etc.

Secret Self Defence Squads

Secret squads are necessary to supplement the open defence, teams, or where, due to repression, it is not possible to form such teams. They too are formed with the broad objective of defending the urban mass movement. One significant form of activity is to participate along with the masses and give them the confidence to undertake militant mass action. Other tasks are to secretly hit particular targets who are obstacles in the advance of the mass movement.

The secret squads require proper military training, and military and political education. The extent and depth of the training will depend on the facilities available, but we must make the best efforts to ensure that the squads are properly trained and armed. The arms used will depend on the situation in the area. As far as possible arms which are not normally used in the area should not be employed.

Due attention should be paid to the discipline of such squads. Selection of members should not be merely on the basis of military abilities, but should consider the political level and discipline of the comrades. All squad members maintain their jobs or other responsibilities and only combine for the purpose of training or actions. They disperse again immediately after that. The squads should function under direct and strict party control, with each squad functioning under a responsible Party comrade. As far as possible no two squads should be combined for performing an action. The knowledge of existence of such squads too should be as restricted as possible. Each squad is a separate entity and there should not be any separate line of command within the self defence squads. All State committees should periodically review the activities of such formations and give guidelines to the committees immediately responsible for them.

Urban Militia

At this stage of the revolution all the open and secret organs of people's defence will maintain a separate identity and the Party will be the only body coordinating their activities. Today there is no scope for bringing together all or many of the self defence teams and squads under a single organisational mechanism to form a militia. This may be possible during certain periods of upsurge when significant sections of the urban population are ready to take up arms either against the fascist militias or against the state. At such times the Party should take immediate initiative to launch urban militia without exposing all its forces. The concrete organisational form of such an urban militia would however depend on the particular situation and the specific forces operating at that time.

Local Intelligence

Intelligence is a much-neglected function in our Party. Very often we suffer severe losses, or lose good opportunities due to the absence of proper intelligence. In the urban areas intelligence is also very necessary to protect and preserve the urban Party as well as the mass movement. Thus the task of information collection and analysis should be taken up from the beginning itself and responsibility should be allocated accordingly. As the organisation grows this task and responsibility should exist at all levels and should be integrated into the functioning of the organisation.

The objectives of our intelligence work should be to learn about and study the tactics and plans of the enemy forces in the area, to study the activities of informers, to prevent infiltration into the organisation, etc. The methods and structure, particularly at the lower levels, should be as simple as possible and should utilise to the maximum the forces available to us from among the masses.

Help to the Rural Armed Struggle

There are numerous ways through which the urban movement can assist the rural armed struggle and particularly, the base areas and the guerilla zones. Some involve direct and immediate help in terms of materials and personnel; others involve the long-term preparation for the decisive battles in the later stages of the peoples' war.

Work in Key Industries

Some industries like transport, communications, power, oil and natural gas, defence production, etc. can play a crucial role in the peoples' war. Disruption of production in these industries has an immediate impact on the enemy ability to fight the war. If struggles in such industries are coordinated with developments in the peoples' war they can provide direct assistance to the PGA/PLA. Party led units within such industries can also perform industrial sabotage actions, which would provide effective assistance during certain points in the war. It is thus the responsibility of the urban organisation to establish a presence and influence in such key industries.

The key industries have normally been in the public sector. Now however with the policy of privatisation, many of the old units are being privatised and new units are being set up directly in the private sector. Thus some of these industries, like the electricity boards and telecommunications department, are experiencing many militant struggles in opposition to the privatisation policies and there has been a significant revival of the trade unions. In the context of the general upswing of the workers' movement, the workers of other key industries too are resorting to struggle. We can therefore make use of this situation to try and influence the workers in these industries.

Infiltration into the Enemy Camp

It is very important to penetrate into the military, para-military forces, police, and higher levels of the administrative machinery of the state. It is necessary to obtain information regarding the enemy, to build support for the revolution within these organs, and even to incite revolt when the time is ripe. Other types of technical help are also possible.

The cities are the strongholds of the enemy and have a large concentration of enemy forces. It is, therefore, from the cities that attention must be given to this task. Such work can be done by following up contacts obtained from the civilian sphere, or by directly allocating comrades to penetrate the enemy ranks. Whatever be the method, the work is of a very special type which requires a high degree of political reliability, skill and patience. Such work should be without the knowledge of the lower level committees and the details of the work should only remain with the comrades directly responsible.

Associated with this task is the need for a plan to work in the cantonment towns spread out throughout the country. Such work even among the civilian population of these towns can give us valuable information and openings for penetration in the enemy ranks.

Sending Cadre to the Rural Areas and the PGA/PLA

A steady supply of urban cadre is necessary to fulfill the needs of the rural movement and the people's war. This is necessary for providing working class leadership, as well as technical skills to the people's war.

To fulfill the need of recruitment from workers in large numbers and sending them to rural areas, we need to work in the unorganised sector where overwhelming percentage of working class is there. While we need to work in key industries which is organised sector for the strategic reasons, we must mobilise and organise millions of workers who are in the unorganised segment. The working conditions are horrendous in this sector and militant struggles are bound to come up here. Most of the working class has live connections with backward rural pockets, in some of which already armed struggles are going on. If we work patiently we can get good recruitment whom we can send to the areas of armed struggle zones.

Logistical Support to the Armed Struggle

The enemy gets all its logistics support from the urban areas. The People's Army however relies as far as possible on the rural areas and the rural masses. However for certain crucial things there is need for support from the urban areas. Depending on its strength, the urban organisation should make all efforts to provide such support.

Supplies or contacts for supplies of certain types are only available in the urban areas. Examples of such supplies are arms and ammunitions, spare parts, certain types of medical supplies, etc. Helping the People's Army to establish the supply lines in this regard is a task that the urban organisation can perform. However once such a supply line is established it is best maintained by the rural organisation. As the needs of the base areas and guerilla zones grow there will be even a need to establish a separate supply and transport wing in this regard.

Medical networks of sympathetic doctors and use of hospital facilities to treat PGA/PLA fighters are also necessary in the urban areas. This is necessary for certain cases which cannot be treated with the facilities available in the guerilla zone areas. Here too the urban Party should always be on the lookout for sources and contacts to set up such a network in various cities. Once a network has been established however it should be separated from the Party bodies leading the urban mass work.

Technical help in the form of repairs and maintenance of fighting, communication and other equipment of the PGA/PLA is another area where the urban organisation has to provide assistance. This is best done by preparing comrades with technical, electrical, electronic and other skills to go and take up such responsibilities in the countryside. It can also be done be sending city comrades to conduct training courses for the PGA/PLA. In some cases where necessary the repair of some equipment can be done in the urban areas. Providing the contacts to help set up a network for production of certain items in the urban areas is also another area of necessary help.

Development of new technologies for the People's War is another crucial area. With the daily advance of technology, there are numerous new devices that could be adapted in the service of the people's war. Since the large metropolitan centres are the points where such technologies or the information regarding such technologies are obtained, it would be the responsibility of all comrades in such areas to be ever alert to any opportunity in this regard. Proposals and devices obtained or developed should be sent to the higher committees for consideration and implementation. Since it would in the future be necessary to set up separate research and development wings in this regard, it would be the task of the urban organisation to develop suitable comrades for such work.

Urban Military Operations under Central Direction

Though the countryside is the main area of operations of the People's Army, there are certain military objectives that need to be performed through operations in the urban areas. This even requires the setting up of permanent structures of the PGA/PLA in the cities and towns.

City Action Teams

These action teams are small secret teams of disciplined and trained soldiers of the PGA/PLA who are permanently based in the cities or towns to hit at important, selected, enemy targets. Such targets may be annihilation of individuals of military importance or sabotage actions like the blowing up of ammunition depots, destroying communications networks, damaging oil installations, etc. These action teams which form part of the main force of the PGA/PLA, perform these actions under the guidance and orders of their respective command. Thus these teams should have no connection whatsoever with the local urban Party structure. The selection of targets and timing of operations too would be based on the overall political and military needs of the people's war. However the secret team should have some broad understanding of the schedules and plans of the programmes of the open mass organisations. This could where possible help prevent problems due to clashing between the open and secret plans.

Details regarding the role, tasks, training and education of the city action teams should be undertaken by the Central Military Commission (CMC).

Central Intelligence

Since the enemy is centred in the big cities, it is very important that our Party develops a network to obtain and analyse political and military intelligence at higher levels. Besides human intelligence, we can make use of the Internet and other modern electronic means for gathering information by entering the enemy's networks. For this it is necessary to allocate separate responsibility. Urban Party organisation may provide contacts and individuals for this work. However once they are assigned to this work they do not maintain any links with the local organisation. Such networks are led and directed by the highest bodies of the Party.

Cyber Warfare

We should, to the extent possible, make use of computers and the Internet ... to further the military objectives of the revolution. Though we are today quite distant from this possibility, we should have the perspective of setting up units with the task of damaging the military and other important networks of the enemy. The possibility of setting up such a structure however depends primarily on the development of the urban mass movement and the ability of the urban Party organisation to draw in and consolidate comrades with the required skills for such work.

Domestic Terriorist Organisation in India (As Declared by Central Government on June 22, 2009)

1. United Liberation Front of Assam (ULFA)
2. National Democratic Front of Bodoland (NDFB) in Assam
3. Peoples Liberation Army (PLA)
4. United National Liberation Front (UNLF)
5. Peoples Revolutionary Party of Kangleipak (PREPAK)
6. Kangleipak Communist Party (KCP)
7. Kangli Yaol Kanba Lup (KYKL)
8. Manipur Peoples Liberation Front (MPLF)
9. Revolutionary People's Front (RPF) IN Manipur
10. All Tripura Tiger Force (ATTF)
11. National Liberation Front of Tripura (NLFT) in Tripura
12. Hynniewtrep Natioanal Liberation Council (HNLC)
13. Achik National Volunteer Council (ANVC) in Meghalaya
14. Babbar Khalsa International
15. Khalistan Commando Force
16. International Sikh Youth Federation
17. Al-Umar Mujahideen
18. Jammu and Kashmir Islamic Front
19. Student's Islamic Movement of India

20. Deendar Anjuman
21. Communist Party of India (Marxist-Leninist) Peoples War Group
22. Maoist Communist Centre (MCC)
23. Dukhtaran-E-Millat (DEM)
24. Tamil Nadu Liberation Army (TNLA)
25. Tamil National Retrieval Troops (TNRT)
26. Akhil Bharat Nepali Ekta Samaj
27. Communist Party of India (Maoist)

Bibliography

Periodicals and Daily Newspapers

1. *Frontline,* August 5-18, 1989 "Fading Thunder".
2. New Delhi September 29-October 12, 1980 "Is India Waiting for Naxalites"?
3. *Telegraph,* June 2, 1987 "Spring Thunder and after" article by Shri A.K. Roy.
4. *The Times of India*, October 12, 1981, "Resurgence of Naxalites" by A.S. Abraham.
5. *The Statesman*, April 18, 1984, "Naxalites Shadow Over Bastar Tribal Area" by Taroon Kumar Bhaduri.
6. *The Hindustan Times*, May 5, 1980, "Splits Shatter Naxalite Dream of Capturing Power."
7. *The Week*, July 20-26, 1986, "Two Weeks in the A.P. Jungles" by G.S. RadhaKrishnan.
8. *India Today*, June 1-15, 1979, "Naxalite Movement."
9. *The Statesman,* October 21, 22, and 23, 1987 "Revolt that Failed" by G.S. Bhargava.
10. *The Times of India*, May 17, 1986, "A.P. Naxalite far from Crippled" by V.G. Prasad Rao.
11. *The Indian Express*, July 24, 1987, "Bane of Naxalism in Bihar" by Sri Vatsa.
12. *The Times of India*, March 27, 1981, "Naxalites Bid for National Stir."

13. *The Illustrated Weekly of India*, July 6, 1986, "The Grapes of Wrath" by P.R. Rajgopal.

14. *The Times of India*, December 29, 1987, "Cops Their Special Targets".

15. *The Times of India*, October 17, 1980, "CPI-ML Considers Russia Main Threat to Peace."

16. *The Illustrated Weekly of India*, July 10, 1988, "The Uprising" by K.P. Sunil.

17. *Frontline*, November 6, 2009.

18. 30 years of Naxalbari : An Epic of Heroic Struggle and Sacrifice in (Down loaded from Internet) www.maoism.org/misc/India/cpiml/cpiml-pw/30 years/30/30-years.html.

19. *Outlook*, November 9, 2009.

Books

1. Red Sun (Travels in Naxalite Country) by Sudeep Chakravarti.
2. *The Naxalite Movement in India* by Prakash Singh.
3. *The Naxal Challenge (Causes, Linkages and Policy Options)* edited by P.V. Ramana (contains articles by different writers).

Index

C

O

R